The Way of the Kenotic Christ

The Way of the Kenotic Christ

The Christology of Jürgen Moltmann

Samuel J. Youngs

 CASCADE *Books* · Eugene, Oregon

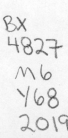

THE WAY OF THE KENOTIC CHRIST
The Christology of Jürgen Moltmann

Cascade Books
An Imprint of Wipf and Stock Publishers
199 W. 8th Ave., Suite 3
Eugene, OR 97401

www.wipfandstock.com

PAPERBACK ISBN: 978-1-5326-6190-7
HARDCOVER ISBN: 978-1-5326-6191-4
EBOOK ISBN: 978-1-5326-6192-1

Cataloguing-in-Publication data:

Names: Youngs, Samuel J., author.

Title: The Way of the Kenotic Christ : The Christology of Jürgen Moltmann / by Samuel J. Youngs.

Description: Eugene, OR: Cascade Books, 2019 | Includes bibliographical references and index.

Identifiers: ISBN 978-1-5326-6190-7 (paperback) | ISBN 978-1-5326-6191-4 (hardcover) | ISBN 978-1-5326-6192-1 (ebook)

Subjects: LCSH: Jesus Christ—Person and offices. | Jesus Christ—Messiahship. | Jesus Christ—Divinity. | Moltmann, Jürgen.

Classification: BX4827.M6 Y68 2019 (print) | BX4827.M6 (ebook)

Manufactured in the U.S.A.   10/24/19

Contents

Acknowledgments

IT HAS BEEN SAID that "theology is biography," and this sentiment, whatever its other merits, distills the humbling truth that every endeavor to speak about God is molded by the life experiences of the one who attempts the speaking. My teachers, colleagues, friends, and family have all shaped me fundamentally, and thus they are all, in their own way, my coauthors.

My theological journey began, as most of ours do, in my home and among my parents. They have both shaped me in innumerable ways—my likes and dislikes, my outlooks and attitudes. From my mother, Kelly, I learned the supreme worth of pursuing faithful truth without dogmatism. From my father, Dale, I was tutored in the value of hard work and dedication to the tasks that God has set before us. Without them I would not be a theologian.

I learned to take my first theological steps when I was shown that an academic mind need not be separate from a generous, joyous heart, and also when I realized that good thinking emerges from well-posed and fearless questions. The former I was taught by Raymond Hundley, my first professor of religion and theology, whose broad erudition was matched only by his care for students and sense of humor. The latter I was taught by Ben Williams, a true friend and mentor, whose encouragements to my passions and challenges to my assumptions are gifts that have "kept on giving" for quite a long time now. Without these men, I might still be a theologian, but certainly one less brave and less inquisitive.

I adopted my theological posture from my two most influential seminary professors: Adonis Vidu and Patrick Smith. Adonis showed me the deep and unavoidable interface between theology, culture, and philosophy, and this has colored my scholarship and teaching ever since. Pat modeled as a teacher and exhibited as a friend the inestimable virtue of circumspection; his genuine humility and appetite for nuance opened wide the vistas of dialogue and exploration. Without Adonis and Pat, I might still be a theologian, but not one who values looking deeply and seeking the many sides of every issue.

Much gratitude is justly owed to my two doctoral supervisors. Paul Janz has, through years of invigorating conversation, tireless editing, and incisive commentary, taken the molten rawness of my theological excitement and funneled it through the fissures of rigor, academic charity, and acuity of expression. Paul is a rare mentor, unafraid of providing censure where needed and only granting praise when truly warranted. Oliver Davies has lent much to my critical investigations, not only through his boundless energy and insight, but in his deep conviction that theology's momentum must always be a constructive one in the midst of humanity's cultural shifts and discoveries. While I may still be a theologian without Paul and Oliver, my thinking would be much impoverished and its horizons far more limited.

There are innumerable other voices that have contributed to my theological growth, academic pursuits, and the formation of the ideas in this book. Jeremy Liddell and Jonathan Xavier are my oldest friends, and they have borne the cross of having a theologically exuberant (and often longwinded) friend with forbearance and good humor. My pastors, past and present—Glenn Gardner, the late Paul Harshbarger, Bruce Quackenbush, Patrick Gray, Chris Sorensen, Ben Ferguson—as well as my parents-in-law, Phil and Susy Downer, have all ministered to me in various, significant ways and have encouraged me to apply my academic vocation in the service of Christ's church.

Through heartfelt conversations that have been both life-giving and stimulating, Joey Schlabs, Paul Downer, Dr. Jud Davis, and many of my students (Jeremy Eastwood, the late Christopher Nitzband, Aaron Pendergress, and Dakota Thacker, among others) have helped forge the principal ideas and insights that animate this book. And of course I am grateful to Jürgen Moltmann, my closest "theological companion" of the past half-decade and the subject of this book, for his personal story of darkness overcome and his fertile theology of Christ-centered hope. By all of these I have been shaped, and to all of these I owe much gratitude.

But the most praise flows most assuredly to my wife Anna. There is no one else who has endured my theological permutations with more grace and genuine understanding. There is no one else who has encouraged and supported me more fruitfully. There is no one else who has chastened my rationality by more beautifully enflaming my heart with love for Jesus Christ and those he came to save. And there is no one else who has, quite simply, taught me more about theology and the Christian life, for our marriage and the parenting of our children have shown me in clearest daylight things of God I only knew as shadows before. Without Anna, I might be a theologian, but only one who lives and thinks at a tragic distance from the world. Without her, I would be a theologian who speaks of false things, rather than real things.

Abbreviations

STANDARD ENGLISH TRANSLATIONS OF Moltmann's major works, having been completed in the original author's lifetime and typically finalized with his approval, are readily referenced and quoted throughout this book. Bibliographic information and corresponding abbreviations for the relevant English editions are provided here. The German originals have also been utilized throughout the study and at certain points the German text is brought into the English quotations in order to help clarify or further specify Moltmann's intended meaning or his unique deployment of theological terminology. When such citations are made, they are from the corresponding German editions below.

ABP   *A Broad Place: An Autobiography*, trans. by Margaret Kohl, Minneapolis: Fortress Press, 2009.

     = *Weiter Raum: Eine Lebensgeschichte*, Gütersloh: Gütersloher Verlagshaus, 2006.

CG   *The Crucified God*, trans. by Margaret Kohl, Minneapolis: Fortress Press, 1993.

     = *Der gekreuzigte Gott: Das Kreuz Christi als Grund und Kritik christlicher Theologie*, München: Chr. Kaiser, 1972.

CoG   *The Coming of God*, trans. by Margaret Kohl, Minneapolis: Fortress Press, 2000.

     = *Das Kommen Gottes: Christliche Eschatologie*, München: Chr. Kaiser, 1996.

CPS   *The Church in the Power of the Spirit,* trans. by Margaret Kohl, Minneapolis: Fortress Press, 1993.

= *Kirche in der Kraft des Geistes,* München: Chr. Kaiser Verlag, 1975.

EG   *Experiences of God,* trans. by Margaret Kohl, Minneapolis: Fortress Press, 2007.

= *Gotteserfahrungen: Hoffnung, Angst, Mystik,* München: Chr. Kaiser, 1979.

ET   *Experiences in Theology,* trans. by Margaret Kohl, Minneapolis: Fortress Press, 2000.

= *Erfahrungen theologischen Denkens,* Gütersloh: Chr. Kaiser Verlag / Gütersloher Verlaghaus, 2000.

EthH   *Ethics of Hope,* trans. by Margaret Kohl, Minneapolis: Fortress Press, 2012.

= *Ethik Der Hoffnung,* Gütersloh: Gütersloher Verlagshaus, 2010.

FC   *Future of Creation: Collected Essays,* trans. by Margaret Kohl, Minneapolis, MN: Fortress Press, 2007.

= *Zukunft der Schöpfung: Gesammelte Aufsätze,* München, Chr. Kaiser, 1977.

GC   *God in Creation,* trans. by Margaret Kohl, Minneapolis: Fortress Press, 1993.

= *Gott in der Schöpfung: Ökologische Schöpfungslehre,* München: Chr. Kaiser, 1985.

GSS   *God for a Secular Society: The Public Relevance of Theology,* trans. by Margaret Kohl, Minneapolis: Fortress Press, 1999.

= *Gott im Projekt der modernen Welt: Beiträge zur öffentlichen Relevanz der Theologie,* Gütersloh: Chr. Kaiser / Gütersloher Verlagshaus, 1997.

HG   *Humanity in God,* New York: The Pilgrim Press, 1983.

HTG   *History and the Triune God*, trans. by John Bowden, London: SCM Press, 1991.

      = *In der Geschichte des dreieinigen Gottes: Beiträge zur trinitarischen Theologie*, München: Chr. Kaiser, 1991.

IEB   *In the End, the Beginning: The Life of Hope*, trans. Margaret Kohl, Minneapolis: Fortress Press, 2004.

      = *Im Ende—der Anfang*, Gütersloh: Chr. Kaiser / Gütersloher Verlagshaus, 2004.

JCTW *Jesus Christ for Today's World*, trans. Margaret Kohl, Minneapolis: Fortress Press, 1994.

      = *Wer ist Christus für uns heute?*, München: Chr. Kaiser, 1994.

PL   *The Passion for Life: A Messianic Lifestyle*, trans. by Douglas Meeks, Minneapolis: Fortress Press, 2007 ed.

      = *Neuer Lebensstil. Schritte zur Gemeinde*, München: Chr. Kaiser, 1977.

SoL   *The Source of Life: The Holy Spirit and the Theology of Life*, trans. by Margaret Kohl, Minneapolis: Fortress Press, 1997.

      = *Die Quelle des Lebens: Der Heilige Geist und die Theologie des Lebens*, Gütersloh: Chr. Kaiser/Götersloher Verlagshaus, 1997.

SpL   *The Spirit of Life*, transs. by Margaret Kohl, Minneapolis: Fortress Press, 2001.

      = *Der Geist des Lebens: Eine ganzheitliche Pneumatologie* (München: Chr. Kaiser, 1991.

SRA   *Sun of Righteousness, Arise! God's Future for Humanity and the Earth*, trans. by Margaret Kohl, Minneapolis: Fortress Press, 2010.

      = *Sein Name ist Gerechtigkeit: Neue Beiträge zur christlichen Gotteslehre*, Gütersloh: Gütersloher Verlagshaus, 2009.

SW   *Science and Wisdom*, trans. by Margaret Kohl, Minneapolis: Fortress Press, 2003.

= *Wissenschaft und Weisheit: Zum Gespräch zwischen Naturwissenschaft und Theologie*, Gütersloh: Chr. Kaiser / Gütersloher Verlagshaus, 2002.

TH   *Theology of Hope*, trans. by James W. Leitch, Minneapolis: Fortress Press, 1993.

= *Theologie der Hoffnung*. München: Chr. Kaiser, 1965.

TK   *The Trinity and the Kingdom*, trans. by Margaret Kohl, Minneapolis: Fortress Press, 1993.

= *Trinität und Reich Gottes: Zur Gotteslehre*, München: Chr. Kaiser, 1980.

WJC   *The Way of Jesus Christ*, trans. by Margaret Kohl, Minneapolis, Fortress Press, 1993.

= *Der Weg Jesu Christi: Christologie in messianischen Dimensionen*, München: Chr. Kaiser, 1989.

Introduction

The Christological Lacuna in Moltmann Studies

JÜRGEN MOLTMANN IS ONE of the most important Protestant voices of the twentieth century. He shares space in the theological firmament with the likes of Niebuhr, Pannenberg, and Rahner, and his global (rather than merely Western) impact exceeds all of them. Over thirty years ago, in 1985, Miroslav Volf noted that more than 130 dissertations had been written on Moltmann's theology, standing as a striking testimony to both the "fecundity" and "attractiveness" of his thought.[1] In a more recent *festschrift* for Moltmann, Volf and Michael Welker put the number of dissertations on Moltmann at "over two hundred" and claim that Moltmann has "shaped the international theological conversation in the twentieth century more than any other Protestant theologian since Karl Barth, Dietrich Bonhoeffer, and Paul Tillich."[2] The extent of Moltmann's influence beyond his native Germany only serves to illustrate the expanse of his theological endeavors,[3] an expanse that has dealt with both age-old doctrinal axioms and emergent challenges to Christian faith. His contributions concerning eschatology and trinitarian theology have received the fullest attention in secondary scholarship,[4] but these areas have been complemented by

1. Volf, "Queen and a Beggar," ix.

2. Volf and Welker, "Preface," xiii.

3. Well noted by Müller-Fahrenholz, *Kingdom and the Power*, 12, 15; see also Moltmann's own discussion in *ABP*, especially chapters 10, 13–15, 18, and 23.

4. Moltmann's prodigious influence is admitted even in the midst of strong criticism of his theology, e.g., Grenz and Olson, *20th Century Theology*, 172. Concerning his trinitarian contributions, Joy Ann McDougall states quite rightly that "no theologian has played a more pivotal role in revitalizing trinitarian doctrine and its implications for Christian praxis than Jürgen Moltmann" (*Pilgrimage of Love*, 6). See also Grenz, *Rediscovering the Triune God*, 73–87.

robust interaction with Moltmann's ethics (spurred in no small part by his long-awaited *Ethics of Hope*[5]), as well as his ecological, cosmological, and anthropological ideas.[6]

However, if one examines the topical range of major secondary works on Moltmann's thought, one thing emerges quite strikingly: *no work in English is wholly dedicated to expounding or interacting with his Christology*. Many studies touch on his Christology in some way, but none offer more than a few scattered sections, or perhaps one focused chapter, on whichever isolated aspect of the Christology they have deemed most pertinent to the other theological locus that they are investigating. Any robust, detailed analysis that attempts to sum the varied contours and themes of Moltmann's christological thought is conspicuously absent in contemporary engagement with his thought.[7] The prominence of this lacuna is exacerbated not only by the fact that the longest writings in both his original trilogy and his six-volume "Contributions to Systematic Theology" are, in fact, devoted to Christology,[8] but also by the fact that Moltmann, throughout his career, has unflinchingly asserted that his theology is christological in foundation and implication, a fact not always recognized by those who comment on his thought.[9]

Moreover, and pivotally, the uniquely *kenotic* trajectory of Moltmann's Christology has been overlooked. This neglect has typically assumed one of two forms: either a single aspect of Moltmann's Christology is focused

5. As *EthH*, appearing in English in 2012. Such a book was "on Moltmann's agenda" immediately after the publication of his initial "trilogy" (*Theology of Hope, The Crucified God*, and *The Church in the Power of the Spirit*), but various issues inhibited its composition (see *ABP*, 292; see also *EthH*, xi).

6. Some of the most significant of these recent books and monographs include: *God Will Be All in All*, edited by R. Bauckham; Van Prooijen, *Limping but Blessed*; McDougall, *Pilgrimage of Love*; Chester, *Mission and the Coming of God*; Beck, *Holy Spirit and the Renewal of All Things*; Wright, *Disavowing Constantine*; Neal, *Theology as Hope*; Bonzo, *Indwelling the Forsaken Other*; Guttesen, *Leaning Into the Future*; Harvie, *Jürgen Moltmann's Ethics of Hope*; Lee, *Celebrating God's Cosmic Perichoresis*; Chung, *Jürgen Moltmann and Evangelical Theology*; Ansell, *Annihilation of Hell*; Bingaman, *All Things New*.

7. Note also that the interactions with his Christology that do exist, while often informative and rigorous, are only chapter-length and moreover are spread over two decades of scholarship. This highlights the lacuna effectively, especially when compared with the large number of books and monographs (not to mention chapters and articles) that have focused acutely on other areas of Moltmann's theological program.

8. *CG* and *WJC*.

9. Bauckham rightly recognizes it: "Jürgen Moltmann," 157; he's followed in this recognition by Bingaman, *All Things New*, 45.

on in isolation, with little exploration of kenosis or other dimensions of his Christology, or kenosis is discussed as an overarching cosmological or trinitarian theme in Moltmann's theology, but without much discussion of its specifically christological expression or ramifications.

The need for these lacunae to be thoroughly addressed forms the principal motivation for this book. I aim (1) to present a far more detailed elucidation and systematization of Moltmann's doctrine of Christ than it has yet received and (2) to constructively argue for a "kenotic reading" of that Christology, highlighting ways in which the theme of kenosis centers Moltmann's christological thought and also casts light on its broader doctrinal and practical implications.

Chapter 1 initiates the study. Before engaging in an exposition of his christological "content" as such, I thoroughly analyze Moltmann's theological methodology (which is unique in and of itself) in order to equip and orient our exploration of his Christology's myriad themes and developments.

In chapter 2, I turn my attention to systematizing what I call Moltmann's "christological thematics." This terminology highlights the fact that, although Moltmann's Christology is spread across several major and minor works emerging in the course of decades of theological development, it bears within it several arrangements of tightly related themes that mutually inform one another. Therefore, in order to have a sense of the Christology's full orbit (which will be necessary for us to argue for its essentially *kenotic* character), a synchronic analysis of its varied expressions, as well as a synthesis of them, will be important.

Chapter 3 engages the topic of christological kenosis in arguably the most direct way possible: by exploring Moltmann's relation to, and application of, the "kenosis hymn" found in Phil 2. Through a multi-layered analysis of past and contemporary interpretive approaches, I contextualize, define, and distinguish Moltmann's own approach, revealing a unique understanding of kenosis that varies from a great many other "kenotic" approaches to Christology.

Chapter 4 proceeds to analyze Moltmann's Christology at its most basal (and perhaps most controversial) level: his standing as regards the Chalcedonian Definition and "two natures" Christology. Since most discussions of christological kenosis hinge importantly on these issues, this portion of the study serves to beneficially reveal the sometimes obscure christological motivations and intuitions of Moltmann, building on key points about his method and his hermeneutics that have been established in the foregoing chapters.

Chapters 5 and 6 proceed to delineate Moltmann's doctrine of Christ by exploring what will be shown to be its true orienting center: *the kenosis of Christ*. Stated briefly, I argue in these chapters that kenosis in Moltmann's thought is a deeply *relational* reality that defines Christ's existence and activity across four major, defining relationships: *relation to the Father*; *relation to the Spirit*; *relations with social realities*; and *relation with Jesus' flesh itself.*

The book's final chapter culminates in an integrated, systematized articulation of Moltmann's Christology that is *multifaceted, biblical, and correlational, but also deeply and pervasively kenotic*. A final and brief section highlights the "horizons" of Moltmann's kenotic Christology, pointing toward ecclesial and practical issues where it may be helpfully applied.

Before leaving this Introduction, a few comments are needed concerning Moltmann as a source of academic theology. Anyone who has taken the time to read and understand Moltmann recognizes that his thinking is characterized by thematic arrangement and present-day challenges rather than systematic exposition. This has frustrated some commentators, but it is fully consistent with Moltmann's theological and methodological suppositions.[10] My approach has been to concentrate my primary research on Moltmann's major published books and on the essays that appear in book-form collections, as these are the sources that represent his most consistent and robust exposition of his ideas. Moreover, my argumentation does not consist in describing Moltmann's "christological development" in a diachronic fashion, but rather in allowing his various mature statements to throw mutual light upon each other in synchronic reciprocity. This approach is justified since, even though there are certainly "phases" to Moltmann's career, as far as his Christology goes there has been very little recanting of earlier positions on his part; rather, there has been a continuous expansion and clarification of his christological reflections along thematic lines.[11]

Furthermore, concerning my treatment of Moltmann, I have taken up the task of systematizing and integrating various—and sometimes latent—themes or ideas that are disseminated throughout his major works. This means that my account of his thought will occasionally make connections, or present systematizations, that he himself does not espouse explicitly (though they will be shown to be fundamentally rooted in his work and

10. This will be demonstrated at some length in chapter 3.

11. See Moltmann's comments in *WJC*, 1–5, 151–53.

implied in his positions). This has been standard practice in constructive interactions with Moltmann's thought, and he himself has not objected to it.[12] Also, given that secondary literature on Moltmann, as mentioned above, is presently quite vast in scope, I have judiciously focused on the range of interlocutors who have concertedly focused on areas of his theology that are most pertinent to an exposition of his Christology.

Finally, then, a closing note on the "tone" of this study, especially as regards the work of Moltmann. Despite the general admiration for Moltmann among many theologians, he has also, interestingly, been subjected to a fair degree of sharp suspicion and theological censure in the course of his career, with the accusations ranging from crypto-atheist, to unbridled Hegelian, to obvious tri-theist, to sponsor of abusive theology, to participant in slipshod doctrinal rumination that lacks proper analytical discipline.[13] Such appellations have led, on occasion, to certain distortionary analyses and unfounded associations in secondary treatments of his work. Where these have been encountered in the course of research, and where possible in the progress of argumentation, they have been carefully highlighted and charitably challenged.

However, criticisms of Moltmann are far from being universally delinquent, and many of them raise legitimate issues. Thus, where it is both topically relevant and logistically possible, I have sought to acknowledge certain deficiencies in either his method or in his doctrinal elucidations. That said, it should be remembered that the underlying disposition of this work is *critically constructive*. It affirms the positive, creative, and doctrinal value of kenotic thinking in Christology and the contributions of Moltmann's career. With this in mind, I have adopted what could be called a "generously critical" approach to the principal interlocutors in this study.

12. E.g., Moltmann professes to have "not seen" some of the major themes that McDougall draws from his work, but he agrees that the themes and ideas do *follow* from what he has written. See his "Forward," in McDougall, *Pilgrimage of Love*, xi-xiii; as well as his "Foreward," in Bauckham, *Messianic Theology*, vii.

13. For the charge of crypto-atheism, see Otto, *God of Hope*, 1-11, 199-233. On Moltmann's Hegelianism, see Blocher, *Evil and the Cross*, 72-76. For indications of the tri-theism charge, Hunsinger, "Crucified God," 278; O'Collins, *Tripersonal God*, 158. On his allegedly abusive theology, see Feske, "Christ and Suffering," 92-101. On lack of rigor in Moltmann's method, see Bauckham's summary statement in *Theology*, 25.

PART I

Moltmann's Theological Method and Christological Thematics

1

Distinctives of Moltmann's Theological Approach

WE BEGIN BY FIRST identifying what I call the "christological center" of Moltmann's theology. Not only is Moltmann's theology holistically tethered by the centering force of his christological intuitions and arguments, but these are also the real source of the other, oft-assumed "centers" of his theology (such as his eschatology and his views on the Trinity). Once I describe this *properly christological center* in Moltmann, the remainder of the chapter focuses on elucidating various facets of his unique approach to the theological task. This elucidation is, of course, intended to empower our eventual consideration of his unique doctrine of Christ.

The Christological Center of Moltmann's Theology

In his first major work, *Theology of Hope*, Moltmann claims that "from first to last . . . Christianity is eschatology."[1] He thereby establishes the eschatological focus that characterizes his thinking and, seemingly, pinpoints eschatology as the "center" of this thought. But it is immediately thereafter that he gives eschatology its *own* centering content, and that, explicitly, is *Christology*: "Christian eschatology speaks of Jesus Christ and *his* future. It recognizes the reality of the raising of Jesus and proclaims the future of the risen lord."[2] He further states that there "can be no Christology

1. *TH*, 16. See the comments on the eschatological-christological dialectic in Williams, "Moltmann on Jesus Christ," 106; see also Meeks, *Origins of the Theology of Hope*, 121–28.

2. *TH*, 17. Veli-Matti Kärkkäinen sums well the relationship between Moltmann's Christology and eschatology: "Moltmann's eschatology is integrally related to Christology in that Christian faith is grounded in hope for the future based on the cross and resurrection of Jesus Christ" (*Christology*, 148). See also Bauckham, "Future of Jesus

without eschatology and no eschatology without Christology."[3] The two loci are the mutually informing dialectic at the heart of his theological enterprise; his Christology is certainly an eschatologically oriented one, but Christian eschatology is content-less (indeed it could not and would not exist) without *Christology*.

In his next major (and "most enduring"[4]) work, *The Crucified God*, it is the cross of Jesus Christ that is spoken of as "the *center of all Christian theology*. . . . It is in effect the entry to [theology's] problems and answers on earth."[5] Theology's fulcrum for Moltmann hereby comes to balance on staurological affirmations. But staurology, like eschatology, is completely hollow without Christology: "Christ the crucified alone is 'man's true theology and knowledge of God.' . . . God's being can be seen and known directly [*sichtbar und direkt erkennbar*] only in the cross of Christ."[6] Moltmann's passionate rhetoric here echoes the young Luther's *theologia crucis*.[7] But whereas for Luther the cross had tremendous meaning for how we conceive the *Christian life*, for Moltmann it also forges a uniquely Christian path to thinking about *God*. The cross becomes Moltmann's measure and criterion for all statements about divinity and the way in which God relates to the world—Christology and its cross are determinative for all. This is not only a matter of doctrinal content, but also of theological method, as John Webster notes:

> [Moltmann's method] is bound up with a theological and spiritual conviction that the cross is not so much an acceptable part of the conceptual and symbolic apparatus of Christianity as an irritant: the cross is that which refuses to be dealt with, which cannot be rendered harmless and domestic. The cross, far from offering clarity and security to Christian faith and theology, stands as a symbol of the unsettled character of our dealings with God.[8]

Christ," 97–110.

3. *HTG*, 95; see also Moltmann, "Theology as Eschatology," 23–34.

4. *ABP*, 200.

5. *CG*, 204, emphasis added. See also his much later statement in *CoG*, where he states that Christology "is the centre of Christian theology" (100).

6. *CG*, 212 (German: 197); see also Kärkkäinen, *Christology*, 151; Ngien, *Suffering of God*.

7. See Theses 19 and 20 of Luther's Heidelberg Disputation; further, see McGrath, *Luther's Theology of the Cross*, 148–51.

8. Webster, "Jürgen Moltmann," 4.

Moltmann's intense focus on a "crucified Christology" famously provides the base for his wide-ranging critique of classical theism[9] while also springing the floodgates of his burgeoning social trinitarianism. In fact, as early as *The Crucified God,* Moltmann found the centermost point of discussing the Trinity in the cross of Christ,[10] and it is this same sentiment that concludes his preface to *The Trinity and the Kingdom* only a few years later: "[The] cross of the Son stands from eternity in the centre of the Trinity."[11] Significantly, following *Trinity and the Kingdom,* it has been Moltmann's highly dynamic, perichoretic, social model of the triune God that became his heuristic bridge into a vast spread of doctrinal territory.[12] These new explorations were certainly catalyzed by trinitarian theology, but, as I have noted, for Moltmann the Trinity is only properly revealed in Christ and his cross.

Thus we can safely say that Moltmann's Christology fundamentally precedes and constitutes his diverse theological trajectories; Christology is the hinge-point of his unique theological enterprise, as J. Scott Horrell implies:

> Moltmann convincingly argues . . . [that] it is Jesus' suffering and death on the cross that . . . now makes untenable a unipersonal God, especially one who is impassible in the sense of many classical interpretations. The relationship of Jesus Christ with the Father and the Spirit rolls back the roof of our human existence for us to peer into the self-giving love between the Father, the Son, and the Spirit.[13]

Beyond serving as both the origination and framework for his robust trinitarian project, Moltmann's Christology also funds his ethics— through his unique articulation of "christopraxis" and God's kingdom

---

9. See the protracted discussion and critique in *CG,* 207–27; such critique is anticipated by *TH,* 140–42.

10. *TH,* 235–49. In a key passage he quotes and expounds on the following from Steffen (*Das Dogma vom Kreuz*): "The scriptural basis for Christian belief in the triune God is not the scanty trinitarian formulas of the New Testament, but the thoroughgoing, unitary testimony of the cross; and the shortest expression of the Trinity is the divine act of the cross, in which the Father allows the Son to sacrifice himself through the Spirit" (*CG,* 241).

11. *TK,* xvi.

12. The Trinitarian reflections become foundational throughout his remaining work, but most prominently in *GC,* esp. 9–20, 94–104, 258–70; *SpL,* throughout; *HTG,* throughout; *SW,* throughout but especially chapters 3–8.

13. Horrell, "Eternal Son of God," 58.

(which is embodied in Christ's very person, not just in his proclamation or actions)[14]—as well as his ecclesiology, wherein the messianic family of the body of Christ enters into cruciform solidarity with the poor in an open friendship that imitates the other-seeking nature of Christ's social relationships. Ecclesiology presupposes Christology fundamentally in Moltmann's thought:

> The doctrine of the church . . . is indissolubly connected with the doctrine of Jesus, the Christ of God. The name the church gives itself—the church of Jesus Christ—requires us to see Christ as the subject of his church and to bring the church's life into alignment with him. Thus ecclesiology can only be developed from Christology, as its consequence and in correspondence with it.[15]

In light of this evidence of the centrality of Christology for Moltmann's entire theological endeavor, the question I raised in the Introduction becomes yet more pitched: why is there so much scholarly focus on virtually every topic in Moltmann's thought, yet little parallel or sustained focus on his Christology?[16]

A preliminary answer, and one that those familiar with Moltmann might expect, is that his Christology develops over time and through various, often somewhat radically stated, iterations; it is extremely multifaceted, and different eras in Moltmann's career reflect variant emphases within it. Thus, when viewed in isolated chunks, Moltmann's Christology can seem disjointed and unwieldy—evocative, but less than coherent.[17] Such a state of affairs, however, begs for a careful analysis of Moltmann's christological statements and themes *in toto*. This is one of the key tasks for the present and following chapters: providing crucial topographic data in the hopes of systematizing the diverse terrain of Moltmann's doctrine of Christ.

---

14. *WJC*, xiv, 41–43, 116–36; also *JCTW*, throughout. See also Harvie, "Living the Future," 150–53.

15. *CPS*, 66. See further 67–132. Bauckham, *Theology*, 122–23; Moltmann, *Power of the Powerless*, 110–12.

16. I gladly note the exception in Watson, *Towards a Relevant Christology.*

17. This variety of criticism emerges in Cowdell, *Is Jesus Unique?*, 23–46; as well as in Williams, "Moltmann on Jesus Christ," 117–21.

Situating Moltmann's Christology: Methodological Considerations

Moltmann's Christology is diffused across a wide range of works and at least forty years of theological development. Over such a stretch, even among the most systematic of thinkers, one would expect progression, change, and even revision—and Moltmann is not renowned for his systematizing propensities.[18] (In fact, Moltmann has shown few qualms about admitting when commentators are better at tracking systematic structures in his thinking than he is himself![19]) Though the full breadth of the Christology is difficult to delineate, there are certainly key *loci* in Moltmann's major published works that contribute pivotal and complementary aspects to his christological vision. These major focused discussions are found in: *The Crucified God* (chapters 3–6); *The Church in the Power of the Spirit* (chapter 3); *The Trinity and the Kingdom* (chapter 3); *The Way of Jesus Christ* (chapters 3–7); *History and the Triune God* (part 1, chapter 4); and *Jesus Christ for Today's World*.[20] Besides a general awareness of the principal works wherein Moltmann develops his christological ideas, it is important also to bear in mind the methodological distinctiveness of Moltmann. In very many cases, it will not be enough to isolate discrete chunks of the Christology and simply repeat *what* Moltmann says; we must always inquire after *how* he is saying it—his approach, his method, is just as "theological" as his doctrinal statements themselves.

18. Cowdell (*Is Jesus Unique?*) and Williams ("Moltmann on Jesus Christ") express frustration with this as it relates to Moltmann's Christology. Though the reality of Moltmann's less-systematic (and less "logical") theology can be counted on to annoy certain interlocutors, many take a favorable view of it, noting that Moltmann's understanding of theology as "conversation" rather than a "dogmatic" or "timeless" system (e.g., *TK*, xi–xiv), as well as his view of the provisionality of theological assertions in light of always-oncoming eschatological reality (e.g., *TH*, 33, 203), seem substantive enough reasons for Moltmann to embrace the somewhat circuitous investigation that he does. See the exposition of Moltmann's theological methodology (below) for further discussion on these points.

19. See, e.g., his comments concerning Bauckham's first attempt to systematically explain his theology: "[Bauckham] demonstrates the consistency and coherence of the thought even where I myself had the feeling of being led by spontaneous inspiration or of only being carried back and forth" ("Foreward" in Bauckham, *Messianic Theology*, vii).

20. In his relatively brief exposition of Moltmann's general Christology, Kärkkäinen gives a rather strange listing of christological *loci* in Moltmann, including *Theology of Hope* but neglecting *Trinity and the Kingdom*, *History and the Triune God*, and *Jesus Christ for Today's World* (see Kärkkäinen, *Christology*, 147). Ryan Neal offers a list close to that presented here, although it also oddly neglects *Trinity and the Kingdom* (see Neal, *Theology as Hope*, 153).

In the final essay collected in *History and the Triune God* (1991), Moltmann attempts to sum up his method: "I would have at least to say that I am attempting to reflect on a theology which has: a biblical foundation, an eschatological orientation, [and] a political responsibility."[21] This passage is sometimes cited in commentary on Moltmann's methodology, but his next (and concluding) sentence of the essay is often not: "In and under that it is certainly a theology in pain and joy at God himself, a theology of constant wonder."[22] We will be taking each of these four statements as keys for unfolding the varied aspects of Moltmann's approach to theology.

Moltmann's "Biblical Foundation"

What could "biblical foundation" mean for Moltmann? If one pursues a short trek through secondary scholarship on his work, it will be noted that his relationship to and use of scripture can often be singled out as a point of critique.[23] Some interlocutors have exhibited concern with an alleged surplus of speculative theological *construction*, accompanied by a lack of detailed *exegesis*. Matthew Bonzo has presented a standard version of this criticism in reference to Moltmann's ethics: "Moltmann's ethical insights do not rely directly upon exegesis. Rather, they emerge from his understanding of the doctrine of Trinity, itself more a construction than a result of exegesis. . . . Moltmann's references to scripture are used more as prooftexts for his particular philosophical position than in sustained exegetical analysis."[24] Such criticism concerning exegesis and "proof-texting" could readily be raised, in some form or fashion, against many systematic and doctrinal theologians, and Moltmann has responded to such criticism only by referencing other important thinkers who have handled scripture in much the same fashion as he does.[25]

But the other and more important dimension of this critique is the implication that in place of "proper exegetical analysis" the ideas of the given theology are assembled *apart* from scripture, and then forced onto it, like an inorganic interpretative brace, driving scripture into a particular

21. "My Theological Career," 182.

22. "My Theological Career," 182.

23. E.g., Chung, "Moltmann on Scripture," 1–16.

24. Bonzo, *Indwelling the Forsaken Other*, 9–10.

25. Moltmann notes that some scholars "have ironically criticized my use of the Bible as a 'use *a la carte*,' although it is no different in principle from the way Karl Barth or Basil the Great used Scripture" (*ET*, xxi).

(ideological) framework. Richard Clutterbuck has referred to this purported tendency as an "instrumentalist use of doctrine."[26] Focusing in particular on Moltmann's trendsetting (and contentious) social trinitarianism,[27] Clutterbuck claims that this doctrine, in Moltmann's hands, "is *instrumental in promoting and justifying a particular form of society*"[28] and later commenting that it is "unclear" if Moltmann's position grows out of Christian doctrine proper or whether it is motivated by "the alien claims of something exterior to Christianity."[29]

Moltmann, for his part, has not addressed such concerns in much detail, especially as they relate to his social doctrine of the Trinity. A possible reason for Moltmann's lack of engagement with the critique is that it often takes its primary force simply from a flat denial of what Moltmann himself claims: that his doctrine of the Trinity derives "from the biblical history."[30] Beginning very early in his career, Moltmann has made it quite clear that he thinks "Christian theology must be *biblical* theology."[31] This is a key point. When Moltmann describes his social Trinity model, he maintains that it is the *history* of Jesus and the early church, as recounted in the narratives of the gospels and Acts, which provides the major point

26. See Clutterbuck, "Jürgen Moltmann," 489–506.

27. Moltmann inaugurated what has been called "the new trinitarian thinking" (Grenz, *Rediscovering*, 83–84) primarily in his promulgation of three themes: (1) A social model of the Trinity, whereby the persons of the Trinity are all independent centers of will, but that are unified in volitional agreement and self-sacrificial love (*TK*, esp. 17–20, 198–99; *SpL*, 309); (2) a "trinitarian understanding of history," describing the Trinity's relationships in constant movement throughout historical and revelatory events, with different trinitarian persons assuming differing roles and directives at different times (*TK*, 89–96); and (3) the social Trinity also being an "open Trinity" insofar as it (a) exposes itself to the world through its changing interactions with history and (b) draws the world evermore into its divine life through the mediation of the Son and Spirit (*TK*, 89–96)—this process will be consummated at the eschaton. See also the summary of the "objectives" of "Christ's history" and the "Spirit's history" in *SpL*, 233–34. Moltmann eventually takes to using the term "primordial Trinity" to refer to the Trinity "from eternity"—but there is no effective difference between this primordial Trinity and the open Trinity except the progression of time (see *SpL*, 294–95, 299). For a short summary of Moltmann's view that also conveys some of the more common criticisms, see John Thompson, *Modern Trinitarian Perspectives*, 33–34.

28. Clutterbuck, "Jürgen Moltmann," 492, emphasis added.

29. Clutterbuck, "Jürgen Moltmann," 501.

30. Most clearly in *TK*, 64–90; also *CPS*, 53–56; Moltmann, "Trinitarian History of God," 82–85.

31. Moltmann, "Christian Theology and Its Problems Today," 6, emphasis added.

of departure for his theological reflections.[32] It is the concrete specificity of Jesus' life and death and resurrection, as mutually constitutive events in time and space, rather than abstract ontological considerations, which gives direction to his statements about Christ.[33] It is from the movements of the specific Jesus-focused history of the gospels that Moltmann draws and shapes his conception of the trinitarian persons and their interactions within history.[34] As Moltmann says:

> The new trinitarian thinking, in contrast [with foregoing trinitarianism focusing on God's differentiated subjectivity], starts from the interpersonal and communicative event of the acting persons about whom the biblical history of God tells. It has to do with Jesus the Son, and with God whom he exclusively calls "Abba, my dear Father," and with the Holy Spirit who in fellowship with him is the giver of life.[35]

Joy Ann McDougall, in her important work on divine love and trinitarian theology in Moltmann, refers to this as Moltmann's "biblical-narrative approach," and notes that while it does resist "tidy schematization," we should expect nothing less, since Moltmann often explicitly grounds himself not in systematizing speculation but in the economic (historical, bodily, material) interactions of God with history.[36] In a representative passage on his approach to scripturally informed doctrine, Moltmann states that he is pursuing

> [The] special experience and the particular practice in the context and in the movements of the history of God. That cannot be called "abstract." To be abstract rather means isolating a single

---

32. *CG*, 241–43; *TK*, 64–65; Moltmann, "Creation, Covenant, Glory," 131; Moltmann, "Trinitarian Story of Jesus," 70–89.

33. *TH*, 141–42.

34. Stephen Williams, in discussing Moltmann's Trinity and its relation to scripture, claims that it is characterized by "meticulous adherence to the biblcal narrative, albeit interpreted . . . in the context of New Testament theology" ("Jürgen Moltmann," 111).

35. *SRA*, 149–50.

36. Moltmann often places himself in firm opposition to speculative modes of theologizing, especially as it concerns the doctrine of the Trinity. Schleiermacher and Kant both serve as shields that Moltmann uses to guard against speculating "in heavenly riddles" (*CG*, 207) as well as combatants when Moltmann seeks to demonstrate the practical relevance of the doctrine of the Trinity (*TK*, 2–3, 6–7). See McDougall, *Pilgrimage of Love*, 12–13. Though Matthew Bonzo is aware of McDougall's work (see *Indwelling*, 17) and, as we've seen, would disagree with McDougall on this point, he does not address her statements on this aspect of Moltmann's method (nor the similar points of John O'Donnell in *Trinity and Temporality*, 115).

> event from its history, the special experience from the context of life to which it belongs. . . . Abstract, isolating thinking [*abstrakte, isolierende Denken*] must hence be set aside by integrated thinking [*integrierende Denken*] and must be guided into life.[37]

While certainly admirable as a methodological principle in theological construction, it must be stated that Moltmann has not always lived up to this non-abstract standard that he has set. Bauckham in particular has praised Moltmann's historical and concrete focus in the biblical narratives while also rightly lamenting various dimensions of Moltmann's trinitarian thinking that do at times verge on needless and ungrounded speculation.[38]

That said, Moltmann has positioned himself to treat doctrine in a thoroughly economic key ever since he adopted Karl Rahner's dual-principle: "The Trinity *is* the nature of God and the nature of God *is* the Trinity. . . . The economic Trinity *is* the immanent Trinity and the immanent Trinity *is* the economic Trinity."[39] (Far from claiming that God is a purely immanent force in the unfolding of world history, Moltmann's more assertive declarations of such an economic priority are simply meant to safeguard the following double-axiom: "statements about the immanent Trinity must not contradict statements about the economic Trinity. Statements about the economic Trinity must correspond to doxological statements about the immanent Trinity.")[40] Since the trinitarian relationships are rooted and expounded in this economic key, and the unfolding of those loving relationships in the midst of this-worldly history are a major red thread for Moltmann's overarching theology,[41] a good number of his seemingly speculative reflections are anchored in concrete details of the biblical history—its

---

37. *CPS,* 51; I have modified Kohl's translation slightly.

38. Bauckham, *Theology,* 163–70.

39. *CG,* 240. See also *TK,* 147–60; Moltmann, "Theology of the Cross Today," 76. By the time he began work on the second half of his "Contributions to Systematic Theology" (the volumes on pneumatology, hermeneutics, and eschatology) Moltmann's use of this Rahnerian principle was more developed. The exposition in *SpL,* 291–94, represents its clearest application to Moltmann's notion of "trinitarian history." It is also within this more-developed discussion that we find his approving reference to Congar's mitigation of Rahner: "The economic Trinity thus reveals the immanent Trinity—but does it reveal it entirely? There is always a limit. . . . The infinite and divine manner in which the perfections that we attribute to God are accomplished elude us to a very great extent" (*SpL,* 291n42, citing Congar, *I Believe in the Holy Spirit,* 3:16).

40. *TK,* 154. See also *CPS,* 54–55; Bauckham, *Theology,* 174.

41. A "discovery" that he generously attributes to McDougall; see Moltmann, "Foreward," in McDougall, xiii.

accounted events, its space-time contexts. This will be important for us as we explore his Christology: Moltmann is not firstly concerned with deductive speculation from general or *a priori* philosophical reifications, nor with re-conceptualizing doctrine in mere definitional self-reference; he is concerned with the biblical trajectory, historical narrative, and embodied realities. This separates him from many other christological approaches and lies at the root of many of his more unusual maneuvers.

But here I should take pains to avoid distortion. Moltmann is not a straightforward "biblicist" who concerns himself simply with "what the text says" and sees in that text a series of propositions that must simply be affirmed or intellectually reconciled. It is true that, on his own admission, and in the contours of his doctrinal developments, Moltmann is fundamentally *directed* by the biblical texts, particularly the narrative histories of Jesus. But his handling of scripture itself is dynamic, and continuously looks to this-worldly realities in unfolding diverse aspects of the revelatory materials.[42] Theological work, in Moltmann's view, should not be abstracted from historical vicissitudes, and likewise giving due place to real and lived history does not undermine the integrity of theological assertions.[43]

It is here that we must come to grips with what I will refer to as Moltmann's *promissory-messianic hermeneutic*. Moltmann's wide-ranging and deep-reaching theological journey begins and ends with eschatology. This has long entailed an understanding on his part of revelation *as promise*.[44] God acts in history; in that acting he promises changed circumstances, novelty, liberation, and life; he promises newly creational and redemptive movements.[45] We see in scripture God's promises to the Israelites and others, and we see them fulfilled by God in history (this is thus *promissory*), but we also find promises that have yet to be fulfilled, and that now will

42. He is particularly concerned to trace liberating and healing motifs as they are developed through scripture's unfolding witness, understood with a strong sense of "progressive" revelation (which is necessitated by his eschatology). See his detailed discussion in *ET*, 87–133. For an appropriation of Moltmann on this score, see Vidales, "How Should We Speak," 148–50.

43. See *WJC*, 69. Cowdell accuses Moltmann of inconsistency, as well as "fideism" and "literalism," on this point (*Is Jesus Unique?*, 38–39, 46), the substance of such objections being that Moltmann is not "critical enough" in his theological use of scripture.

44. See Olson, *Journey of Modern Theology*, 458–63.

45. Bauckham (*Messianic Theology*, 112) emphasizes that this fundamentally anchors Moltmann in this-worldly concerns—revelation is not about the conveyance of propositional truth from "out there" somewhere, but is rather about acts of God in the midst of people in history and space-time contexts.

only be fulfilled under the auspices of the continuing lordship of Christ and work of his church (this is thus *messianic*).[46] But going even beyond this, Moltmann will sometimes read key biblical events in *both* a promissory and messianic way;[47] they are *fulfillments* of past promises that posit *still further* promises for God's work in the world.[48] Relatedly, Moltmann also emphasizes the certain key events of the Christian faith (especially in the life of Jesus) will need to be read both "historically" and "eschatologically" in order to unravel their full significance in both origin and trajectory.[49] This is certainly important for understanding Moltmann's Christology, as it allows him to pursue and affirm multiple meanings for a single fact or event, meanings that can sometimes give the impression of not cohering in any straightforward fashion. However, when some of these facets are read as "fulfilled promise" and others are read as "oncoming messianic fulfillment," many such tensions readily dissipate.[50] In noting this salient hermeneutical movement we have hereby crossed from Moltmann's "biblical foundation" over to his "eschatological orientation."

Moltmann's "Eschatological Orientation"

Moltmann's interpretive approach to scripture and history, while not immune from critique,[51] is fundamentally tied to categories of real sensible-embodied experience in which true novelty is available via the advent of decided action (or enacted decision). Eschatology is not about detached truths concerning the world's political and religious future (fundamentalism) or moral ideals that dawn upon the human heart (romanticism) nor about radical self-actualization under religious impetus (existentialism). All of these approaches cleave the world into a dualistic schema: either

46. E.g., *TH*, 50–58; *CG*, 162; *ET*, 125–30; *HTG*, 67, 182; *SpL*, 39, 51–53.

47. He will refer to this, for instance, as "anticipations of the remembered future" (*CoG*, 141).

48. "The Word of the gospel makes Christ present. . . . It thrusts through the times of history and makes its way to us because it carries with it the promise of his presence. . . . The gospel is remembered promise" (*SpL*, 232).

49. See Bauckham, *Messianic Theology*, 64, 70–71; Olson, *Journey of Modern Theology*, 461–62; Watson, *Towards a Relevant Christology*, 145–50.

50. For an underappreciated example of Moltmann employing this approach in his Christology, see the discussion in "Theology as Eschatology," 24–34.

51. Chung raises several issues from an evangelical perspective: "Moltmann on Scripture," 5–6, 10–16.

between God and creation, or between rationality and intuition, or be-tween interior meaning-making and exterior realities. Moltmann's escha-tology pursues a line that differs from all of these—it is reality-grounded and forward-looking; indeed, it is "messianic" insofar as time's progression and the changes that are wrought thereby are seen as *fundamental* to the redemptive shaping of reality.[52] As Olson correctly says, "If anything is axiomatic for Moltmann, it is that the future is new and not an extension of the past."[53] Such an outlook has received validation from many quarters in late-modern theology, not least of which includes the ever-burgeoning scholarship of N. T. Wright, which continues to see eschatological cat-egories and the inbreaking, oncoming kingdom as the irreducible axis around which the gospel hope revolves.[54] In discussing his self-designated "hermeneutics of hope," Moltmann writes,

> Every promise thrusts towards the fulfilment of what is prom-ised. Every covenant with God thrusts towards God's all fulfilling presence. From the standpoint of the fulfilment, every promise is therefore literally a *pro-missio*, a sending-ahead [*eine Voraus-schickung*] of what is to come, in the way that the daybreak takes its colours from the rising sun of the new day. In this respect God's promise is "gospel" in the heralding of his coming (Isa 52:7: "How beautiful upon the mountains are the feet of him who brings good tidings . . ."). . . . For all the differences, there must already be an identification between what is to come and the promise in which what is to come is announced. As the one who will come, Christ is present now in his word and Spirit. In the present promise, the future is made present [*die Zukunft vergegenwärtigt*].[55]

This hermeneutical openness, relating quite clearly to what I have termed his promissory-messianic outlook, conditions Moltmann's handling of biblical texts and orients his entire treatment of doctrine: "Throughout history as the biblical writings tell it, God's history of promise runs like a scarlet thread of hope. It is at once a history in word and a history in act. Talk about 'the mighty acts of God' is not the language of acts which

---

52. See, e.g., *CoG*, 22–46.

53. Olson, *Journey of Modern Theology*, 459.

54. See, e.g., Wright, *Resurrection*; *Surprised by Hope*; "New Creation"; and "That the World May Be Healed."

55. *ET*, 102 (German: 99).

are finished and done with; it is future-promising history [*zukunftsverheißender Geschichte*]."[56]

Importantly, Moltmann employs this eschatological hermeneutic to counter the very notion of reality as something that can, in all its travail and complexity, be known in an absolute or definitive way. Current worldly reality, seen eschatologically, cannot be resolved or defined by any series of *self-enclosed concepts*. A purely inferential or deductive approach to understanding life, doctrine, or God is, for Moltmann, untenable in light of a faith that is truly future- and kingdom-oriented. Deductive and inductive modes of reasoning—if employed to the exclusion of all other insights— cut against an eschatological faith in a devastating way: *they rely on the past to know the "truth" of the present.*[57] Now, the past can certainly *help* us to understand some dimensions of the present, but for the Christian the promised *future* also sheds light on, and indeed shapes, the meaning of the present. The world is always being revised and transformed under the continuing lordship of Christ, and thus it is God's future that has final say, *not any past definition, theorem, grammar, or system.*[58] Olson conveys well the implications for theological method: "Because he holds to such an eschatological epistemology, it is no wonder that Moltmann does not elevate rigid rational consistency and systematic coherence as theological virtues."[59] Moreover, Moltmann states,

> [P]romise reaches out beyond what is existently real into the sphere of what is not yet real, the sphere of the possible, and in the word anticipates what is promised. In so doing it opens up what is existently real for the futurely possible, and frees it from what fetters it to the past: if things are fixed and finished (*rebus sic stantibus*) reality can be reduced to a concept, and defined; if they are in process (*rebus sic fluentibus*) they can be influenced only through anticipations of a possible future.[60]

---

56. "Future-promising history," (*ET*, 56 [German, 62]. Cf. also 126–28, wherein Moltmann relates these ideas to the "kingdom of God" and refers to this also as the "scarlet thread" of "biblical theology." See also Olson, *Journey of Modern Theology*, 459.

57. Deduction relies on rules of logic established in the *past*; induction relies on *past* observations.

58. *ET*, 102–6.

59. Olson, *Journey of Modern Theology*, 459.

60. *ET*, 102–3.

In short, if the so-far-agreed rules of our finite reason, or the dogmatic pronouncements of our theological past, were to hold ultimate sway in theology, Moltmann is unabashed about referring to such a condition as "petrification" and seeing it as opposed to the onward-coming (and still-being-revealed) nature of God's kingdom.[61] Conserving, fundamentalist, and legalistic forces always draw Moltmann's suspicion for this reason.[62]

Moltmann's consistent opposition to such "petrifying" forces also comes to the fore quite clearly whenever he detects them in currents of thought proceeding from Enlightenment anthropocentrism. In his analysis of such currents, Moltmann doggedly works to break down dualistic structures of thought which, in the wake of modernity, served to resolve history, humanity, and the divine into discrete, controlled dichotomies that are subject to analytic "objectivity" and allow for their definitions and speculative relations to be called upon in the construction of various self-referential systems of reason or doctrine. I will note briefly a few examples of Moltmann's reactions to such tendencies. In *Theology of Hope* he signals his opposition to Enlightenment and Neo-Protestant arrangements that oppose *history to theology* as such, advocating for a new understanding of history beyond the pale of an enclosed metaphysical system and more engaged with the true possibility of emergent novelty as a result of God's acts.[63] Later, he starkly confronts two dominant modernist polarities: the metaphysical opposition between *humanity and nature*[64] (critiquing this is at the root of Moltmann's

61. *ET,* 102–3. Similar themes were being enumerated as early as *TH,* 203. After his "pneumatological turn" (coinciding in significant ways with his cosmological turn in the mid-1980s), Moltmann also emphasizes the devaluing of diversity and plurality as a sign of such petrification: *SpL,* 184.

62. See, e.g., Moltmann, "Christian Theology and Its Problems Today," 1–2.

63. *TH,* esp. 174–80; Moltmann, "Theology as Eschatology," 2–3; Moltmann, "Gottesoffenbarung und Wahrheitsfrage," 149–72. Moltmann writes that Christian thinkers should allow the resurrection to be the determinative element in their understanding of history, and that they "[need] no longer regard the historical method and its view of history as being final and inescapable in its substantio-metaphysical form, and thus veer off into the subjective decision of faith, but that we seek new ways of further developing the historical methods themselves. . . . [We] must divest ourselves of all hard and fast presuppositions about the core or the substance of history and must regard these ideas themselves as provisional and alterable" (*TH,* 179). Such themes are resounded elsewhere, e.g., *JCTW,* 76–82.

64 "We shall only be able to reduce history to human and natural dimensions if [modernity's] anthropocentrism is replaced by a new cosmological theocentrism. The creatures of the natural world are not there for the sake of human beings. Human beings are there for the sake of the glory of God, which the whole community of creation extols"

turn to cosmology with the 1985 publication of *God in Creation*[65]), and the anthropological dualism between *mind and body*.[66] Finally, in his mature pneumatology especially, Moltmann advocates for a disintegration of the conceptual dualism between *spirit and matter*.[67] In the face of these problematic dichotomies, Moltmann praises the "new psychosomatic view of the human being, and the ecological viewpoint which stress the continuity between nature and civilization."[68]

With the Enlightenment's advent of Neo-Protestant Liberalism generally, and the many conservative reactions to it specifically, Christian theology gave up its roots in *history* (for that became the sphere of historical critics), *enacted and embodied human life* (which became the sphere of the social sciences), and the *natural world* (the sphere of the hard sciences).[69] Moltmann thoroughly rejects these ground-giving tendencies, seeking to reclaim much of the territory that doctrine has vacated over the past two centuries and abolish the dualistic thinking that has facilitated such an evacuation.[70] Alongside eschatology, the arenas of discourse in which Moltmann most readily combats these trends are in his pneumatology and Christology, and perhaps nowhere more fiercely than at their interface.[71] In fact, it can be said with little reserve that it is nearly impossible to understand Moltmann's opposition to things like divine impassibility and the immanent/ economic distinction in theology without reference to his anti-dualistic concerns: the former notion (impassibility) encourages a thoroughgoing

---

(*GC,* 139). Consider also his concern to not perpetuate a dualism between "nature and history," *CoG,* 136.

65. This turn had been anticipated by numerous developments in his thinking during the 1970s—see *ABP,* 211–12.

66. Chapter 10 in *GC* bears the title (quoting Friedrich Oetinger) "Embodiment is the end of all God's works." Throughout this chapter Moltmann continually returns to embodiment, that is, "human reality in the history and surrounding field of God's creation, reconciliation, and redemption" (244). Moltmann argues that all the works of God in the midst of his people are aimed at increasing (not decreasing) and reshaping (not removing) bodily, sensible, material reality (244–46).

67. See *SpL,* 226–29.

68. *EthH,* 61, see further 61–62.

69. Paul Janz refers to these developments as the "ungrounding" of Christian doctrine; see his "What Is 'Transformation Theology?'" 16–22.

70. See, e.g., Moltmann, "Theology as Eschatology," 5–6.

71. *WJC,* 73–78; also *SpL,* 65–73. Here it becomes evident why McGrath pinpoints Moltmann's Christology (alongside Jüngel's) as the "end of the Enlightenment" and its various christological impasses (*Making of Modern German Christology,* 202–11).

and radical dualism between the world and God, and the latter (immanent/ economic distinction) often foments a bitter polarity between faith and history.[72] Moltmann wants to see these surmounted—most especially due to the negative ramifications for the life of the church that arise out of such dichotomies[73]—and takes bold steps in his attempts to do so.

This thoroughly *holistic* orientation to history, nature, and human life itself naturally causes a pitched ethical focus to arise in Moltmann's work and, given his situation as a German theological voice after WWII, that ethical dimension consistently assumes political overtones.[74]

Moltmann's "Political Responsibility"

In light of his eschatological orientation, it is no surprise that Moltmann's work on political and ethical issues is consistently oriented toward the transformation of the *status quo*.[75] This is in fact how he understands *messianic* as the central category in Christian eschatology—*messianic* refers to that which disrupts the "power of history," which is Moltmann's oblique reference to the manner in which the ideology of the powerful conditions their view of the future as unchanging and fixed. Messianic realities, then, are the emergence of God's liberating "possibilities" in the midst of ideologically frozen power structures and visions of history.[76] Moreover, Moltmann believes that current ethical and political realities ought to inform theology and determine the way in which it engages the principal objects of its study.[77] The contemporary context must hold weight and have a say; the-

72. A very similar stance against dualism in Christology is prominent in the work of Colin Gunton. See, e.g., Gunton, *Yesterday and Today,* chapter 4.

73. See his denunciation of "false alternatives" in Christian thinking and acting: "Problems Today," 4–6.

74. Two of the most recent and important monographs on Moltmann's ethical contributions and political outlooks are, respectively, Harvie, *Moltmann's Ethics of Hope* (2009) and Wright, *Disavowing Constantine.*

75. Moltmann, "Christian Theology and Its Problems Today," 8.

76. *CoG*, 45–46; see also Müller-Fahrenholz, *Kingdom and the Power,* 167–68.

77. Clear examples abound: in *CG,* the Holocaust loomed large in Moltmann's theological psyche, as well as the response of protest atheism to theodical issues, see esp. xi–xii, 249–52, 273; *GC* emerged out of a sustained meditation on the reality of nuclear weapons and industrialism, see esp. 12–13, 136–37; owing in no small part to the contribution of his late wife to feminist theology, Moltmann has also been preoccupied with the theological rootings of patriarchalism and power politics, see *TK,* 162–66; *SpL,* 239–41; *ET,* 289–92.

ology must be a *correlational* enterprise.[78] In his Christology for instance, as I will show in subsequent chapters of this study, it is very clear that ecology, Judaism, and feminism (among other concerns) are given significant weight, which shapes both his theological attentiveness and his interaction with tradition. His correlative approach is unique in its coupling of both historical and political interest, again, growing out of his situation as a post-Auschwitz German.[79] He describes these inclinations by saying that his theology has its "face toward the world" [*Gesicht zur Welt*].[80]

Correlational models of theology always run the risk of compromise or assimilation;[81] the questions and themes encountered in prevailing cultural and academic environments can turn theology away from its fundamental rootedness in the history and accomplishment of Christ.[82] But Richard Bauckham rightly states that Moltmann does not often succumb to this possibility in his correlational movements:

> [For Moltmann] Christian theology does not become relevant by allowing itself to be determined by its contemporary context, but by being faithful to its own determining centre and criterion, which is the crucified Christ. . . . Moltmann's method . . . aims to find the contemporary relevance of the Christian faith in doing justice to the theological heart of the Christian faith.[83]

---

78. Olson explicitly compares Moltmann's correlational tendencies to Tillich's: *Journey of Modern Theology*, 459–60. Of course, Tillich's understanding of this was heavily determined by his brand of existentialism, which is not shared by Moltmann (see Loomer, "Paul Tillich's Theology," 150–56). Note Jeroncic's characterization of Moltmann as a "theologian of the moment" in "Peaceable Logic of Self-Integration," 46.

79. Well illustrated in the first two chapters of *GSS*.

80. *ET*, 115–16 (German, 110): "[The] programme of 'talk about God with a face turned to the world' and 'talk about God in our own time' became for us the painful task of talking about God with a face turned to the Jews and to Auschwitz" (115–16). Moltmann attributes this "directional thrust" to Johann Baptist Metz (*ABP*, 156).

81. Moltmann, "Christian Theology and Its Problems Today," 2–3.

82. Olson notes a version of this criticism as applied to Tillich: *Journey of Modern Theology*, 384.

83. Bauckham, *Messianic Theology*, 62. This is evident early in Moltmann's career: "The relationship is indeed a dialectical one: Christians exist, act, suffer, and speak in the present, with the open Bible in their hands, as it were. Whoever closes the Bible in order to speak more effectively and contemporaneously no longer has anything new to tell his age. Whoever breaks off the conversation with the present in order to read the Bible more effectively merely engages in sterile monologues" (Moltmann, "Towards the Next Step," 157).

Fundamentally, this aligns Moltmann with theological motifs that are both "act-oriented" and rooted in historic (or we might say "concrete") Christology. For Moltmann, *Christ, praxis, and changed existence in the world* are all interlocking strands of the ongoing pilgrimage of the church and form the true contours of engaged correlational theology:

> Every meditation on Christ is a submitting to this alteration [in one's own existence.] That is why *it is this first of all that permanently changes the practice of life in the world.* Meditation about the hard fact of Christian faith cannot become a flight from practice, nor can practice become a flight from this fact. In this way meditation and practice, *turning to Christ and turning to the world,* belong together, just as, in extreme cases, Christian mysticism and martyrdom do. We turn to the *meditatio crucis,* in order to experience the salvation of the broken world and to participate in it.[84]

This orientation in Moltmann's theological method can then be described along the lines of a *correlational praxiology*; he does not correlate theology with contemporary concerns for the sake of trendiness—he explicitly claims that Christian thought should produce "an anti-chameleon theology" that retains prophetic power by not blending into any given cultural milieu[85]—but for the sake of effecting transformative circumstances in the contemporary world,[86] such transformations being fundamentally originated in Christ and what he has done and continues to do. Thus, there is no disentangling concern for current life in the world, Christology, and eschatological transformation in Moltmann's thought.[87] It is in line with this ethos that he can say, adapting Trotsky, that theology is a "permanent reformation" that remains "breathless with suspense. . . . [A] story that is constantly making history, an event that cannot be concluded in this world, a process that will come to fulfillment and to rest only in the Parousia of

84. Moltmann, "Trinitarian History of God," 81–82. Non-Latin italics are mine.

85. Moltmann, "Christian Theology and Its Problems Today," 3.

86. Moltmann states, "I am not so concerned with correct doctrine as I am with concrete doctrine; and thus not concerned with pure theory but with practical theory," ("An Autobiographical Note," 204, quoted in Grenz, *Rediscovering,* 74).

87. Bauckham highlights that "the strength and appropriateness of these [methodological] structures lie in their biblical basis, their christological centre, and their eschatological openness. They give Moltmann's theology a relevance to the modern world that is achieved not only without surrendering the central features of biblical and historic Christian faith, but much more positively by probing the theological meaning of these in relation to contemporary realities and concerns" (*Theology,* 26).

Christ."[88] Moltmann makes this point ecclesially significant whenever possible; theology serves the church insofar as it provides direction and insight for genuine Christian acting in the world: "[Christians should] become men and women who can think independently and act in a Christian way in their own vocations in the world."[89]

What then of tradition? Consistently this question emerges in the secondary literature, with many thinkers taking exception to Moltmann's alleged lack of focus on traditional theological schemas or creedal affirmations. There are at least two key points to highlight here. First, Moltmann prioritizes his theology of the cross and makes it a determinative criterion for theological expression. (He adopts the axiom *theologica crucis dicit quod res est*—the theology of the cross says what is truly the case.[90]) He treats *theologia crucis* in opposition to *theologia gloriae* and, in so doing he perceives a God who, in the freedom of his own love, sovereignly chooses to enter into the suffering of the cross on behalf of humanity—this means that God suffers in solidarity with the oppressed and is not defined in abstract categories of power, control, or passionlessness, but is rather known in terms of sacrificial, transformational, and other-seeking love.[91] This pronounced critique of certain facets of "classical theism"[92] means that, respecting tradition, Moltmann is highly critical of forms of theology that have aligned with God's immutability and sovereign power and from these attributes derived corollary justifications of oppressive political/social realities, or fostered inhuman conditions under the auspices of divine imperturbability.[93] This gives Moltmann's theology of the cross a critical edge with which he confronts several foregoing developments in Christian

88. Moltmann, "*Theologia Reformata et Semper Reformanda*," 121.

89. Moltmann, "Christian Theology and Its Problems Today," 11.

90. *ET*, 83; *CG*, 213.

91. This will be a theme to which I return many times, as it is key to deciphering Moltmann's view of christological kenosis. The most important and fullest expressions of this outlook on divine suffering are in *CG*, chapter 6, and *TK*, chapter 2. See also *JCTW*, chapter 2, and Moltmann's essay "The Crucified God and Apathetic Man."

92. This term was of course popularized by Charles Harteshorne (*Omnipotence*, xi, 1, 6)—Moltmann does not apply it himself (and he certainly disagrees with process thought on several fronts), but he does use other, similarly-intended terms, e.g., "the god of Parmenides" (*TH*, 84), the "apathetic god" (*TK*, 25, 218; Moltmann, "Theology of the Cross Today," 68).

93. *CG*, 321–29. In *TK*, the range of this political critique will take on trinitarian dimensions, with any lack of emphasis on God's sociality seen to justify what Moltmann calls "political and clerical monotheism" (192–202).

thought.[94] Proceeding in tandem with this line of critique, Moltmann is also quite harsh with any form of the church that inhabits a realized chiliasm, merges political aspirations with religious triumphalism,[95] or neglects communal ecclesiology in favor of hierarchical authoritarianism.[96]

Second, and directly related to Moltmann's promissory-messianic hermeneutic, no systematization in the past can ever be seen as definitive in light of the eschatological future. Whereas this focus, as we have seen, allows Moltmann to resist and combat detrimental strains of Enlightenment-birthed ideology, it also provides yet another critical edge that he applies to past formulations of Christian thought. In his early work, Moltmann referred to this as an "eschatologizing approach to tradition [*Eschatologisierung des Traditiondenkens*]."[97] However, it has been noted by Clutterbuck that "Moltmann's own practice as a theologian shows that it is not possible to be as radically independent of tradition as he suggests."[98] Clutterbuck is right about this, as any perusal of Moltmann's major works will demonstrate. Almost all of his formulations, even those that are stated in the most striking terms, arise out of some engagement (often constructive) with theological tradition. Graham Buxton has commented lucidly on this score, stating that "[Moltmann] is acutely aware that he offers suggestions—not dogma—within the *communio sanctorum*."[99]

On my reading, then, the motif of *conversation* is the most productive way of viewing Moltmann's interactions with past theology. This is, in fact, the motif that he himself regularly employed once he had progressed through the more radical phase that produced *Theology of Hope* and *The Crucified God*:

> My intention was not a new system and not a dogmatics of my own or another theological textbook; I wanted to make my

94. Moltmann's exposure to the Frankfurt School further fortifies this aspect of his methodology. See *CG*, 221–27; Bauckham, *Messianic Theology*, 66–67. Jon Sobrino, in his analysis and appropriation of Moltmann's Christology and staurology, also makes these connections (*Christ the Liberator*, 265–69) but does not notice that these elements were already emerging in nascent form in *Theology of Hope* (e.g., 28–33).

95. The most resonant, and historically wide-ranging, discussion of these tendencies appears in *CoG*, chapter 3, esp. 131–84.

96. This latter point Moltmann perceives as deriving from an insufficient view of God's triunity, *CG*, 183; *TK*, chapters 5 and 6; *CPS*, chapter 6.

97. *TH*, 298 (German: 274).

98. Clutterbuck, "Jürgen Moltmann," 496. See further, 495–96.

99. Buxton, "Moltmann on Creation," 49. See *CoG*, xiv.

"contributions" to the ongoing dialogue of theology over the centuries and continents. My contributions to theology presuppose an intensive *conversation* between theologians past and present, and take part in this conversation with proposals of my own. Human theology is theology on the road and theology in time.[100]

This conversational posture is animated by Moltmann's constructive-yet-critical stance toward a myriad of thinkers throughout the course of his major works.[101] Examples are numerous, but to take one: in an article on the proper trajectory of Christian hope, Moltmann refers to both Joachim of Fiore and Thomas Aquinas as his "theological contemporaries in the only church,"[102] and then participates in theological dialogue with each of them as though they were living peers. It is thus appropriate to refer to Moltmann as a "critical ecumenist"—engaging in ongoing discussion with historical developments in theology as well as seeking to work through critical present-day divisions and controversies in theology. His dialogical approach to tradition lends his discussions a vitality that can, admittedly, sometimes be clouded by the dismissive handling of some important past theological formulation or nuance.[103] So, as he is critical with tradition, so Moltmann's own method invites critical reading.[104]

100. *ABP*, 286. His first major employment of this "conversation" motif appears in *TK*, xii–xvi; see also *GC*, xv–xvi.

101. E.g., with Luther in *CG*, 207–14, 222–35; Augustine and Gregory of Nazianus in *GC*, 234–40; Schleiermacher in *SpL*, 221–26; Barth in *HTG*, 125–40; Calvin, A. A. Van Ruler, and Dorothee Sölle in *CG*, 256–67; Moltmann, "Theology as Eschatology," 26–27. We can also note the ecumenical interactions with present-day theology (e.g., with representatives of the Eastern Orthodox Church on the Trinity: *TK*, 178–85; *ABP*, 85–87, 291–93; with liberation theologians concerning social justice and solidarity, *ET*, 217–48). See also the conversation concerning political and ecumenical dialogue in *HTG*, 176–80.

102. Moltmann, "Christian Hope," 92.

103. Though somewhat critical of Moltmann's handling of traditional doctrine, Clutterbuck eventually states, "By insisting that 'Athanasius, Augustine, Luther, and Schleiermacher' become our conversation partners, Moltmann is at least implying that successive expressions of Christianity are not incommensurate with each other and that, because they point towards a common future, signs of continuity should be expected and looked for" (Clubberbuck, "Jürgen Moltmann," 499, 502).

104. When writing forewords for new works on his theology, Moltmann often praises other thinkers when they "take him to task" or critically engage with his thought; in this sense, not only does he engage in a critical conversation with other theology in his own work, but in fact welcomes it from other thinkers; see Moltmann, "Foreword," in McDougall, *Pilgrimmage of Love*, xi–xiv; Moltmann, "Foreword," in Harvie, *Jürgen Moltmann's Ethics of Hope*, ix–x.

Moltmann's "Constant Wonder"

Finally, and briefly, I note that though the charge of "undisciplined specula-tion" has sometimes been leveled at Moltmann's theology,[105] there are two significant ways in which this charge is deflected with relative consistency throughout his work.[106] The first has already been mentioned, but it bears repeating: Moltmann is imminently concerned with *practicality*, in the sense that his theology is a theology turned toward the world and the circum-stances of the church within it. Stephen Williams has noted that, at its core, "Moltmann's thought is anything but abstract in its intention."[107] In assessing his own theological legacy, Moltmann confesses his past concern that the simple act of writing a book on trinitarian theology (referring to *The Trin-ity and the Kingdom*) would cause people to think he had "[acquired] the odour of abstract and unpractical theological speculation." However, to his satisfaction, "the opposite proved to be the case" as his trinitarian outlook was both investigated in the biblical history and found relevant in a variety of contemporary ecclesiological contexts.[108] As both Michael Cook and Simon Cowdell have observed: "Moltmann's Trinity concerns the cross and is not about 'thinking'; it is not a matter of speculative metaphysics."[109]

Alongside his practicality, which concerns the concrete nature of many of Moltmann's theological proposals and reflections, we need to note his emphasis on doxology, which often concerns the areas of his thought that do verge closely to speculation. Again, we look to his social, eschato-logical understanding of the Trinity. Rather than seeking to thematize God within any self-enclosed systematization, Moltmann comments,

> In ordering these doctrinal tenets in theology, it is not a question
> of one schematic arrangement over another. The doctrine of the
> Trinity has *a doxological form*, since it expresses the experience

---

105. Bauckham mentions the recurrence of this charge: *Theology,* 25.

106. This is not to say that the charge is completely without merit. However, Stephen Williams, who is an appreciative-yet-critical interpreter of Moltmann, has consistently emphasized areas that are often touted as speculative in Moltmann but which are, under close examination, grounded in either the historical revelation of God or the present realities of his church. See Williams, "Jürgen Moltmann," 79–124, esp. 95, 97, 116.

107. Williams, "Jürgen Moltmann," 77. Of course, Williams believes that Moltmann sometimes espouses perspectives that cannot be fully demonstrated by the events re-corded in the Bible. See, e.g., his points about Moltmann's understanding of God's rela-tionship to history, 110–11.

108. *ABP,* 231.

109. Cowdell, *Is Jesus Unique?*, 35—drawing on Cook, *The Jesus of Faith,* 181.

of God in the apprehension of Christ and in the fellowship of the Spirit. This means that in this doctrine no definitions are permissible which simply pin something down as a way of "mastering" it. [*keine Definitionen zulässig die etwas feststellen, um es beherrschen zu wollen*]. . . . "Concepts create idols. Only wonder understands," said Gregory of Nyssa. And this wonder over God respects God's unfathomable mystery, however great the delight in knowing.[110]

The doxological backdrop to Moltmann's theology hints at the genuinely blurry boundary between "speculation" and "theological wonder," or what Moltmann calls in one place "theo-fantasy."[111] The texts and traditions and liturgies of the Christian tradition drive the theologian's mind to pursue more deeply the ways and acts of God.[112] It is in this context that Moltmann, when verging on speculation, can claim that theology-as-worship might go beyond the explicit testimony of the scriptures or the concrete experiences of the church today, though without ceasing to be fundamentally *rooted* in these things.

Having traversed a detailed, though cursory, survey of Moltmann's methodological tendencies, I can now summarize them as well as note their significance for studying his Christology:

Promissory-Messianic Hermeneutic—This is the real source of most perceived "dialectic" in Moltmann, and any christological construct should be passed through this hermeneutic in *both directions* (from the past as promise, from the future as messianic) in order to fully understand its implications.

Anti-dualism—The dichotomizing schemes of many Enlightenment philosophies are starkly opposed by Moltmann; in christological interpretation it will force Moltmann to consider Christology within new fields of thought and fresh affinities (ecology, relational and developmental psychology, psychosomatic anthropology, etc.).

Correlational Praxiology—In an attempt to echo Bonhoeffer's pressing query: "Who is Jesus Christ for us *today*?" Moltmann has said that to turn toward the world cannot be separated from turning toward Christ and considering, once again and always, his significance for the church and the cosmos.

---

110. *SpL*, 73 (German: 86); also *SpL*, 301–6; *ET*, 26; *TK*, 152–53.

111. *ET*, 25.

112. This is perhaps nowhere more clearly perceived, or experienced, in examining the doctrine of the Trinity in general in the life of the church, which has given rise to the greatest heights of doxological insight as well as speculative abandon. See *TK*, 151–54.

Critical and Conversational Ecumenicism—All areas of theological inquiry are shaped by those who have spoken in the past. Moltmann's Christology seeks, fundamentally, to dialogue with creed and canon and theologians of historical import, but also to correlate christological insights with the questions of the present day.

Doxological Tendency—Again, the line can be blurry between doxology and speculation, but one wonders if this is avoidable. Regardless, in his more abstract formulations, it will be worth noting what is most key for Moltmann's point, and to see if it cannot be articulated in a more grounded, less speculative tenor. Furthermore, we should note that Moltmann has never been afraid of overemphasis in the interest of making a point in a given context (especially in his early work),[113] and he appreciates the *evocative and poetic capacities of theology* in a way that few other theologians of his standing do.[114] Thus, in thinking through his christological doctrine as we proceed through our next chapter, "doctrine" might be better replaced by "portrait" or "tapestry"—a series of brushstrokes or threads, all contributing to the whole, but needing to be "stood back from" if they are going to be adequately taken in.

Conclusion: Christological Preliminaries

This discussion has served a straightforward initial goal for my upcoming examination of Moltmannian Christology. Moltmann's theological methodology has been presented and will be referred to often as I set about the

---

113. On overemphasis as a deliberate aspect of his theologizing: *TH*, 11–12; "My Theological Career," 173–74. Even balanced commentators can find such overstatements to be a serious methodological liability at times; e.g., Neal, *Theology as Hope*, 55n79. Some commentators, however, run to this well too often rather than engaging with the clear and dominant lines of Moltmann's thematic progressions—e.g., Antony Clarke's persistent references to Moltmann's "imprecison" and "inconsistency" (*Cry in the Darkness*, 69, 70, 72, 78–79, 89).

114. On the value of the poetic and even pictorial articulation and representation of ideas, see Moltmann, *Experiences in Theology*, 162(n137); Moltmann, "Foreword," in McDougall, *Pilgrimage of Love*, xiii–xiv. There is a further unmined topic in Moltmann studies relating to the importance of art and iconography for this theological method, e.g., Andrei Rublev's classic picture of the Trinity (*TK*, xvi; *ET*, 305); medieval "mercy seat" images of the Trinity at the cross (*ABP*, 195; *ET*, 305); Joachim of Fiore's specifically pictorial representation of the three interlocking rings of trinitarian history (see Moltmann, "Christian Hope," 102–6; *CoG*, 143–44; *SpL*, 297–98 and the references there). Further references to significant artwork that motivated and inspired Moltmann can be found in *ABP*, 191; *CG*, 6.

task of unfolding the diverse aspects of his christological program. The next chapter will focus on the thematic range of Moltmann's Christology, detailing the various lines of thinking about Christ that he uniquely interrogates and synthesizes throughout his major works.

2

Themes in Moltmann's Christology

THIS CHAPTER CONTINUES OUR exploration of Moltmannian Christology by engaging in what I will call a *thematic analysis*, which aims at delineating the themes that animate the Christology's pluriform expression throughout Moltmann's career. I will demonstrate through synchronic expositions how these different dimensions of the Christology all play a pivotal role in Moltmann's fully mature, integrated thinking about Christ.

In doing so, I will be making use of some thematic categorical designations that are helpful in organizing Moltmann's christological thought. Only a few of these designations are explicitly used by Moltmann himself (e.g., "messianic Christology" and "pneumatological Christology"); others are my own heuristic invention for the purpose of organizing and drawing together key themes (e.g., "promise Christology," "firstborn Christology"). As discussed in chapter 1, Moltmann resists hard-and-fast categorical breakdowns of his theology. Regardless, this strategic survey of his thought, as it emerges from a critical reading of his major works, is important for determining the contours of his Christology and, crucially, sets the stage for the important role of kenosis.

Moltmann's Messianic/Promise Christology[1]

Messianic Christology as a category is quite at home with Moltmann; after all, his own title for his six-volume "contributions" to theology is "messianic theology,"[2] and the subtitle for his largest work on Christology is "Christology in Messianic Dimensions." But what precisely does Moltmann mean by

---

1. "The doctrine of the Christ is the doctrine of the anointed Messiah. . . . Christology is nothing other than messiology," (Moltmann, *On Human Dignity*, 100).

2. *GC*, xvii; *WJC*, xiii.

this? On the simplest level, the category arises from Moltmann's *promissory* outlook on revelation, hence the additional term for this facet of his Christology: promise. Like "hope," "promise" is a simple term of deep salience for comprehending Moltmann's thought. God's revelation, knowledge of God, indeed, even God's very divinity, are understood within the framework of *promises that break into the present and contradict it (or renovate it) in light of a future or eschatological reality.*[3] God's making of promises that contradict the transience and death of the present world, and God's faithfulness and wisdom in bringing those promises to fruition, provide the principal providential framework that bookends Moltmann's conception of theology and history, and they serve this role from the earliest stage of his thought.

This logic of promise has significant implications for Moltmann's Christology. Promises naturally contain a twofold sense: the past (in which the promise is made, requiring trust in the promise-maker) and the future (in which the promise is fulfilled, vindicating the character and capability of the promise-maker). Moltmann emphasizes that, as messiah, Jesus possesses *both* dimensions in distinct array: he is the fulfillment of many messianic promises (and he is thus the future of those past promises) and he is himself an eschatological promise for the oncoming future of redemption (thus standing, for us, in past history as that which promises a future reality). This important interplay constitutes the greater part of "the dialectic of Christology and eschatology" in Moltmann's thought.[4]

Promised Messiah

"Are you the one who is to come?"[5] This question reverberates powerfully within Moltmann's Christology; he deems it the "earliest question about Christ."[6] Moltmann clearly perceives in Jesus of Nazareth the forceful emergence of a reality that comes up against the expectations of the Old Testament:

> In terms of open questions of the Old Testament and the apocalyptic promises, and the existential experience of Israel in exile and alienation, Jesus is revealed as the one who fulfills these

---

3. E.g., God's revelation: *TH,* 42–45; knowledge of God: *GC,* 60–65; God's divinity: *TH,* 143.

4. E.g., Moltmann, "Trinitarian History," 86–88.

5. Matt 11:3 and pars.

6. See *CG,* 98, 99; *WJC,* 28; *JCTW,* 119.

promises. . . . If we start from this point, it is no longer a matter of indifference or chance that Jesus was a Jew, appeared in Israel, came into conflict with the guardians of his people's law, and was condemned and handed over to the Romans to be crucified.[7]

And such expectations are not general, but grounded in the distinctly messianic range of Israel's prophets:

Isaiah 61.1ff. puts [the] gospel into the mouth of the end-time messianic prophet, who is filled with the Spirit of the Lord and brings about salvation through his word. In relation to God, [the promised messiah] proclaims the direct lordship of Yahweh without limits and without end, and in relation to human beings, justice, community and liberty. His message is addressed to the poor, the wretched, the sick and the hopeless, because these are the people who suffer most from God's remoteness and human hostility.[8]

It is thus of paramount importance that Jesus was a Jew, and that he manifested particular realities that were promised by Yahweh, the God of Abraham, Isaac, and Jacob, the God of the Jews in the Old Testament. Jesus' specifically situated humanity is not a result of historical happenstance; it has abiding significance for all christological thinking, for it indicates that whoever Christ is, he stands in the auguring light thrown by the Old Testament, taking its "law and promise" as both his "presupposition [*Voraussetzung*]" and his "conflict [*Konflikt*]."[9] It is at the intersection of the promises and the law that we see Jesus' distinct teaching and vision for the kingdom emerge, as well as his unique vision for his own person as the inaugurator of the kingdom. As Moltmann puts it, "On the basis of the identification of his message with his person Jesus can be called 'the incarnation of the promise of the kingdom.'"[10]

In Jesus' response to the question (posed by the followers of John the Baptist) about whether or not he was the one to fulfill the promises of old, Matt 11:4–6 indicates that the "events which took place around Jesus and his word speak on his behalf, for they are signs of the messianic age."[11]

7. *CG*, 141. See also *JCTW*, 119.

8. *WJC*, 96.

9. *TH*, 141–42 (German: 127). By this, Moltmann foreshadows his more cogent explication later in his work; Jesus simultaneously fulfills those promises of Israel and confounds their expectations in relation to those promises as the suffering, dying messiah.

10. *CPS*, 82. Moltmann here cites Käsemann, "On the Subject," 122.

11. *CG*, 98.

Moltmann does not stress that Jesus was the fulfillment of OT prophecies (nor does he deny it) but rather that Jesus consciously brought into effect messianic realities: "I am assuming that Jesus understood himself and his message in the expectation categories of this messianic hope, and that his followers saw him in these categories too, so that Jesus is linked with the messianic hope in a primal and indissoluble sense [*ursprüngliche und unablösbare Weise*]."[12]

For Moltmann, the messianic "secret" of Jesus emerges in the face of two questions. The first we have already noted: "Are you he who is to come?" The second comes from Jesus himself, to his disciples: "Who do you say that I am?" (Mark 8:29 and parallels). To both questions, Moltmann avers, Jesus either answers to the messianic role "indirectly" or without "affirming or denying."[13] Though Jesus stands in the light of the OT, he also will cast light of his own, for this is not simply a new-but-predictable reality—it is something unexpected. The disciples and those surrounding Jesus wanted to identify him analogically with something known and foretold, but Jesus instead gives

> himself and the disciples an answer of his own: *the announcement of his suffering* [Mark 8.31ff.]. . . . Whether [the peoples'] yardstick is Elijah or John the Baptist, the figure of the messiah or the Son of man, ideas of this kind, if they lead to preconceived judgments about what is to come, make the experience of what is new impossible or contradictory. Jesus does not reject the titles. He suspends them, and takes the path of suffering that leads to the cross.[14]

Thus, in his clear role of fulfilling the promises of the Old Testament faith, Jesus also introduces a staggering new reality: the reality of the messiah's cross. In this sense, Jesus both fulfills and redefines "messiah"—this is a key point for Moltmann, because it intrinsically binds together one of

---

12. *JCTW*, 110–11 (German: 97); further, *WJC*, 137. The evaluation of Jesus' self-consciousness that sees him deliberately acting in a messianic fashion has appeared in scholarship since the original "quest for the historical Jesus" but has received some of its most forceful recent articulation in the work of N. T. Wright; see *Jesus and the Victory*, Parts I & II.

13. *CG*, 98; *WJC*, 138.

14. *WJC*, 138, emphasis added. Further: "Jesus' true 'messianic secret' is therefore *the secret of his suffering*. He did not 'claim' the messiahship; he suffered it" (139, emphasis original).

his most directive christological categories, the *messianic*, with the pivotal Christic praxis of self-sacrificial *suffering*.[15]

Messiah's Promise

Not only does Jesus bring promise to pass in himself, but *he is also himself a promise of what is to come*. As fulfillment of past promises, he is an inaugurating fulfillment that promises still something more:

> If the Christ event contains the validation of the promise, then this means no less than that through the faithfulness and truth of God the promise is made true in Christ—and made true wholly, unbreakably, for ever and for all. . . . "All the promises of God in him are yea, and in him Amen" (II Cor. 1.20). . . . On the other hand, the gospel itself becomes unintelligible if the contours of the promise are not recognized in itself. It would lose its power to give eschatological direction . . . if it were not made clear that the gospel constitutes on earth and in time the promise of the future of Christ.[16]

The emergence of the "new promise" of Christ's gospel is made manifest in the resurrection, and thus the two promises (the promised messiah and messiah's promise) must be seen dialectically, or, in the spirit of some of Moltmann's later work, *perichoretically*—past and future, promise and what-is-to-come, cross and resurrection, all mutually interpreting and informing the other as interrelated moments.[17]

But what is the *content* of this promise made in Christ and brought through Christ? "Christ's resurrection has an added value and surplus of promise [*Mehrwert und einen Verheißungsüberschuß*] over Christ's death. . . . It promises a 'new creation' which is more than 'the first creation'

---

15. In *SpL* Moltmann states that Jesus offers "a new definition to the notion of the messiah. This idea is now newly defined through Jesus' own experiences. . . . The *fact* of Jesus' messiahship was derived from his endowment with the Spirit in baptism; but now its *content* is defined through the vista that stretches forward towards his death. What is known as 'the messianic secret' is unveiled in Jesus' sufferings and his dying" (63).

16. *TH*, 147–48.

17. See Moltmann, "Theology as Eschatology," 25–27. Again, as discussed above, it should be emphasized that Moltmann does not do away with the harshness of dialectic, but that the dialectic is always between the brokenness of the current state of affairs and God's redeeming *eschaton*. As far as other realities are concerned, Moltmann is often concerned to demonstrate a dualism-dissolving coinherence and mutual formation, not a paradoxical, eschatologically resolved dialectic.

(Rev 21:4: 'For the first . . . has passed away')."[18] The resurrection presents a new hope in the midst of the world, and it confirms Jesus as not only a promised person, but as a person who brings another promise, the promised (and renewing) end of the old world order.[19] He is both the messiah of past prophecy and of eschatology: "[The] gospel is not a utopian description of some far-off future. It is the daybreak of this future in the pardoning, promising word that sets people free."[20]

Moltmann's Solidarity/Firstborn Christology[21]

Moltmann's overall theology hinges on the "crucified God." The cross stands as the revelatory linchpin around which all else revolves.[22] (More precisely: the cross shows that God is *open to suffering, historically involved, and relational*,[23] and this doctrinal step undergirds the later-expanding orbit of Moltmann's theology; the cross is clearly primary when it comes to his controlling theological hermeneutic.) If viewed from the hill of Golgotha, Moltmann claims to perceive that "a mild Docetism runs through the Christology of the ancient church."[24] This latent docetism, in Moltmann's view, can be primarily perceived in the early church's unwillingness to attribute any measure of suffering to God, due to an allegiance to the Platonic *apatheia* axiom.[25] The logic of the ancient church was (ac-

18. *WJC,* 186 (German: 208); see further, 215, 223; *TH,* 202–15; *ET,* 100: "The promised life becomes lived promise and living hope, and the life lived in hope becomes the *real promise* of its own fulfillment in 'the life of the world to come.'"

19. Moltmann also lends this a trinitarian dimension, speaking of the Holy Spirit's procession also as a promise of the new creation, see *TH,* 212; *SpL,* 7, 155, 280—but Moltmann makes it clear that the Paraclete itself was *promised* by Jesus (158, 232).

20. *WJC,* 96; "The gospel is remembered promise" (*SpL,* 232).

21. "Jesus' cross requires Christology . . . but it is also the mystery behind all Christologies, for it calls them into question and places them in constant need of revision" (*CG,* 86).

22. Alan Lewis artfully refers to Moltmann as a "Holy Saturday theologian," due to the fact that he is unafraid of testing Christian convictions "against the reality of suffering, death, and doubt" (*Between Cross and Resurrection,* 215).

23. "We are bound to talk about God's vulnerability, suffering, and pain, in view of Christ's passion, his death on the cross and his descent into hell. God experiences suffering, death and hell. This is the way he experiences history" (*CPS,* 64).

24. *CG,* 89, see also 227–28. Latent docetism in Christology is a theme to which Moltmann returns: "Theology of the Cross Today," 75n47; *SpL,* 250.

25. This is the initial point-of-departure for Moltmann's "revolution in the concept of

cording to Moltmann): God cannot suffer; humanity can suffer; ergo the humanity of Christ diminishes in emphasis, to safeguard his deity from any hint of suffering. But, Moltmann counters, if the cross is not to be "evacuated of deity,"[26] then worldly suffering must have *some genuine effect* on God, and therefore God must truly be able to experience some measure—or some dimension—of suffering.[27]

Christ Crucified

So, Moltmann argues, famously, that the divine Son genuinely experienced suffering at the cross, and that this suffering affected the Trinity itself. The Son suffered the death of the person of Jesus on the cross; the Father suffered on account of the suffering of the Son; the Holy Spirit served as the bond of suffering, co-willing love that held them in unity even in the midst of their most profound separation, the separation of the cross.[28] "God himself is involved in the history of Christ's passion"[29] becomes the staurological truism for Moltmann. Instead of seeing on the cross a disunity between the divine and human aspects of Christ, he powerfully declares a unity of divinity with the hellish realities of pain, abandonment, and loss. Just as the identity questions are key for the messianic and promissory aspects of Moltmann's Christology, here it is the experiences of Gethsemane and Golgotha—and Christ's own words in the midst of those human experiences—which form, quite literally, the crux of Christology's *agon*:

> [In Gethsemane] comes the prayer that in its original version sounds like a demand: "Father, all things are possible to thee; remove this cup from me" (Mark 14.36). . . . Is the prayer for deliverance from death? I think it is fear of separation from the Father, horror in the face of "the death of God." . . . This *unanswered prayer*

God" (see *CG*, 187–207), and it is well-illustrated across the following protracted discussions: *CG*, 267–74; Moltmann, "Theology of the Cross Today," 67–71; *TK*, Ch. 2.

26. *CG*, 214.

27. "'*What does the cross of Jesus mean for God himself?*' . . . A serious fault of earlier Protestant theology was that it did not look at the cross in the context of the relationship of the Son to the Father, but related it directly to mankind as an expiatory death for sin" (*CG*, 201).

28. *WJC*, 172–75; *CG*, 240–47; *TK*, 80–83.

29. *TK*, 21.

is the beginning of Jesus' real passion—his agony at his forsakenness by the Father.[30]

> "My God, why has thou forsaken me?" (Mark 15.34). He hung
> nailed to the cross for three hours, evidently in an agony which
> reduced him to silence, waiting for death. Then he died with a loud
> cry which is an expression of the most profound rejection [*tiefste
> Verworfenheit*] by the God whom he called "Abba," whose mes-
> sianic kingdom had been his whole passion, and whose Son he
> knew himself to be.[31]

Thus, the sufferings of Christ, from the garden to the grave, must be seen
(in Moltmann's view) as "the history of the passion which takes place between the Father and the Son."[32]

This aspect of his Christology occasioned a famous critique by Dorothee Sölle. In short, Sölle's reading of *The Crucified God* led her to see a
sadistic movement of the Father against the Son on the cross—a sort of
"divine child abuse." Moltmann's response to this (oft-recurring) critique
has always been to repeat, rather than correct, what he argued in *The Crucified God*: Jesus willingly accepted the cup of suffering ("Not my will, but
thy will be done") and, given his own predictions of his suffering and his
commitment to the Father's will, was not coerced in any way to the cross.
And the Father is not remote from Christ's passion, but out of love for the
Son the Father suffers also as the Son dies.[33] Such trinitarian co-suffering,
says Moltmann, is hardly the locus of sadism.[34] This sort of "trinitarian
theology of the cross" is what forms the connection between Moltmann's

30. *TK*, 76. The language here is just as strong as Luther's own, see *TK*, 77. Also see
Luther, "Meditation on Christ's Passion," 126–31.

31. *TK*, 78 (German: 93).

32. *TK*, 76. There are times when Moltmann seems to imply that the Trinity is constituted in history via the cross (see *CG*, 239–47). This led to substantial criticism, as it
definitively imperiled numerous facets of creedal orthodoxy and smacked heavily of a
staurological Hegelianism—Bauckham's early work on Moltmann highlights these issues
well: see *Messianic Theology in the Making*, 106–10. With his later addition of a robust
social doctrine of the Trinity, however, Moltmann is able to treat the cross as the key
revelatory event of the trinitarian relationships and the trinitarian shape of history, rather
than the constituting origin of the Trinity (see *TK*, 62–83; Chapter XII in *SpL*).

33. *CG*, 241–46.

34. Moltmann on Sölle's criticism: *ABP*, 198–200; *WJC*, 175–77. Feske has reiterated
a more modern version of this criticism, see "Christ and Suffering." However, even some
sympathetic Moltmann interpreters will get uneasy at this point and reiterate some form
of the criticism; see Fiddes, *Participating*, 238.

assault on impassibility and his promulgation of a social trinitarian framework.[35] In Ryan Neal's words: "For Moltmann, the historical activity of God in the life of Jesus governs one's view of the Trinity. . . . Thus, a proper theology of the cross, removed of the philosophical presupposition of impassibility, avoids merely allowing divine passibility: it elevates it to a constitutive element of God's experience."[36]

This facet of Moltmann's Christology—its original offense, one could say—has caused no end of consternation and no end of inspiration.[37] The crucified Christ, apart from any predetermining metaphysical axioms, allows Moltmann to explore fresh horizons. In connection with our previously examined dimension of the Christology, it is this cross—this "revolution in the concept of God"[38]—that not only counters the Aristotelian deity of apathetic detachment, but also the zealous, militaristic messianic outlook of first-century Jewish hope. The promised messiah brings a twist to the picture—he is the suffering (genuinely suffering, in robust trinitarian terms) Son of God.[39]

What are the consequences of the cross's revelation of such a passionate God? What does this suffering *mean*? This is the key question of Christ's *Leidenschaft*—"Why was it necessary for the Christ to suffer these things?" (Luke 24:26),[40] or as Moltmann has alternatively phrased it, "What can knowledge of the 'crucified God' mean for helpless and suffering men?"[41]

---

35. See the connections initiating in *CG*, 235–49, then fully articulated in *TK*, 61–90.

36. Neal, "Jürgen Moltmann," 375.

37. For consternation: Blocher, *Evil and the Cross*, 72–76, 81–82—Blocher focuses acutely on the alleged Hegelian tendencies in *Crucified God*, though he aligns Moltmann and Hegel more closely than the evidence allows—see the lucid and rigorous discussion in Siu-Kwong Tang's published disseration, *God's History*, chapter 4. For those inspired by this dimension of Moltmann's thought, we can note especially the work of Sobrino, *Christology at the Crossroads*, 28–33, 179–235.

38. "This is where the revolution in the concept of God is to be found which makes faith in the crucified God necessary. For here a God did not merely act outwards, out of his untouchable glory and his supreme sovereignty. Here the Father acted on himself, i.e., on the self of his love, his Son; and therefore the Son suffered from himself, the self of his love, his Father. . . . [This] overcomes[s] the apathetic God who cannot be touched or troubled either by the human history of suffering or by the passion of Christ" (Moltmann, "Theology of the Cross Today," 67).

39. *WJC*, 153, 178–79; Moltmann, "Trinitarian History," 93–94; *SpL*, 299; *TK*, 22–23.

40. *CG*, 181; Moltmann, "Justification and New Creation," 158; *WJC*, 171.

41. *CG*, 252.

The next theme of his Christology is specifically focused on an answer to this question.

Christ in Solidarity: The Suffering Brother

To what nadir does the humiliation of the Son of God plummet? For Moltmann, it is only by internalizing the particular, real, and deeply human face of Christ that we understand the true horror and beauty of the cross: Christ *with us*, a co-experiencer of life's tragedies, even to the point of *knowing what it feels like to be apart from God* in the despair of death. This is an idea drawn not only from that enduring statement of Bonhoeffer's—"Only the suffering God can help"[42]—but also from Moltmann's own experiences as a guilt-ridden prisoner of war:

> I read Mark's Gospel as a whole and came to the story of the passion; when I heard Jesus' death cry, "My God, why have you forsaken me?" I felt growing within me the conviction: this is someone who understands you completely, who is with you in your cry to God and has felt the same forsakenness you are living in now. I began to understand the assailed, forsaken Christ because I knew that he understood me. The divine brother in need [*der göttliche Bruder in der Not*], the companion on the way, who goes with you through this "valley of the shadow of death," the fellow-sufferer [*der Leidensgenosse*] who carries you, with your suffering.[43]

In his earthly life, but especially on the cross, Christ is intensely identified with the lowly. For Moltmann, this is identification *pro nobis* and *per se*; Christ experiences the feelings and pain that belong to the poor, the sick, the abandoned, and the despised of society. God himself comes close; he does not remain "mysterious, incomprehensible"; he is revealed as "the human God, who cries with him and intercedes for him with his cross where man in his torment is dumb."[44] Here Moltmann broaches no theodicy—he dares not; the atheism of protest weighs too heavily on his mind and theology.[45] Instead he speaks of Christ's identification in our pain, his understanding

42. A phrase which Moltmann calls on often: e.g., *CG*, 47; *JCTW*, 40; *IEB*, 70.

43. *ABP*, 30 (German: 41).

44. *CG*, 252.

45. *CG*, 219–27, 249–52. Stephen Williams notes that Moltmann's loyalty to the concerns of protest atheism could be rendered a bit more critically, insofar as Moltmann never "seems to question the 'good faith' of 'protest atheism'" (Williams, "Jürgen Moltmann," 114).

of our situation because he himself has made it a part of the divine history. Moltmann states: "The Father has become different through his surrender of the Son, and the Son too has become different through the experience of his passion in the world . . . . God 'experiences' something which belongs essentially to the redemption of the world: *he experiences pain*."[46]

The motif of Christ as the suffering brother, or as the companion, is pervasive in Moltmann's Christology,[47] and it is hugely integral for his christological ethics (or "christopraxis").[48] But this is not the final depth of the incarnation, for Moltmann will eventually resound the claim, following his "cosmological turn" in the 1980s,[49] that Christ identifies even with the created order of nature itself, suffering for its sufferings, and bringing those sufferings to a proleptic, apocalyptic end on Golgotha. Christ, in taking on flesh, the "stuff" of the order of this world, is able to die representatively not just for poor humanity, with whom he has identified, but also for the sighing creation, liberating it all through his identification with wretchedness:

> As an anticipation of universal death, Golgotha is the anticipa-
> tion of the end of this world and the beginning of a world that is
> new. . . . What has already happened to Christ is representative
> of what will happen to everybody: it is a happening *pars pro toto*.
> Consequently he has suffered vicariously [*stellvertretend erlitten*]
> what threatens everyone. . . . He did not suffer the sufferings of
> the end-time simply as a private person from Galilee, or merely as
> Israel's messiah, or solely as the Son of man of the nations. He also
> suffered as the head and Wisdom of the whole creation, and died
> for the new creation of all things. . . . "Jesus will be in agony until
> the end of the world," wrote Pascal. But the reverse is also true. In
> the agony of Christ this world finds its end.[50]

46. Moltmann, "Trinitarian History," 93, emphasis added.

47. It is in fact the first answer he gives to the question of "why did the Christ have to suffer these things?" in *JCTW*, 38–40.

48. *WJC*, 41–43, 118–19, 215. Also *JCTW*: "Acknowledgment of Christ and disciple-ship of Christ are two sides of the same thing: life in companionship with Christ. We need an answer to our questions which we can live and die with. That means that *every Christology is related to christopraxis*." (2, emphasis mine).

49. Moltmann notes that after his earlier preoccupation with time, history, and rev-elation, his theology increasingly turned toward a concern for the categories of space, nature, and cosmology—a shift most clearly marked by his 1985 Gifford Lectures, pub-lished as *GC* (1985). See *ABP*, 211–12.

50. *WJC*, 155 (German: 176), 157. This powerful point was made by Moltmann nearly twenty years before as well: see his "Theology as Eschatology," 4–5n6, wherein he calls the "rock of atheism" (the presence of suffering) the same thing as the "stumbling

So then, Golgotha is not only identification with people in our sin and desperation; it is identification with the whole created order in its finitude and futility, it is identification with all of the "former things" (Rev 21:4). The agony of the first heaven and the first earth, subject to transience and tragedy, is given its end on the cross, in Christ. This is not simply identification in order to understand or to give sympathy; in Moltmann, Christ becomes part of the broken, creaturely order of the world in order to lead it, as a part of it, into redemption: his is a mission that *transcends, liberates,* and *transforms.* And the picture of such a transformed condition is provided in the vindicating resurrection of Christ—the other side of the dialectic. Here we find the heart of what Moltmann calls his "eschatological Christology"—the Christology of Easter.

Christ Risen

For Moltmann, the empty tomb is not a dead fact of history, but a window into the future of the world—death dead, life alive forevermore. And the empty tomb, the trinitarian nature of God, and the cross of god-forsakenness, must all be held together: "If one conceives of the Trinity as an event of love in the suffering and the death of Jesus—and that is something which faith must do—then *the Trinity is no self-contained group in heaven, but an eschatological process open for men on earth,* which stems from the cross of Christ."[51] This evocative language points to the christological reality that is perhaps the most preeminent in Moltmann's thought—appearing as early as the third chapter of *Theology of Hope:* "The resurrection has set in motion an eschatologically determined process of history, whose goal is the annihilation of death in the victory of the life of the resurrection."[52] In the existential situation of the disciples following the death of Jesus, Moltmann notes that whatever shape their experience of the risen Christ took, it "must plainly be of such a kind that it *compelled* proclamation to all peoples and the continual formation of new christological conceptions."[53] This proclamation, the formation of Christ's very church, constitutes itself in that body that has determined to live in light of Christ's eschatological

---

block" of the cross—perhaps the clearest and most poetic summary of his anti-theodicy sentiments.

51. *CG,* 249, emphasis mine.

52. *TH,* 163.

53. *TH,* 188, emphasis original.

reality. Moltmann has no time for anthropocentric existentialisms or wistful utopia,[54] for these do not treat the historical, reality-bearing encounter with God as something true and necessary. He sees instead a new era inaugurated by the resurrection of Christ, and it is an era in which the church can truly *live*—live a real and different life in contradiction with the present world. Essentially, then, the resurrection is a very *worldly* reality; it is about *this world*: the church thereby is called not to spiritualistic retreat but rather to embodied activity in space and time,[55] shaped by, empowered by, and given hope by the resurrection life of Jesus.[56]

Moltmann's understanding of these transformational realities is quite concrete, and *The Church in the Power of the Spirit* was his first attempt to make clear the practical (ecumenical, social, interreligious) ramifications of this world-transforming view of the resurrection. As his thought turned increasingly to the actual, physical nature of the world, via cosmology and ecological concerns, the new creation became something of significance for nature as well. If Christ *died the death of the old creation* on the cross, then his resurrection serves as the *birth of that new creation*:

> With the raising of Christ, the vulnerable and mortal human nature we experience here is raised and transformed into the eternally living, immortal human nature of the new creation; and with vulnerable human nature the non-human nature of the earth is transformed as well. This transformation is its eternal healing. . . . In Christ's resurrection human nature in its primordial form triumphs over its unnatural imprisonment in transience [*ihre unnatürliche Gefangenschaft in der Vergänglichkeit*].[57]

Christ, then, is both. He is the old and the new. His death, the death of the old. His resurrection, the birth of the new. He is truly "the first and the last" (Rev 1:17).

---

54. *TH*, 167.

55. Such realities have been discussed variously by Moltmann, but come across most clearly in *PL*, chapters 3 and 6. In *TH*, Moltmann emphasizes more the cruciform nature of these realities—"namely, persecution, accusation, suffering, and martyrdom" (195).

56. *CPS*, 192. This is the initial origin of Moltmann's specific terminology of "messianic"—mediating the future rule of God into the broken spaces of the present world; this is a mediation that is "stirred up" by the conditions humanity finds itself beset by; the messianic existence under the cross and in light of the empty tomb strains toward change (see Müller-Fahrenholz, *Kingdom and the Power*, 167–68).

57. *WJC*, 258–59 (German: 281–82).

Christ in Glory: The Firstborn Brother

This eschatological Christology,[58] standing alongside the cross as the dual-event in which the old creation is proleptically dissolved and the new creation nascently erupts, thus moves beyond identification to *transformation*. And though he does not deny some place to individual, interiorized models of "salvation,"[59] Moltmann's soteriological aims are both broader and deeper.[60] The deathly state of humanity, *of all of nature*, is defeated by the resurrection—Christ is the firstborn from the dead.[61] His solidarity, imparting comfort and hope to a seized and broken world, does not end at the cross only to be rendered hollow by a non-bodily resurrection and ethereal continued existence, apart from the lowly continuance of those who follow him. No, Moltmann emphasizes that Christ's firstborn status is such because it is from among "many brothers."[62] As Christ goes, so too the adopted sons and daughters of God will go; it is Christ who makes such transformative adoption possible. Opening a new way of thinking about God and new way of relating to God, Jesus, who without precedent called God "Father" and related to him in continuous and unique intimacy, calls upon the lowly of the world to also possess this depth of relationship (see Rom 8:15; Gal 4:6).[63] This representative Christology is thus not a matter of penal substitution or sacrifice for sin,[64] but a matter of proleptic path-

---

58. *TH*, 192–201; Meeks, *Origins*, 121–28.

59. *WJC*, 45.

60. He speaks about going beyond, or further than, "personal" salvation toward more holistic, liberative, and universal understandings: *CG*, 4; *GC*, 35.

61 "The process of the resurrection from the dead has begun in him, is continued 'in the Spirit, the giver of life,' and will be completed in the raising of those who are his, and of all the dead. The eschatological question about the future of the dead is answered christologically" (*CoG*, 69).

62. See *TK*, 120–21; Moltmann, "I Believe in Jesus Christ," 35–43.

63. *WJC*, 142–150; Moltmann, "I Believe in God the Father," 10–18.

64. For an excellent recent discussion on atonement and sin in Moltmann, see Mc-Dougall, *Pilgrimage*, 147–51. Moltmann has asked: "Is atonement necessary?" and replied with "I believe that it is." But the atonement that he goes on to discuss is not Anselmian (between people and God) but social (between human beings); Christ suffers for the sake of the victims and pays for the sins of the oppressors against the victims; see *JCTW*, 40–42. It is interesting that scholarly opinion divides here: Schweitzer sees in Moltmann an "Anselm-like emphasis on the efficacy of Jesus' death" (74) and Schmiechen sees in Moltmann a completely "tables-turned" version of Anselm, where God has to provide some "satisfying" answer to stricken humanity (305–6). Both outlooks correctly name aspects of Moltmann's integrated outlook, but both miss the larger, christo-thematic

clearing—Christ makes a way, a cruciform way, and the church is made up of those who follow him on that way:

> Believers enter into the fellowship of Christ's sufferings and take the impress of the cross—become cruciform [*werden kreuzförmig geprägt*]. They hope to become of like form with the transfigured body of Christ in glory (Phil. 3:21). That is why we can talk about both "our crucified Brother" and "our risen Brother." What is meant is the whole form of existence which is lived by Jesus Christ and which takes its stamp [*geprägte*] from him. Fellowship with Jesus the brother means ultimately participation in the liberation of the whole enslaved creation, which longs for the "revealing of the liberty of the Sons of God" (Rom. 8:19, 21) and for the experience of the "redemption of the body" (Rom. 8:23).[65]

But this is not all, and we can see the addition waiting to be made at the end of the just quoted passage. Moltmann's reference to the "enslaved creation" here precipitates his much fuller understanding of cosmological rebirth in Christ that appears in *The Way of Jesus Christ*.[66] We must remember that soteriological concerns (i.e., the dreads and anxieties of the present moment) are, for Moltmann, always pressing in on Christology, forcing it to say more and to say it differently, perhaps, than it has before. The nuclear threat to the fabric of the world, as well as the ecological destruction wreaked by pollution and depletion, increasingly has pushed a cosmological consciousness onto the forefront of the public scene. Moltmann, seeing himself as a practically-oriented, dialogical, theologian-of-the-moment, feels that the salvific nexus of Christianity can respond to this threat, and thus doctrinally should direct attention to it. Such is the function of a Christology that is truly "postmodern," according to Moltmann.[67] This is the root of Moltmann's "cosmic Christology," and it is nowhere more cosmic than in Christ's redemptive, transforming headship over creation.[68]

---

picture that I am here describing.

65. *TK*, 121 (German: 136).

66. See 252–63; see also the simplified discussion in *JCTW*, 82–87.

67. "Postmodern" for Moltmann means a Christology that is not ancient (metaphysically focused) or modern (historically focused), but one that understands humanity's place in the world *relationally* (ecologically, socially, etc.). See *WJC*, xv–xvi.

68. Moltmann in his early theology eschews the use of the term "Logos" and utilizes more mystical, Jewish categories to discuss this aspect of his Christology, identifying Christ as primordial Wisdom. On occasion, one can find him making explicit his identification of the Logos and Wisdom: *ET*, 339. In his later, more pneumatologically textured

The key passage below ties together these myriad themes—solidarity with humans and nature, redemption through resurrected transformation—that I have presented in this section:

> [Christ] died in solidarity with all living things, which have to die although they want to live. . . . If his resurrection is the death of death, then it is also the beginning of the annihilation of death in history, and the beginning of the annihilation of death in nature. It is therefore the beginning of the raising of the dead *and* the beginning of the transfiguration of the mortal life [*der Verklärung des sterblichen Lebens*] of the first creation in the creation that is new and eternal. Christ is then in person not merely "the first born" from among the dead who will be reborn through the eternal Spirit of life. He is also "the first born" of the whole re-born creation (Col 1:15). In raising him, God brought not merely eternal life for the dead but also the first anticipatory radiance of immortal being for mortal creation.[69]

The suffering messiah and the eschatological promise—these are the entwined dimensions—concern Christ's past and his future, and they concern Christ's cross and his resurrection. But we have said little thus far about Christ's birth, baptism, life, teaching, or purported miracles. This has been deliberate, as it reflects the actual pacing and focus in the diachronic development of Moltmann's Christology. His earliest works (*Theology of Hope* and *The Crucified God*) focused intently on the resurrection and the cross, respectively—though Moltmann always emphasized that they needed to be read in the course of Christ's entire earthly life. But it is in *The Way of Jesus Christ* that Moltmann most fully illustrated the thematic interconnection between Christ's "messianic mission" and his sufferings and resurrection.[70] The next dimension of his Christology is the most focused on these themes.

---

thinking, Moltmann became more comfortable using the term "Word" to refer to the second person of the Trinity, and worked out his trinitarian history in a complex inter-weaving of Word, Spirit, and Wisdom in *SpL*, chapters 2–3.

69. *WJC*, 253, translation slightly modified (German: 404). See further *CoG*, 92.

70. See Linahan, *Kenosis of God,* chapter 3, e.g., 128n2.

Moltmann's Pneumatological/Developmental Christology[71]

At the beginning of *The Way of Jesus Christ*, Moltmann, with characteristic candor, says the following:

> I have not based this Christology on the christological dogma of the patristic church but—as far as I was able—have cast back historically and exegetically to the histories of the biblical tradition, in order with their help to arrive at new interpretations of Christ which will be relevant for the present day. So this Christology is also a *narrative* Christology.[72]

It is in this volume that Moltmann finally articulates a thoroughly trinitarian Jesus—not just at the cross, but all the way through his earthly life. And here is where Moltmann fully posits, elaborates, and defends his "Spirit Christology." Pneumatology, it should be noted, was the last piece of his trinitarian theology to mature, but as concerns his Christology it had been brewing for some time: in *Theology of Hope,* the Spirit is explicitly linked with Christ's *resurrection;*[73] in *The Crucified God,* the Spirit's christological range was expanded to the *crucifixion* as that event took on its deeply trinitarian form;[74] and in *Trinity and the Kingdom* it is mentioned that Jesus' *ministry* took place through the Spirit, but the details are sparse.[75] These threads come together in his mature pneumatological Christology—exhibited clearly in *The Way of Jesus Christ* and *The Spirit of Life*—to which we now turn.

---

71. "In the power of the Spirit Christ is sent from God . . . into this divided world" (*ABP*, 172).

72. *WJC*, xv, emphasis mine.

73. *TH*, 57, 68, 84.

74. Moltmann is still not tremendously clear on the Spirit's role at this juncture though; see the points concerning the Spirit in *CG*, 245–48. McDougall is right to see at this stage of his trinitarian thinking a quite Augustinian account of the Holy Spirit—as the *vinculum caritatis*, the bond of love between the Father and the Son. "Moltmann also inherits the weak points of Augustine's model, namely, whether this understanding of the Spirit . . . can assure the Spirit's full personhood." (McDougall, *Pilgrimage,* 48). See also Bauckham, *Theology,* 152–54.

75. *TK*, 66, 74.

The Christ in the Power of the Spirit

From birth to resurrection Christ is seen as a man thoroughly dependent on the Spirit. He is born of the Spirit, baptized with the Spirit, and he ministers and heals via his endowment with the Spirit.[76] So pervasive is Christ's reliance on the Spirit, according to Moltmann, that at Golgotha it is not that Christ chooses not to supernaturally come down from the cross, but rather that he *cannot* do so. The obedient Son has gone to his death, and must bear it in powerlessness (*Ohnmacht*) and forsakenness (*Verlassenheit*),[77] and this serves to intensify the recounting of Christ's suffering and abandonment even beyond its stark portrayal in *The Crucified God*.

Such a pneumatological outlook accomplishes at least two salient tasks: (1) it renders the trinitarian dimensions of Moltmann's Christology more well-rounded and coherent (and also, as it turns out, biblical—note simply the number of biblical citations in *The Way of Jesus Christ* compared to the central chapters of *The Crucified God*); (2) it allows Moltmann to articulate the eschatological promise in Christ in a more clear way, for the Spirit is the bridge, the *mediation*, between Christ's mission and the mission of the church:

> Through Jesus Christ, the Spirit is sent upon the gathered community of his followers, so that its efficacy spreads. . . . This shows that Jesus was not baptized into the Spirit as a private person, but *pars pro toto*, representatively, as one among many, and as one for many. He received the Spirit for the sick whom he healed, for the sinners whose sins he forgave, for the poor whose fellowship he sought, for the women and men whom he called into his discipleship. He received the Spirit . . . as the messiah of God's new creation.[78]

In this sense we can see that though the Spirit is the animating and empowering force in the life of Jesus, it is also a thematic that stands in continuity with the eschatological, re-creative outlook of the Christology's other dimensions.

I must here briefly address the issue of Christ's *divinity*. It is, after all, a potential of pneumatological Christologies to lean toward "degree Christology" or even "adoptionist Christology." And the language that we have noted thus far from Moltmann would hardly seem to resist such a reading,

76. *WJC*, 73–94.

77. *WJC*, 109–10 (German: 130).

78. *WJC*, 94.

especially when we consider his discomfort with the tradition of the virginal conception of Jesus.

But, in light of our upcoming discussion of two-natures Christology and Logos Christology in chapter 4, I will not overly exercise the topic here. Three points will be concisely made. First, all questioners about Moltmann's view of traditional Christology must understand his hesitancy to use patently "incarnational language" in light of his expressed theological concerns. The following passage needs to be quoted at length to illustrate this:

> The differentiation between the two natures bears the mark of incarnation Christology, and does not derive from the particular history of Jesus himself. It is drawn from a general metaphysics of the world. Attributes are ascribed to the divine nature of Christ which the God of Abraham, Isaac and Jacob, "the Father of Jesus Christ," never knew. His faithfulness is transformed into a substantial immutability, his zeal, his love, his compassion—in short his "pathos," his capacity for feeling—are supplanted by the essential apathy of the divine. The passion of his love and its capacity for suffering [*Die Leidenschaft und die Leidensfähigkeit seiner Liebe*] can no longer be stated. . . . It is more appropriate, then, to start from Jesus' special relationship to God, whom he called Abba, dear Father, in order to elicit from this mutual relationship between the messianic child and the divine Father what is truly divine and what is truly human.[79]

In short, insofar as the two-natures conception has functioned as merely a defense mechanism for a classical conception of an impassible God, Moltmann finds it faulty.[80] Moltmann does not "deny" the role of metaphysics in Christology; his point is that the New Testament history does not formulate

---

79. *WJC*, 53. The quote continues to make additional pivotal qualifications: "By first of all developing Christology and the doctrine of God in specifically Christian—which means trinitarian—terms, we are not denying the task of Christology in the framework of metaphysics in general. But the New Testament is not concerned about the relationship between Christ's human and his divine nature. It is concerned with Jesus' relationship as child to the Father, and with God's relationship as Father to Jesus" (German: 71). See also Pannenberg's similar discussion: "Frühchristlichen Theologie," 296–346.

80. Mentioning the heritage of Aristotelian impassibility, Moltmann notes that it raises "the difficult problem of the two-nature Christology: the divine nature is incapable of suffering, the human nature is capable of suffering. But what then really happened on the cross?" (Moltmann and Lapide, "Dialogue," 63).

such metaphysical axioms for us, and we should be exceedingly cautious about importing such notions into our understanding of God.[81]

Second, this point on Moltmann's part does not entail that he denies the "divinity" of Jesus. At the risk of stating the obvious, many of Moltmann's most enduring contributions to contemporary theology have been bound up with *trinitarian* themes. If the Son is not divine, he is not a member of the divine Trinity. If the Trinity is missing the Son, then it is not the Trinity. Without the Trinity, quite literally, there is no Godhead.[82] Regardless of Moltmann's sometimes imprecise language—appearing, we note, in a work that is self-consciously focused on a non-metaphysical, narrative-shaped, dialogical-with-Judaism Christology—the inner nexus of his theology simply comes undone if Jesus is merely a divinely adopted man or a man who is gradually divinized.[83] Moltmann cannot allow for this, and never does.

Third and finally, Moltmann presents numerous passages in which the divinity, or divine status, or latent divinity, of Jesus is affirmed. To wit: "The one God whom all men seek in their finitude and transitoriness became man in Jesus [*in Jesus Mensch geworden*]."[84] In speaking of the cross Moltmann calls it an event between "the Father and the Son" and then qualifies this as being between "God and God."[85] He can discuss a perichoretic relationship between the Father and the Son that "is constitutive [*konstitutiv*]"

81. Elsewhere, Moltmann will be quite clear that he *does* assume a metaphysical reality for Christ's divinity: "Understood in metaphysical terms, Jesus' divine Sonship means his eternal divine nature" ("I Believe in Jesus Christ," 31).

82. Moltmann is unambiguous about this; see "I Believe in Jesus Christ," 38–39. On balance, I note that with the publication of *CG*, Moltmann appeared to argue, in certain infamous places, that the Trinity itself was actually historically constituted by the event of the cross, or that the Trinity "emerged" from that "eschatological" happening (most notoriously at 247–55). Not surprisingly, endless critical questions emerged in response to Moltmann's language here, and he has responded in several forms—see the series of essays, *Diskussion über Jürgen Moltmann*. Moltmann has taken care not to reiterate such troublesome language, preferring to speak of the cross as *revealing* the Trinity: "The cross is at the centre of the Trinity. This is brought out by tradition, when it takes up the Book of Revelation's image of 'the Lamb who was slain from the foundation of the world' (Rev. 5:12). Before the world was, the sacrifice was already in God. No Trinity is conceivable without the Lamb, without the sacrifice of love, without the crucified Son" (*TK*, 83). Tang, *God's History*, makes similar points: 127–36.

83. See also *CG*, 245.

84. *CG*, 88 (German: 84). Moltmann makes this affirmation in the midst of critiquing the immutability-impassibilitiy framework for the divine, but he is not critiquing this affirmation as such.

85. *CG*, 151.

and "equally primal [*gleichursprünglich*]"[86] for both, and he discusses how the Son is "eternally begotten" of the Father, an "eternal" member of the Trinity, and the only member of the Trinity who had to "become man [*Mensch werden*]."[87] It is perhaps in *The Way of Jesus Christ*, which, as we've seen, contains some of the least traditional christological statements, where Moltmann makes his viewpoint the most clear: Christ is "divine," but that divinity ought to be understood in terms of relational, self-giving trinitarianism, not in terms of an ancient vision of metaphysics:

> [We shall examine] the shifting facets of the divine person Jesus Christ which reflect his relationship to God—Spirit, Son, Logos, Wisdom, Kyrios, and so forth. We understand these, not as hypostases of the divine nature, but as trinitarian relations in God; or in other words: divine self-relations [*Selbstverhältnisse Gottes*] in which Jesus discovers and finds himself, and through which believers delineate his divine mystery.[88]

This quote not only serves to conclude this initial discussion of the "divinity" of Jesus Christ in Moltmann's thought, but it also leads us to the final element of the Christology that I will highlight in this chapter: the developmental progression of Christ's past and present life.

The Christ in Development

For Moltmann, remarkably, the dependence of Christ on the Spirit and the Father entails not just a lack of self-originating power for miraculous acts; his depth of humanity also entails a self-consciousness in which Jesus, quite literally, must *come to know* who he truly is. Jesus develops; he changes; he grows. Not just in his understanding of his person, but in his very person itself.[89] Here, perhaps more than anywhere else in the Christology, Moltmann is driven by a plain reading of numerous biblical texts: texts wherein Jesus lacks knowledge; texts which explicitly state that Jesus "grows" and "learns"; and texts which seem to imply genuine alterations in his self-understanding.[90] These texts, which Moltmann handles with profound seriousness,

---

86. *WJC*, 143 (German: 164).

87. *TK*, 166–67 (German: 184).

88. *WJC*, 71–72 (German: 91).

89. Among recent commentators, Bingaman is one of the few to give this dimension of the Christology any examination: *All Things New*, 62.

90. Moltmann points either implicitly or explicitly to: (1) the numerous passages

indicate to him that Jesus is, in his early life and early stages of ministry, "not yet the messiah"—rather, he is "on his way to being the messiah."[91] This "way" is one of the chief meanings that Moltmann identifies for the title of his central christological work, *The Way of Jesus Christ.*[92] Jesus is on his way to a goal, and that way possesses stages of genuine development in which Jesus grows in the midst of his social and trinitarian relationships:

> The more modern (and especially feminist) concepts about Jesus' being as *being-in-relationship* take us a step further [than the older models of nature and substance]. But they do not yet enter into Jesus' being as a *being-in-history*, and the "learning process" of his life and ministry, his experience and his suffering. Here we shall try to take up the different christological concepts of person and integrate them, so as to arrive at a fuller, richer portrait of the person of Jesus Christ. We shall look at the divine person, the person in his messianic ministry, the public person commissioned by God, the person in the warp and weft of his relationships [*im Beziehungsgeflecht ihrer Gemeinschaften*], and the person in the emergence and growth of his own life history [*im Werden ihrer Lebensgeschichte*].[93]

This is not to say that Jesus ever necessarily perceives himself in *ordinary* terms, but it is to say that Jesus' self-understanding *grows*—he is not seen by Moltmann as being perfectly cognizant of his divine status, fully inhabiting his Lordship, and or to be merely "condescending" or "accommodating" or "testing" when he asks questions or learns things. He is truly the messianic person in his becoming, and Moltmann perceives at least five stages in the messianic journey of Christ: (1) the "mediation of creation" before his earthly life;[94] (2) his earthly life, constituted by the "messianic mission of Jesus to the poor"; (3) the "apocalyptic passion of Jesus" on the cross; (4) the "transfiguring raising [*verklärenden Auferweckung*] of Jesus

---

where Jesus asks questions to gain information, (2) statements that Jesus "grew in favor with God and with man" (Luke 2:52) and that he "learned obedience through suffering" (Heb 5:8), and (3) pericopes (usually involving women) where Jesus is seemingly challenged and appears to alter his thinking (e.g., Matt 15:1–28).

91. E.g., *WJC*, 111.

92. *WJC*, xiv.

93. *WJC*, 136–37 (German: 158).

94. *WJC*, 288–90.

from the dead";[95] (5) and finally, after the earthly life, "the coming One" of God's eschatological kingdom.[96]

This genuine place for progressive growth on the part of Christ is key for both Moltmann's narrative Christology and his trinitarian, panentheistic eschatology. Taking the biblical histories and traditions of scripture, and the true humanity of the Son, in such a sweepingly serious way causes Moltmann to perceive a development in the second person of the Trinity— a true journey and real progression of work and experience, which only concludes at the reconciliation of all things.

This developmental aspect of Moltmann's Christology is, implausibly, almost never discussed at length in the secondary literature on his thought.[97] Thus, it has not been explored in what manner this element of his Christology might (or might not) cohere with the other thematic facets. In fact, the question of his Christology's praxiological import and conceptual unity remains yet to be robustly addressed in Moltmann scholarship. This is owed, I suggest, to the fact that Moltmann's unique view on Christ's kenosis has been so little examined and that the Christology itself has resisted systematization and organization. The role of kenosis within his Christology is key, and each of the categories addressed in this chapter conceals an element of great import for understanding it.

Conclusion: Looking Toward Moltmann's Kenotic Christology

As I have noted in the introductory section and chapter 1 already, Moltmann's Christology has been one of the least examined aspects of his overarching theology, with many of the core thematics delineated in this chapter being hardly discussed at all, even among prominent commentators. This present chapter has thus differed from nearly all other interactions with Moltmann's Christology, the vast majority of which isolate only one or two of Moltmann's christological themes, with the aim of using them to explicate some other dimension of his theology.[98] Moreover, in order to see

95. *WJC*, 71 (German: 90).

96. *WJC*, 321–26.

97. Excepting Bingaman, *All Things New,* 61–62, but even there the discussion is limited.

98. Representative recent examples would include: Bingaman, *All Things New,* 45–62, which briefly highlights some unique dimensions in Moltmann's christological thought, but only as necessary background for a study of his anthropology; Bonzo, *Indwelling the*

how Moltmann's conception of kenosis functions in its full christological application, it has been important for us to circumscribe the myriad themes of Moltmann's Christology more generally.

This chapter's work in establishing a preliminary understanding of the major themes of Moltmann's Christology can be summarized as follows: *The divine Son becomes human, and as such he is the pneumatologically empowered, promised messianic person, who, through his suffering-in-solidarity and eschatological resurrection, develops into his divine Lordship as the firstborn of the new creation, carrying all the world with him toward redemption.* This is an effective initial rendering of the basic contours of Moltmann's doctrine of Christ. It is thorough, insofar as it takes account of the varied streams he consistently propounds in his writing about the history and significance of Christ. However, it admittedly remains a somewhat disparate array of christological topics; its consistency in terms of theological vision or narrative remains questionable. Thus, we are still compelled to ask: What binds these compelling, yet scattered, themes of Moltmann's messianic Christology together?

It is my contention that *kenosis* fundamentally undergirds the logic of all other Moltmannian christological tropes and progressions. So, fittingly, we now turn our attention in Part II of this study to the location and articulation of christological kenosis in Moltmann's thought. This will be accomplished over two chapters that each tackle salient issues in the articulation of any form of kenotic Christology: How is the "kenosis hymn" in Phil 2 to be understood? And how does kenosis relate to the traditionally construed "two natures" of Christ?

Forsaken Other, 52–68, details with admirable insight the cosmic dimensionality of Moltmann's Christology, but does so in service to his overarching examination of Moltmann's trinitarian ethics of discipleship; Müller-Fahrenholz, *Kingdom and the Power*, 167–81, gives an admirable look at the notion of the messianic in Moltmann's Christology for the sake of developing an outlook on Moltmann's views of the kingdom, but leaves the Christology's other dimensions untouched.

PART II

Locating Christological Kenosis in Moltmann

3

Moltmann's Hermeneutics of the Kenosis Hymn

WE ARE NOW EMBARKING on the centermost venture of our study. The task before us is not only to show that Moltmann *is* a kenotic thinker when it comes to Christology, but also to display the *unique* dimensions of his kenotic Christology. Now, in order to avoid any abstract or *ad hoc* definition of kenosis that would be forced inorganically onto Moltmann's thought, this chapter focuses on an examination of the "kenosis hymn" in Phil 2, taking stock of its most prominent interpretations across theological history before presenting a contextualized analysis of Moltmann's own outlook on the passage and his christological applications of it.

Philippians 2:5–8 and Its Christological Interpretations

The text of Phil 2:5–8, often surmised to be part of a hymn of the early church, reads as follows in the NRSV:

> Let the same mind be in you that was in Christ Jesus, who, though he was in the form of God [*morphē theou*], did not regard equality with God [*einai isa theōi*] as something to be exploited [*harpagmon*], but emptied himself [*heauton ekenōsen*], taking the form of a slave [*morphēn doulou*], being born in human likeness. And being found in human form, he humbled himself and became obedient to the point of death—even death on a cross.

The passage is early (if not pre-Pauline), evocative, theologically weighted, and linguistically difficult. Every form of Christology, kenotic or not, has had to come to terms with this passage, and its treatment in exegetical history is worth analyzing for the light that it will cast on Moltmann's thought concerning the "kenosis" of Christ.[1]

---

1. Kenosis derives from the verb *ekenōsen* in v. 7.

There are three general trends in the interpretative history of the passage, and we can identify them heuristically as follows: the *traditional* interpretation (which sees the kenosis as *concealing* the divine qualities in Christ), the *radical* interpretation (in which kenosis consists in the *abandoning* of divine qualities in Christ), and a *contemporary* interpretation that has lately become quite prominent in exegetical scholarship (wherein the kenosis has been viewed as *revelatory* of God's character and action). I survey all of these outlooks in the following sections, and this survey will pay dividends when we turn to the question of which of these three exegetical trajectories aligns most readily with Moltmann's own view.

Concealment (Traditional) Interpretation

In the earliest days of christological creed and controversy, the passage was appropriated to specific doctrinal ends. Responses to Arian forms of Christology defined the initial patristic theologizing of the Phil 2 hymn. Athanasius in particular standardized the understanding of the passage's terminology. "In the form of God" [*morphē theou*] was taken as parallel with "equality with God" [*einai isa theōi*] and thereby glossed as the divine substance of the Second Person of the Trinity (Athanasius called it "the essential nature of the Word"[2]). This reading of the "form of God," when combined with the Hellenistic assumption of divine immutability,[3] meant that the "self-emptying" (*heauton ekenōsen*, v. 7) was seen to entail a hiding or concealing of divine qualities in the midst of the human nature's assumption: "'[the Word] humbled himself' with reference to the assumption of the flesh."[4] Pannenberg notes that "Origen, Athanasius, Gregory of Nyssa, Cyril of Alexandria, Augustine, and others who connected Phil 2:7 with the coming of the Logos in the flesh meant by the term 'self-emptying' (*kenōsis, exinanitio*) the assumption of human nature."[5] Further, this meant that *harpagmon* ("grasped" or "exploited," v.

---

2. Athanasius, *Orationes contra Arianos*, 1.41.

3. Dawe notes: "In the Greek conception the essence of divinity was existence beyond change and suffering and death. . . . [The] acceptance of passion or change in God was tantamount to saying that God was no longer divine. For the essence of divinity was unchangeableness" (*Form of a Servant*, 16, 53).

4. Athanasius, *Orationes contra Arianos*, 1.41.

5. Pannenberg, *Jesus*, 308. For Augustine's view on the passage, see *Sermon* 4, 5, 41, 21–22.

6) could only mean that Christ did not need to "grasp" for equality with God "because he *already* possessed it."[6]

In essence, then, the hymn was taken to refer to an "obscuring of the divine glory during the earthly ministry of Jesus. . . . Kenosis was the assumption by the Second Person of the Trinity of a veil of human flesh by which incarnation was possible."[7] Gregory of Elvira stated this interpretation perhaps most clearly: "Note that when the sun is covered by a cloud its brilliance is suppressed but not darkened. The sun's light, which is suffused throughout the whole earth . . . is presently obscured by a small obstruction of cloud but not taken away. [Christ] does not lessen but momentarily hides the divinity in him."[8]

Augustine lent his pen to this perspective when he wrote: "It was thus that he emptied himself: by taking the form of a slave, not by losing the form of God; the form of a slave was added, the form of God did not disappear."[9] This line of theological reasoning was followed thereafter for centuries of christological reflection. It can be seen also to underlie the thinking of Reformation luminaries like Calvin:

> [Christ] suffered his divinity to be concealed under a veil of flesh. Here, unquestionably, [Paul] explains not what Christ was, but in what way he acted. Nay, from the whole context it is easily gathered, that it was in the true nature of man that Christ humbled himself. For what is meant by the words, he was "found in fashion as a man," but that for a time, instead of being resplendent with divine glory, the human form only appeared in a mean and abject condition?[10]

Martin Luther's Christology also made a clear "tapeinotic" application of the kenosis hymn, wherein the "[self]-humbling" [*etapeinōsen*—v.8] is taken as a synonym for *ekenōsen* in v.7: "Christ did not empty himself once for all; rather he constantly emptied himself throughout his earthly life."[11]

6. See Athanasius, *Orationes contra Arianos,* 1.40, emphasis added; see also Dawe, *Servant,* 30.

7. Dawe, *Form of a Servant,* 30.

8. Gregory of Elvira, *On the Faith,* 88–89, in Corpus Christianorum, 69:244.

9. Augustine, *Sermon* 4, 5, Corpus Christianorum, 41, 21; see also Kasper, *God of Jesus Christ,* 189.

10. Calvin, *Institutes,* 2.13.2.

11. Althaus, *Theology of Martin Luther,* 194 (see further 194–97 for relevant quotations from Luther to this end). Coakley also presents the basic shape of a tapeinotic reading of the hymn: "*Kenosis* and Subversion," 7–8. The term "tapeinotic" is my own.

These two complementary ideas—(1) kenosis as the hiding of divinity in the assumption of the flesh manifested in (2) the humble bearing of the human life of Christ—in large part dominated traditional understandings of the passage.[12]

Abandonment (Radical) Interpretation

When the first wave of modern kenotic Christology burst onto the Continental scene (most distinctly in the work of Gottfried Thomasius and Wolfgang Gess), fresh exegetical directions were brought to bear on the passage's interpretation. For these more-properly kenotic schools of thought the "kenosis of Philippians 2:7 and context (vv. 6–11) was . . . taken as a real self-relinquishing, limiting, or emptying of divine attributes, powers, prerogatives, and/or glory by the pre-existent Logos upon the event of the Incarnation."[13] For Thomasius in particular, the assumption of human nature and the simultaneous generation of the *una persona* entails, of logical necessity, a giving-up (a self-divestment— *Entäußerung*) of certain divine attributes in order to make manifest a truly human life. Thus, what is "emptied" in the Phil 2 hymn are those attributes of divinity that could be abandoned without negating the divine nature in its essence:

> [Thus] we shall have to posit the Incarnation itself precisely in the fact that he, the eternal Son of God, the second person of the deity, gave himself over into the form of human limitation, and thereby to the limits of a spatio-temporal existence, under the conditions of human development, in the bounds of an historical concrete being, in order to live in and through our nature the life of our race in the fullest sense of the word, without on that account ceasing to be God.[14]

Thomasius famously distinguished between what he termed the "immanent" attributes (which are divinely essential and necessary) and the "relative" attributes (which are not essential, because they only relate to the governing of the contingent created order). It is this second category of attributes, which includes omnipotence, omniscience, and omnipresence, that Thomasius saw to be relinquished by the assumption

---

12. See the summative material in Dawe, *Form of a Servant*, 53–83; Brown, *Divine Humanity*, 25–30; Coakley, "Does Kenosis Rest on a Mistake?"

13. Thompson, "Nineteenth-Century Kenotic," 75.

14. Thomasius, *Christi Person und Werk*, 48.

of humanity.[15] Thus Thomasius felt he could say that though Christ truly abandoned certain divine properties upon becoming incarnate, he still "lacks nothing which is essential for God to be God."[16] The immanent attributes of the Godhead—love, faithfulness, holiness, etc.—are retained fully in the incarnation.[17]

Subsequent reflection on this phase of kenotic Christology has seen a "real *novum*" introduced into christological discourse by Thomasius, who was willing to fully embrace some literal understanding of divine self-limitation (while simultaneously foregoing any allegiance to the notions of divine simplicity and immutability).[18] But the self-emptying of the Logos in the kenotic Christology of Gess was yet more extreme. Whereas Thomasius supported the abandoning of some attributes possessed in the pre-existent state, Gess argued for their complete abandonment in order for the Logos to be transformed, quite literally, into a human person.[19] As Gerald Haw-

---

15. See Welch, *Protestant Theology*, 238.

16. Thomasius, *Christi Person und Werk*, 73; see also 94.

17. See Thompson, "Nineteenth-Century Kenotic," 83; Brown, *Divine Humanity*, 49–51; cf. Welch's comments in *God and Incarnation*, 67–69n10, as well as the classic summary in Bruce, *Humiliation of Christ*, 179–87. As seemingly simple as the christological formulation is in Thomasius, commentators often verge on distorting it—see, for instance, Pannenberg's critique in *Jesus—God and Man*, wherein he accurately describes Thomasius' kenotic Christology (310–11) but thereafter posits the following critique: "Attributes *essential to his divinity* cannot be absent even in his humiliation unless the humiliated were no longer God" (312 [emphasis added], cf. too 315); Pannenberg is staging this as a critique of Thomasius, though it is something with which Thomasius manifestly would agree, which is why he posits the division between the immanent and relative attributes in the first place. Arguably, Barth commits the same kind of misrepresentation when he sums up all radical kenotic models as "self-limitation or *de-divinisation*" (*Church Dogmatics*, 4:183). Again, this fairly attains, perhaps, to Gess or Godet, but less so to Thomasius. Thomasius had argued that immutability was inappropriately described in foregoing theology, and this consideration alone, if granted, defangs many of the usual critiques of him. If not granted, then the immutability point should be the subject of critiques of Thomasius, rather than his rendering of the kenosis itself. Hans Urs von Balthasar sees this more clearly than most: *Mysterium Paschale*, 31. Sarah Coakley is also more balanced in her interaction with Thomasius: "*Kenosis* and Subversion," 18–19.

18. Coakley, "*Kenosis* and Subversion," 19. Anna Mercedes disagrees, strangely, and claims that Thomasius is simply expositing an extension of his Reformation heritage, see *Power For*, 30. Mercedes thinks that Thomasius does not revise his classical doctrine of God enough, for he still sees God as free from dependency on the world (29).

19. On Gess's radical model of kenotic Christology, see Brown, *Divine Humanity*, 62–65; cf. Bruce, *Humiliation*, 187–97.

thorne states, for Gess, "the presence of any divine attributes would destroy the reality of Jesus' humanness."[20]

Revelatory (Contemporary) Interpretation

The "concealment" and "abandonment" schools of thought represent two stark variations in the dogmatic interpretation of Phil 2:5–8, and they serve as a remarkable cautionary tale for both biblical scholars and theologians. David Brown well conveys the fact that the passage's vexed interpretation should "alert us to the difficulty of keeping the question of exegesis distinct from our own particular theological prejudices."[21]

For the ancient Christologies, the majesty of God in Christ as the immutable, transcendent, almighty deity had to be preserved in the face of ancient challenges like Arianism, and so the hymn was appropriated to those ends. For the ninenteenth-century kenoticists, the radical humanity of the incarnation had to be emphasized in the face of ever-growing post-Enlightenment critiques of dogmatic history. Ultimately, however, in both cases, there seems to have been a certain determinative sense in which the passage was commandeered by foregoing doctrinal concerns, rather than being used to formatively direct those doctrinal concerns.[22] Gratefully, much contemporary scholarship has studied the passage with more critical awareness of such ingrained presuppositions, and this more neutral work has opened new avenues in understanding.

Thus we now turn to a spectrum of scholarship on the passage that is both recent and integrative, encompassing many of the foregoing interpretive issues into a fresh outlook on the passage. This interpretation takes the kenosis of Christ to be not a concealment of divinity, and not an abandonment of any foregoing aspect of that divinity, but rather a *revelation* of the divinity's character and nature. Hence we can call this the "revelatory" interpretation. The major interlocutors who have contributed to such an understanding include Gerald Hawthorne, N. T. Wright, Richard Bauckham, Gordon Fee, and Michael Gorman.

But before discussing the philological and grammatical specifics of this line of exegesis, we need to render a baseline understanding of the "logic" of the kenosis hymn. In its most basic sense, the hymn is serving a

20. Hawthorne, *Presence and the Power,* 206.

21. Brown, *Divine Humanity,* 10.

22. See the comments in Coakley, *"Kenosis* and Subversion," 105.

strongly practical (even ethical) role in the letter to the Philippians. Commentators as diverse as Hawthorne, Hurtado, Wright, David Brown, and James Dunn recognize that the hymn is calling the Philippians to account using the example of Christ's sacrificial humility as a kind of paraenesis.[23] Thus the basic logic appears as follows:

> *Have this mind among you (v.5) . . . That though he was in the form of God (v.6) . . . He . . . did not . . . grasp at . . . equality with God (v.6) . . . But rather emptied himself (v.7)*

Interpretative debate abounds about each of the underlined phrases, and each of them are key to the passage's intentional force overall. Thus we engage each of them in turn.

morphē theou—the form of God (v. 6)

Hawthorne notes the sizable diversity of interpretations that have attended the use of *morphē* here.[24] James Dunn and other thinkers have seen *morphē theou* as a "near synonym" for *image of God*, and have used this alleged linguistic association to fund their perception of an Adam-Christology in the passage.[25] Dunn's reading has been contested on multiple grounds,[26] his equivocation between *form* and *image* perhaps most forcefully. The principal difficulty with his reading, according to Fee, is simply that the Philippians hymn features no "*verbal* correspondence with the Genesis account" at all.[27] Furthermore, the synonymity of *morphē* and *eikōn* has been questioned effectively enough[28] to beg the question of why, if Paul intended an overt Adam-Christ correspondence, *eikōn* was not the word employed rather than *morphē* (especially when Paul has no reservations about using

23. Dunn: "the hymn serves the purpose of illustrating or commending a habit of mind," ("Christ, Adam, and Preexistence," 74); Hawthorne: "[the] Christ-hymn presents Jesus as the supreme example of the . . . self-giving service that Paul has just been urging the Philippians to practice (*Philippians*, 79); Brown speaks of the text primarily as an "ethical injunction" (*Divine Humanity*, 8–9, 13) and notes the agreement by Oliver Quick on this point ("An Ethical Sermon," 82); Hurtado, "Jesus as Lordly Example," 113–26; Wright, *Climax of the Covenant*, 87.

24. Hawthorne, *Philippians*, 81–84.

25. Dunn, "Christ, Adam, and Preexistence," 77.

26. Many of them well-summed in Wanamaker, "Philippians 2:6–11," 179–93.

27. Fee, "New Testament and Kenosis," 31.

28. See Fee, "New Testament and Kenosis, 31n12; Steenburg, "Case Against the Synonymity," 77–86.

eikōn in relation to Christ elsewhere, e.g., 2 Cor 4:4). Furthermore, the equation between *eikōn* and *morphē* "comes to grief fundamentally in the fact that it cannot be adopted for the second occurrence" of *morphē* in the passage (*"form* of a slave" v.7).[29]

Another chief candidate for the meaning of *morphē* here has been "status" or "condition,"[30] which certainly seems to make contextual sense, but is, according to Hawthorne, simply unattested in the wider Greek literature.[31] However, concerning both these contested interpretations there is diversity, with N. T. Wright joining Dunn in seeing at least some degree of an Adam-Christ correspondence at work in the passage;[32] and though Bauckham disagrees with this (claiming that Wright is "trying to have his cake and eat it too"[33]), he does appear to favor an understanding of *morphē* along the lines of status or condition, and he also takes the strongest reading of an Isa 53 background to the hymn, over and against an Adam-Christ reading.[34] Clearly, then, even among the scholars who, as we will see, all favor what we are calling the *revelatory interpretation* of the passage, there is some fundamental diversity about the background (i.e., Old Testament) correspondences within the hymn. Regardless, the specific meaning of *morphē* is left open by all of these positions unless additional exegetical information is brought to bear. Thus we will circle back to *morphē theou* after analyzing other aspects of the hymn.

harpagmon—the grasping (v. 6)

A prominent line followed by Dunn, Ralph Martin, and others is that this *grasping* is meant in a *snatching* or *seizing* sense—it is referring to the attempt to get something that is not already possessed (often referred to as the *res rapienda* understanding of the term).[35] On this reading, the "object of this [seizing]" is the *einai isa theōi* in v.7, and for Dunn this clearly recalls Gen 3:5 and the original temptation of humanity (thus furthering

29. Hawthorne, *Philippians*, 82. See also Herbert, *Kenosis and Priesthood*, 93.

30. See Martin, *Philippians*, 96; Martin, *Carmen Christi*, xx.

31. Hawthorne, *Philippians*, 83; also Hawthorne, "In the Form of God," 99.

32. Wright, *Climax*, 57–61.

33. Bauckham, *God Crucified*, 57.

34. Bauckham, *God Crucified*, 57–61; he refers to the notion of an Adam typology in the passage as a "red herring" in the history of interpretation (57). Wright sees the themes of Suffering Servant and Last Adam as mutually contributory: *Climax*, 59–61.

35. Dunn, "Christ, Adam, and Preexistence," 77; Martin, *Philippians*, 96–98.

his reading of the Adam-Christ correspondence).[36] But this notion of grasping after something in order to possess it has been greatly reduced in plausibility due to the work of C. F. D. Moule and Roy Hoover, whose philological investigations have offered a strong reading of *harpagmos* that is more sharply defined by its immediate linguistic context. Moule had originally argued for an understanding like "acquisitiveness" (a disposition of *seeking-to-gain*) and thus importantly understood *harpagmos* as an attitude rather than an action.[37] But Hoover's work went even further and identified the term as part of an idiomatic expression that combines with the verb *hēgēsato* in order to convey the sense of "something to be used for one's own advantage."[38] It is this sense that is agreed upon by a growing contingent of Philippians scholars (Fee, Wright, Hawthorne, et al.), as evidenced by its adoption in the NRSV (reflected in the English translation of v.7 given above).

But what theological weight do these considerations lend to the passage overall? N. T. Wright, building strongly on Hoover's idiomatic understanding of *harpagmos* ("to take advantage of"), makes the point that "the object in question—in this case equality with God—is *already* possessed [by Christ]. One cannot decide to take advantage of something one does not *already* have."[39] In contrast to those views which see the hymn as portraying Christ deciding against trying to *attain* something, Wright argues that what is actually presented is Christ who, though "in the form of God" does not "take advantage of" (or "exploit") this status. This point is strengthened when *morphē theou* is defined not from the wider Greek literature (which, as noted above, is quite difficult) nor from a questionable correspondence with *eikōn*, but from the internal context of the passage itself: letting the passage stand on its own, the phrase "equality with God" might, according to Wright, "even suggest the stronger translation *'this divine equality.'*"[40]

---

36. Dunn, "Christ, Adam, and Preexistence," 76–77. Another way of understanding *harpagmos* is "clinging" (in a greedy or selfish sense—known as *res retienda*), among other slight variations in meaning. See the further discussion in Martin, *Hymn of Christ*, 135–53 and the further critical (and, according to its own estimation, corrective) discussion in Wright, *Climax*, 62–81.

37. Moule, "Further Reflexions," 266.

38. See Hawthorne, "Form of God," 102; Moule's position can be found in "Manhood of Jesus," 95–110. Hoover's solution is presented in his "Harpagmos Enigma," 95–119.

39. Wright, *Climax*, 82. Emphasis mine.

40. Wright, *Climax*, 83, emphasis added. So too Hawthorne, "Form of God," 104.

In short, then, it can be argued that the *form of God* is summed, paralleled, and defined by the phrase "equal with God."[41] Hawthorne well notes that *morphē* ought not be loaded with undue ontological baggage, though it is certainly referring to Godlikeness in a non-philosophical semantic range,[42] and Wright's exegesis here allows this to stand.[43] Thus what we have in the passage is an understanding of Christ's pre-human existence in which equality with God is possessed (thus making Jesus "divine") but where Christ's attitude to that divine equality is not exploitative or self-seeking. Rather than divinity being understood in terms of "taking advantage" it is understood as self-emptying and self-sacrificing in humility.

hyparchōn, ekenōsen—the participle and the emptying (vv. 6, 7)

The final element of this line of exegesis comes into focus when we consider that the participle *hyparchōn* has been argued by Moule (and followed more recently and forcefully by Wright, Gorman, and others) as being causative—"*because* he was in the form of God"—rather than concessive—"*although* he was in the form of God."[44] That is, the self-emptying does not provide any sort of exception to or abandonment of the form of God. Rather Christ's self-emptying is *illustrative* of the fact that he possesses the form of God. This fundamentally shifts the understanding of kenosis in the passage. For, on this interpretation, it is quite correct to say that when Christ *empties himself* he is *demonstrating* his divinity, and not doing something that obscures it (as in the traditional interpretations) or that is an exception to that divine life (as in the radical interpretations). Gorman is emphatic here: "Kenosis, therefore, does not mean Christ's emptying himself of his divinity (or of anything else), but rather Christ's *exercising* his divinity, his

---

41. Fee adopts this reading strongly, *Paul's Letter to the Philippians*, 206–7; as does Bauckham, *Jesus and the God of Israel*, 41–42.

42. See Hawthorne, "Form of God," 104; see also "Form of God," 98, where Hawthorne agrees with criticism of his own earlier phrasing, which leaned more heavily on metaphysical definitions, in *Philippians*, 83–84.

43. Hence why Hawthorne concludes his description of his own position by quoting Wright at-length: "Form of God," 104–5.

44. See Moule, "Manhood of Jesus," 97; Wright, *Climax*, 83; Gorman, *Inhabiting the Cruciform God*, 10, 22–29. (Note that Gorman argues that both senses [causative *and* concessive] are intended simultaneously, as a way of challenging and undermining ancient conceptions of power-focused deity.)

equality with God."[45] Wright expresses it similarly, saying *ekenōsen* "does not refer to the loss of divine attributes but—in good Pauline fashion—to making something powerless, emptying it of apparent significance. The real humiliation of the incarnation and the cross is that one who was himself God, and who never during the whole process stopped being God, could embrace such a vocation."[46]

Such an interpretation—the *kenosis as a revelation of God's divinity rather than an exceptional mode of being undertaken by that divinity*—clearly challenges the radical forms of kenotic Christology, especially in their early German articulations and the more recent resuscitation of these models.[47] This is clearly different than (and actually often staged in contrast to) the radical kenotic school of thought; but, we should ask, is it truly distinct from the more traditional interpretation? The recent exegetical progression challenges this viewpoint as well. Demurring from Calvin, Barth, and other proponents of the traditional "concealment" view of the incarnation,[48] Gorman asks, "But is it really the case that Christ's self-emptying or humility *hides* his divinity? Is it not rather Paul's point that the humility of the incarnation and cross *reveals* the divine majesty, like a *transparent* curtain? 'Look here to see true divinity,' calls Paul. . . . It is the constitutive character of the divine identity that this narrative reveals."[49] Both Gorman and Wright are unanimous, along with Fee and Bauckham, that what the hymn presents

> is not simply a new view of Jesus. It is a new understanding of God. Against the age-old attempts of human beings to make God in their own (arrogant, self-glorifying) image, Calvary reveals the truth about what it meant to be God. Underneath this is the conclusion, all-important in present christological debate: incarnation and even crucifixion are to be seen as *appropriate* vehicles for the dynamic self-revelation of God.[50]

---

45. Gorman, *Inhabiting*, 28.

46. Wright, *Climax*, 84.

47. Feenstra, Evans, Davis, among others, are representative of the contemporary wave of radical kenoticists, most of whom are heavily indebted to Thomasius and Gess; see Evans, *Exploring Kenotic Christology*.

48. We noted Calvin above; Barth follows a line very close to Calvin in his commentary: *The Epistle to the Philippians*, 63–64, referring to the life of Christ as an *incognito* (64), perpetuating the concealment motif.

49. Gorman, *Inhabiting*, 28, 29.

50. Wright, *Climax*, 84, emphasis original. For similarly emphatic affirmations, see Gorman, *Inhabiting*, 25–27; Bauckham, *Jesus and the God*, 45–46; Fee, *Paul's Letter to the*

Wright's own emphasis on the word *appropriate* drives home the key exegetical—and hence *doctrinal*—shift. Becoming man and dying does not conceal divinity and does not entail its abandonment (in either an explicit or tacit sense); becoming man is appropriate or "proper" to the Son; dying is the willing way of expressing divine love. Read in this way, the vexing question of kenosis instead becomes "revelatory of the 'humility' of the divine nature."[51] Graham Ward, quoting F. F. Bruce, concurs, saying that "the implication is not that Christ, by becoming incarnate, exchanged the form of God for the form of the slave, but that he manifested the form of God in the form of the slave."[52] It is in this sense that we can unify also the tapeinotic and kenotic aspects of the hymn, which means that we must go beyond positions that claim "Jesus' kenosis was *sociopolitical* rather than *metaphysical*,"[53] for Christ's "tapeinosis" (humble bearing of his life in the world) is reflective of the kenotic divine economy at large and involves the real suspension of things that had characterized the divine life "prior to" the incarnation (majesty, glory, splendor, etc.—see John 17:5).[54] Here then we find exegetical foundation for discussion of the "humanity of God."[55]

Having examined, then, these three different lines of exegesis and theological interpretation of the passage, we can now turn to Moltmann's use of the passage. This foregoing analysis will help us to see, though Moltmann never delves into at-depth exegetical work, where his hermeneutical appropriation of the passage stands and what its implications are for his christological doctrine.

Exploring Moltmann's View

That Moltmann rarely engages in sustained exegesis is simply a fact of his theological method, a fact often highlighted and critiqued, and one

---

Philippians, 210–11.

51. Coakley, "*Kenosis* and Subversion," 10.

52. Ward, "Kenosis," 22.

53. Murphy and Ellis, *On the Moral Nature*, 177.

54. For an example of a reading of the passage without these exegetical points (i.e., those concerning *morphē* and *harpagmos*) see Gibbs, "Relation Between Creation," 270–83.

55. A key phrase and idea in both Barth and Moltmann; see Barth, *Humanity of God*; and Moltmann, "God With the Human Face," respectively.

conceded by Moltmann himself.[56] Accordingly, we rarely find detailed engagement with the linguistic, philological, or grammatical aspects of pertinent sections of scripture. However, he calls upon certain verses often enough that a sort of assumed exegesis emerges with relative clarity.[57] This is certainly the case with the kenosis material of Phil 2.

Moltmann's earliest significant employment of Phil 2 in a christological context comes in *The Crucified God*. Discussing the notion of "taking up one's cross" Moltmann connects this to an imitation of Christ "who abandoned [*aufgab*] his divine identity and found his true identity in the cross (Phil 2)."[58] This language of *abandoning* the divine "identity" immediately recalls more radical interpretations of the hymn (e.g., Thomasius, Gess), and this trajectory seems at least partially confirmed by Moltmann's later comment that the poor of the world "find in [Christ] the brother who put off [*verließ*] his divine form and took on the form of a slave (Phil 2)."[59] The implication here that the divine form of Christ was somehow vacated or left behind in the kenotic course of the incarnation seems to be following radical kenoticist assumptions.

However, importantly, in that same work Moltmann also makes a clear *distinction* between himself and foregoing radical expressions of kenotic thought:

> God's incarnation "even unto the death on the cross" [Phil. 2.8] is not in the last resort a matter of concealment. . . . When the crucified Jesus is called the "image of the invisible God," the meaning is that *this* is God, and God is like *this*. God is not greater than he is in this humiliation. God is not more glorious than he is in this self-surrender. God is not more powerful than he is in this helplessness. God is not more divine than he is in this humanity. The nucleus of everything that Christian theology says about "God" is to be found in this Christ event. The Christ event on the cross is a God event. . . . So the new Christology which tries to think of the "death of Jesus as the death of God," must take up the elements of truth [*Wahrheitsmomente*] which are to be found in *kenoticism* (the doctrine of God's emptying of himself).[60]

56. Moltmann, "Adventure of Theological Ideas," 104.

57. E.g., Mark 15:34 ("My God, why have you forsaken me?"), 1 Cor 15:28 (". . . that God may be all in all.").

58. *CG*, 16 (German: 21).

59. *CG*, 49 (German: 51). See also *JCTW*, 39; *ET*, 213, 233.

60. *CG*, 205 (German: 190)

This passage is of monumental importance for understanding Moltmann's own brand of kenotic Christology. Here we see several diverse doctrinal hints, all of which allow us to locate Moltmann within our threefold typology of Phil 2 interpretations.

Moltmann clearly states that the incarnation and suffering of Christ are revelatory and "not a matter of concealment," thereby distancing himself from traditional interpretations of Phil 2:5–8.[61] And here Moltmann, in slight contrast to what he seems to have implied earlier, makes the *divinity* of Christ *causative* for the death "even unto the cross"; divinity is expressed in the incarnation—"the meaning is that *this* is God and God is like *this* [*das ist Gott und so ist Gott*]."[62] This presents an interpretation of Christ's self-emptying that is in general agreement with the revelatory interpretation we outlined above, though Moltmann is writing at a time before this interpretation gained such prominence among English authors. His language relating to the passage is admittedly less controlled than what we find among the exegetes, but Moltmann does not often return to the more extreme language of "giving-up" the divine form in exchange for the servant one, preferring in subsequent work to use expressions like "emptying [*Entäußerung*]" and "self-giving [*Selbsthingabe*]."[63] Moreover, it is clear in many passages that Moltmann intends the kenotic servanthood and self-giving suffering of Jesus to be illustrative for the proper understanding of divinity itself: the serving God who seeks the liberation of humanity through self-sacrificial love.[64]

Both Barth and Pannenberg were dismissive of what they saw as the clear heterodoxy and absurdity of radical kenoticism.[65] But, as indicated in the final sentence of the block quotation above, Moltmann adopts a more textured relationship to the mediating kenotic thought of the nineteenth century. Both early in his career, in *The Crucified God*, and in his more

---

61. He takes Paul Althaus to task for advocating this sort of concealment language while simultaneously critiquing the traditional doctrine of divine immutability: *CG*, 206 (discussing Althaus' article on "Kenosis," in *Die Religion in Geschichte und Gegenwart*, 1243ff.).

62. *CG* (German), 190.

63. E.g., *TK*, 81 (German: 97); *WJC*, 173; *SW*, 51.

64. E.g., Moltmann, *On Human Dignity*, 42; *CoG*, 303–4; *TK*, 59–60, 118–19; *CG*, 270–78; *GSS*, 181–85.

65. Barth, *Church Dogmatics*, 176 (see further 175–77); Pannenberg, *Jesus*, 311–12. But Pannenberg may betray a deeper indebtedness to this tradition than his critiques indicate: see the discussion in Brown, *Divine Humanity*, 226–27.

recent work, e.g., *Science and Wisdom*, Moltmann has attempted to sift foregoing kenoticism and dialogically appropriate certain emphases from it.[66] Most importantly for Moltmann, kenoticism tried to "understand God's being in process,"[67] that is, apart from classically defined divine attributes (omnipotence, omniscience, etc., bound together by the immutability axiom), which were derived "from Aristotle's general metaphysics" but that "have very little to do with God's attributes according to the history of God to which the Bible testifies."[68] In kenoticism, the incarnation and the cross do not just mean something for *us* (soteriology) but they also mean something for *God* (theology).[69] But this theological meaning does not, as in Thomasius, consist in an idiosyncratic dividing of the divine attributes and ascribing only some of these to the incarnate Christ.[70] Moltmann is instead driven to see kenosis as a *revelation* of God, and here he seems to have initially been inspired by the thought of Hans Urs von Balthasar.[71] Balthasar interprets the kenotic life of Christ as primarily revelatory in terms of the Trinity; the trinitarian relations are always kenotic in Balthasar's thought—for instance, the Son is eternally obedient to the Father in kenotic love—and thus the kenotic dimensions of the incarnation are, at least partly, a temporal expression of those eternal relations of the Trinity.[72] As Steffen Lösel (erstwhile student of Moltmann) writes of Balthasar: "The extra-trinitarian kenosis of God serves the ever-dramatic inner divine life of the mutual glorification of the divine persons."[73] Moltmann adopts this interpretation whole-heartedly, and his own social trinitarianism eventually comes to depend on an understanding of perichoresis

66. The key passages are *CG*, 200–207; and *SW*, 55–58.

67. *CG*, 206.

68. *SW*, 56; see also *WJC*, 53. Brown agrees that this is the core alignment Moltmann appreciates in the kenotic christologians of the nineteenth century (*Divine Humanity*, 227–28).

69. Moltmann most famously states this notion in *CG*, 201; see also, "Theology of the Cross Today," 62–64, 72; *WJC*, 152; *ET*, 304; *ABP*, 192.

70. Moltmann claims that this brand of kenotic Christology on its own results in "impossible statements" (*CG*, 206) that are "unsatisfactory" (*SW*, 56). In that sense, at least, he aligns with most major twentieth century theologians in relegating the Thomasian model of "dividing the attributes" to theological impossibility.

71. See the praise accorded Balthasar in *CG* (202) and *SW* (57–58).

72. See Balthasar, *Mysterium*, vii–viii, 25; see also Papanikolaou, "Person, *Kenosis*, and Abuse," 46–48; Ward, "Kenosis," 15–68.

73. Lösel, *Kreuzwege*, 158, my translation.

between the three persons that is essentially a *pluriform kenotic relating*, constitutive of the triune identity of the Godhead.[74]

But this is not the whole story. Moltmann's kenotic Christology remains somewhere between this revelatory school of thought and the more radical "abandonment" outlook from the nineteenth century. In order to illustrate the difference, we must first make a critical point in regards to the revelatory interpretation.

The Ambiguity of "Emptying" in the Revelatory View

All of the contemporary exegetes we cited earlier as supporting the revelatory interpretation (Wright, Bauckham, Fee, Gorman, etc.) have maintained that the christological kenosis reveals that God is a God who loves in sacrificial ways and is willing to humble himself for the sake of his creation's redemption. But these same thinkers are so resistant to being identified with the nineteenth-century radical kenoticists that they consistently refuse to follow through on the underlying logical and doctrinal force of their exegetical claims. *What* does the divine Son sacrifice? In what specific aspects of his existence is the divine Son *humbled*? These questions are often treated by this group of interpreters as though their position itself does not necessitate any positive answers to them, as seen in the representative passages below:

> It is not necessary . . . to insist that the phrase ἑαυτὸν ἐκένωσεν demands some genitive of content be supplied [emptied himself *of* something]. . . . Rather, it is a poetic, hymnlike way of saying that Christ poured out himself.[75]

> Christ did not empty himself *of* anything; he simply "emptied *himself*," poured himself out. This is metaphor, pure and simple. . . . Pauline usage elsewhere substantiates this view, where this verb means to become powerless or to be emptied of significance.[76]

74. *TK*, 18–20, 63–64, 149–50, 171–78; see also Moltmann, "Trinitarian Personhood," 312. Lösel notes confluence between Moltmann and Balthasar in these points: *Kreuzwege*, 159.

75. Hawthorne, *Philippians*, 86.

76. Fee, *Paul's Letter to the Philippians*, 210–11. Fee's reasoning here is problematic not only along the lines discussed in the body text above, but also insofar as he banks much of his argument on "Pauline usage" (210, 211), as do the sources he cites (Silva, Hoover, Wright). But the verb in question is *never* used reflexively (emptied him/her/itself) by Paul elsewhere, and, of course, if it is a pre-Pauline hymn, then the wording is

The phrase "emptied himself" in 2:7 should not be read as a reference to the divestiture of something (whether divinity itself or some divine attribute, or even as self-limitation regarding the use of the divine attributes), but "figuratively," as a robust metaphor for total self-abandonment and self-giving.[77]

All of these statements argue that nothing constitutive of Christ's pre-incarnational existence is given up (or, for Gorman, even *limited*) by the incarnational act. But the logic of the Philippians passage does not seem to allow for this; the paraenetic point fails without a sacrifice (a giving-up, a surrendering) of some *ability, status, or capacity* on the part of Christ.[78] Moreover, these same commentators seem to be tacitly aware of this, for they *imply* quite clearly that Christ did, in fact, give up *something*, however vaguely stated, even in the same context in which they deny that he gave up anything.[79] Fee's example, the second quotation above, demonstrates this most immediately: he claims that no genitive of content is required in Phil 2:7, but he then indicates that Paul's usage of the emptying language elsewhere *does* imply some genitive of content—for to become "powerless" (Fee's own language) is to be emptied *of* power, and to be emptied *of* significance (Fee's own language) is clearly indicative of some content ("significance") for the emptying. The other commentators use similarly ambiguous or contradictory phrasing.[80]

The corrective to such inconsistency can be rendered quite simply: to be sacrificial means to sacrifice *something*; to be humbled means to be diminished, limited, or divested in *some way*. Ben Witherington makes the point effectively:

> [*Ekenōsen*] must have some content to it, and it is not adequate to say Christ did not subtract anything since in fact he added a human nature. The latter is true enough, but the text says that he did empty himself or strip himself. . . . The contrast between verses 6b

---

likely *not original to Paul* anyways.

77. Gorman, *Inhabiting*, 21(n54).

78. See Horrell, *Solidarity and Difference*, 210–12.

79. For Hawthorne, "[Christ] set aside *his rights*" (86); for Fee, elsewhere he writes that Christ "limit[ed] certain *divine prerogatives* that . . . seem incompatible with him being truly human" ("New Testament and Kenosis," 34); for Gorman, "[Christ] renounced *all privilege*" (*Inhabiting*, 21n55), all emphases mine.

80. Sykes, who is critical of radical kenotic Christology, still states of Phil 2:7 that "we have a biblical text which affirms that Jesus *divests himself of the glories of heaven* and humbles himself" ("Strange Persistence," 360, emphasis added).

and 7a is very suggestive; that is, Christ set aside his rightful divine prerogatives or status. This does not mean he set aside his divine nature, but it does indicate some sort of self-limitation.[81]

In short, some "genitive of inferred content" seems to be necessitated, though this is certainly not to say that we are thereby permitted to speculate in any sort of detail about the precise nature of that content. But the point remains: one cannot undertake a sacrificial act that does not impose a sacrifice *of something*; sacrifice and humility imply content, else they surrender meaning. Moltmann gets at this quite strongly with his notion of "active suffering" or willing vulnerability. He argues that loving sacrifice-in-relation entails, at the most basic level, the surrendering of some level of security or status or power, because one has opened oneself up to another in relationship—the "other" can "affect" oneself.[82]

Moltmann's Kenosis as Creational and Dialectical

So, the question emerges: does Moltmann supply some genitive of content for the emptying of Christ? The answer is somewhat complex, and requires us to unfold Moltmann's kenotic framework still further. Moltmann will say, somewhat unclearly, that "Christ's emptying of himself is not a partial or ostensible self-emptying, but a whole and genuine emptying of his divine form . . . as well as his divine power."[83] Throughout his discussions on the christological kenosis, Moltmann is concerned to indicate that Jesus does not possess divine *omnipotence*. But this emphasis aligns with Moltmann's more fundamental kenotic logic, which sees God self-electing a non-omnipotent existence (in some sense) upon the determination to create a truly free world: "God permits an existence different from his own by limiting himself. . . . [God] withdraws his omnipotence. . . . God limits and empties [*begrenzt und entäußert*] himself."[84] Thus, for Moltmann, kenosis is not just an incarnational reality, but also a "creational" one; in order to free his creation for genuine relationship, God must limit himself in certain ways—God does not have "all power" once a free creation exists—the freedom of the creation is a natural, but real, limitation on the power of God, and it is

81. Witherington, *Friendship and Finances*, 66.

82. See Moltmann's initial statement in *CG*, 230. See also Hanson, *Christian Theology*, 28–29.

83. Moltmann, "God Is Unselfish Love," 118.

84. *TK*, 118, 119 (German: 134).

a limitation that God has willingly brought into effect. Thus creation and incarnation are reflective of one another: Moltmann is emphatic that the initial creational movement of divine kenosis "reaches its perfected and completed form [*vollendete Gestalt*] in the incarnation of the Son."[85]

Since omnipotence entails both maximality of knowledge (omniscience) and presence (omnipresence), the incarnate Logos is also emptied of these things. But, at this point, it appears to be Thomasius and company all over again. How can Moltmann be affirming the revelatory interpretation of Phil 2 and critiquing the radical kenoticists, and yet sound so much like them in discussing his own kenotic Christology? The reason is twofold. First, as we've noted above, Moltmann sees divinity as having *always* been defined by *kenotic inner-relationships* within the Trinity and *kenotic outer-relationships* to the created order and its freedom. There is even a sense in which the kenosis of God in relation to the world causes a degree of *change* in the divine life. Indeed the trinitarian relationships can even be said to alter through time, insofar as the persons kenotically assume different "roles" in the progression of salvation history.[86] Most importantly for us, omnipotence, omnipresence, and, indeed, omniscience have already, to some extent, been relinquished by God upon the world's creation, in order to "let be" a truly free "other" who can respond to the sacrificial love of God.[87] Thus, for Christ to "radically" give up the exercise of such divine rights/powers/capacities, *is rightly revelatory of the God who already has been self-emptying in such ways.*

This is, then, a significant difference from radical kenoticists who generally see the kenosis of Christ as an *exception* to the foregoing mode of divine-world relations, and it also shifts the grounds of possible criticism. For instance, Sarah Coakley accuses Moltmann of allowing for "seepage" of human properties into his conception of God.[88] But Anna Mercedes effectively responds to Coakley, saying that "[if] God's nature is always kenotic, no seepage has taken place—only an eroding of a classical theology of God's nature. . . . Coakley assumes that the human is

85. *TK*, 118 (German: 133).

86. E.g., *TK*, 174, 210.

87. *TK* argues, "For the sake of freedom, and the love responded to in freedom, God limits and empties himself. He withdraws his omnipotence" (119). *SW* speaks of "a *restriction* of God's omnipotence, omnipresence and omniscience, so that those he has created may have room to live" (63).

88. Coakley, "*Kenosis* and Subversion," 23–24; Coakley, *Powers and Submissions*, xiv–xv.

contaminating the divine rather than that God was always so 'contaminated' by God's love for creatures."[89]

Second, Moltmann has long maintained that there ultimately must be a *dialectic* (an illuminating contrast between two apparently oppositional ideas which leads to a fuller conception beyond either of them) between the divine attributes in their maximal expression and in their kenotic limitation. Stating things simply, Moltmann maintains that "only God can limit God."[90] Only the power of an omnipotent being could willingly invoke the freedom to act in ways that are less than omnipotent. Moltmann draws support for this thesis from Kierkegaard, who states, "Only almighty power can withdraw itself by surrendering itself,"[91] as well as Gregory of Nyssa: "[That] the omnipotent nature should have been capable of descending to the low estate of humanity provides a clearer proof of power than great and supernatural miracles."[92] This, once again, demonstrates that Moltmann is arguing for the "form of God" to be dialectically exemplified in the giving up of that form's maximal expression.[93]

Radical and *Revelatory:* Moltmann's Reading of Kenosis

The beginning of Moltmann's kenotic Christology is thus neither in the concealment nor abandonment camp; his overarching kenotic theology means that his Christology reads Phil 2 as revelatory for divinity itself. Likewise, Colin Gunton (in the midst of a salvo against radical forms of kenotic Christology) writes that "it seems not inappropriate to speak of a self-emptying of God, but only if it is understood in such a way as to be an *expression* rather than a 'retraction' of his deity."[94] This well sums the trajectory that initializes Moltmann's kenotic Christology. Thus, we can call

89. Mercedes, *Power For,* 32.

90. *SW,* 62, but articulated long before in terms of the "active [voluntary] suffering of love" in *CG,* 230.

91. Quoted by Moltmann in *SW,* 64, citing *Gesammelte Werke,* 124.

92. Quoted by Moltmann in *CG,* 205n20, referencing *Or. cat.* 24, 77.

93. There is also a sense in which Moltmann may be following (implicitly) some part of the kenotic logic of Thomasius, for Thomasius posited that to "renounce" the exercise of omnipotence was tantamount to divesting oneself of such power completely: "Renunciation of the use is thus here *eo ipso* divesting of the possession. . . . Thus we say simply: During his earthly state of life the redeemer was neither omnipotent nor omniscient nor omnipresent" (Thomasius, *Christi Person und Werk,* 70).

94. Gunton, *Yesterday and Today,* 172, emphasis original.

the baseline outlook on kenotic Christology that we find in Moltmann a "radical revelatory" model, for it uniquely combines emphases from both the radical interpretation and the revelatory. It entails *real limitations* applied to the divinity of Christ in his becoming human, but these limitations are *extensions and radicalizations* of the already existing kenotic patterns of the God-world relationship. The thematic thrust of this is conveyed by Moltmann in the following key passage:

> [If] the significance of the Son's incarnation is his true human-
> ity, then the incarnation reveals the true humanity of God. That
> is not an anthropomorphic way of speaking, which is therefore
> not in accordance with God's divinity; it is the quintessence of
> his divinity itself [*der Inbegriff seiner Göttlichkeit selbst*]. . . . His
> strength is made perfect in weakness. The traditional doctrine
> about God's kenosis has always looked at just the one aspect of
> God's self-limitation, self-emptying and self-humiliation. It has
> overlooked the other side: God's inward limitations are outward
> liberations [*Einschränkungen Gottes nach innen sind Freisetzungen
> nach außen*]. God is nowhere greater than in his humiliation. God
> is nowhere more glorious than in his impotence. God is nowhere
> more divine than when he becomes man.[95]

And though the kenosis of Christ in Moltmann is revelatory of the way in which God relates to the world, this should not obscure for us the fact that Moltmann perceives this as always involving real sacrifice on the part of God. Whether in the incarnation or in wider contexts in which he carries through the theme, Moltmann's kenotic language consistently embraces this directive element: *God's willing suffering.* We see this reflected in his range of kenotic terminology, which is scattered throughout all of his major works. Margaret Kohl, Moltmann's most prominent English translator, has rendered Molt-mann's kenotic terms variously as self-negation (translating *Selbstnegation*),[96] self-restriction (*Selbstbescheidung*),[97] self-humiliation (*Selbsterniedrigung*),[98] as well as in the more standard kenotic parlance of self-emptying ([*Selbst-*]

---

95. *TK*, 119 (German: 133–34). I have modified Kohl's translation slightly.

96. E.g., *GC*, 87 [German edition, 100]; see Kohl's translation in *SW*, 120.

97. E.g., *TK*, 210 [German: 227]; *GC*, 88 [German: 101]; see Kohl's translations in *CoG*, 282, 332; *SpL*, 61; *SW*, chapter 4.

98. E.g., *TK*, 27–28, 59, 119 [German edition: 42–43, 75, 134]; *GC* 102 [German: 113]; cf. *CoG*, 302–3.

Entäußerung[99] and self-limitation (*Selbstbeschränkung*).[100] These terms and their variants emerge at key junctures in the unfolding of Moltmann's kenotic Christology across his major works.

Conclusion: From Kenotic Hymn to Kenotic Christ

This chapter has laid the groundwork for our continuing exploration of christological kenosis in Moltmann through an analysis of his baseline kenotic logic, rooted in his implicit interpretation of Phil 2. Via a diachronic analysis of three foregoing hermeneutical outlooks on that passage, we were enabled to categorize Moltmann's own treatment of it as a "radical revelatory" model. Moreover, this discovery facilitated our realization of the connection between Moltmann's doctrine of divine passibility and inter-trinitarian kenotic relations with his view of Christ's kenosis specifically. Kenotic Christology, for Moltmann, is thus found to be fundamentally rooted in his broadest theological presuppositions and to be directly expressive of some of his most overt theological concerns. From this conceptual basis in Moltmann's theology, we turn next to examine the doctrinal ramifications this bears for Moltmann's handling of the incarnation.

99. E.g., *GC*, 88 [German: 101]; *TK*, 119, 174, 210 [German: 134, 190, 227]; see also *CG*, 121, 275; *WJC*, 138, 178; *SpL*, 64, 288.

100. E.g., *TK*, 59, chapter 4.2; 119, 174 [German: 75, *Kapitel* 4.2, 134, 190); *GC*, 78, 80, 86, 102 [German: 91, 92, 99, 113]; see Kohl's translations in Moltmann, *Sun of Righteousness*, 91; *EthH*, 122. Other, less common, terms used by Kohl in her translations include "self-surrender," "self-offering," and "self-renunciation."

4

Moltmann's Commitments

Creed and Kenosis

UP TO THIS POINT, I have sought to do the following: establish the christological center of Moltmann's thought, survey his unique theological method, array his diverse christological thematics, and explore his hermeneutical approach to and application of the "kenosis hymn" in Phil 2:5–11. Along the way, however, trained theologians in particular have no doubt been nagged by a battery of issues that I have deliberately delayed until now: *Moltmann's relationship to the Chalcedonian Definition and properly "creedal" Christology.* This particular dimension of Moltmann's thought is both pivotal and controversial, and it is too often addressed without an adequate grasp of the foregoing elements that this study has presented. Having now covered those topics, we are equipped to turn our attention to Moltmann's posture toward Chalcedon and what it means for his conception of both the *incarnation* and *kenosis* of Jesus Christ.

Christology, Context, and Creed

Bauckham has stated that Moltmann's Christology "is one of the few recent Christologies which is capable of reinvigorating christological thinking, expanding its horizons and realigning it with the church's task of witness to the contemporary world."[1] Moltmann has always been concerned with the *kairos* in which his theology emerges and to which it speaks, and this is certainly the case with his Christology—in his view, as soteriological questioning shifts, Christology must shift along with it.[2] Appropriately enough, questions

1. Bauckham, *Theology*, 199.

2. Bauckham, *Theology*, 200. This is quite typical of the correlational approach that Moltmann adopts throughout his work: "If it is correct to say that the Bible is essentially

arise concerning what such a *correlational* view of theology might do with doctrinal *tradition*. Here we recall Moltmann's enduring propensity to see all theology as a provisional conversation; no aspect of tradition is allowed to go unquestioned, but nor should it be summarily or presumptuously tossed aside. The present concerns and past traditions of the church dynamically engage with one another on the road to richer and more applicable formulations of the faith. Christologically speaking, there are plenty of time-ensconced categories to go around. Methodologically speaking, Moltmann champions what he sees as useful and critiques, ignores, or de-emphasizes what he deems less so. But it is very rare—contrary to what is implied by some of his less sympathetic interlocutors—that Moltmann ever issues a flat denial of creedal affirmations. And along the way, it is certainly not always the newest or trendiest forms of theology that receive his approval.[3]

Another characteristic of Moltmann's Christology that deserves, but seldom receives, targeted discussion is his determinative attention to Judaism. As a post-WWII German who became aware of the dawning horror of the death camps only when he was imprisoned as a POW, Moltmann has been clear that the looming shadow of those events has fueled his attention to both human suffering and Jewish categories of understanding.[4] Indeed, Jewish thinkers are hugely important to Moltmann's thought overall,[5] and in his longest work on Christology he emphatically states, "In this Christology . . . I wanted the Christian-Jewish dialogue to be continually present."[6] This sensitivity to Judaism has a two-fold effect on Moltmann's christological work: (1) It intensifies his vision of Christ's particular historical Jewishness, that is, his *developmental and social context*; (2) it is a factor (among several) that causes Moltmann to often *avoid discussion of certain tradition-specific categories* in Christian theology, or

---

a witness to the promissory history of God, then the role of Christian theology is to bring the remembrances of the future to bear on the hopes and anxieties of the present" (Moltmann, "Christian Theology and Its Problems Today," 8).

3. Bauckham rightly highlights that in Moltmann's dual evaluation of patristic Christology and liberal Enlightenment Christology, he favors the cosmological emphasis (though not the substance metaphysics) of the early church and denounces the "Jesusologies" of modernity: *Theology*, 200–201; see Moltmann, *WJC*, 46–63.

4. The horror and shame of the Holocaust is stark across Moltmann's work, e.g., *GSS*, 169–172; *CG*, xi; *JCTW*, 108–109; *ET*, 4, 115–116; *ABP*, 29.

5. Most notably Gershom Scholem, Martin Buber, Abraham Heschel, and Schalom Ben-Chorin.

6. *WJC*, xvi; see also *JCTW*, 108–9.

to discuss them in oblique or creative ways. This second effect will be readily evident as we turn in the next section to consider the question of Christ's two natures specifically.

Conflicting Interpretations of Moltmann and Chalcedon

It should be striking to us that across the writings of serious theologians there are multiple dimensions of disagreement concerning just *how* Moltmann relates to what we might call Chalcedonian Christology (or the traditional "two-natures" framework). Donald Macleod remarks that "[in] *The Way of Jesus Christ* Moltmann achieves the extraordinary feat of writing 300 pages on Christology without once mentioning Chalcedon."[7] Macleod is not quite right about this; Moltmann does discuss Chalcedon and two-nature formulations in that particular work and elsewhere.[8] But it is certainly not a topic on which Moltmann presents an abundance of specific commentary, and other theological voices have aligned with Macleod's concerns insofar as they disapprovingly note Moltmann's neglect of a sustained and careful account of where he stands before the Chalcedonian Definition.[9]

Beyond these voices, however, there is further disagreement. Don Schweitzer holds that though Moltmann focuses on the trinitarian relationships of Jesus, he in fact *assumes* the truth of the "hypostatic union" in Christ.[10] Peter Schmiechen, on the other hand, maintains that Moltmann *qualifies* "the language of two natures . . . though his intent is not to reject these categories but to incorporate them into a larger eschatological perspective."[11] And, different still, Ryan Neal states directly that Moltmann "rejects" two-natures Christology.[12] What are we to make of this plurality of interpretation?

Upon examination of these commentators (and the portions of Moltmann's work which they cite in support of their analyses) it can be seen that all three evaluations have correctly identified certain aspects of Moltmann's

7. Macleod, *Jesus Is Lord*, 145.

8. *WJC*, xiii, 47–53.

9. E.g., Williams, "Moltmann on Jesus Christ," 104–113.

10. Schweitzer, *Contemporary Christologies*, 78.

11. Schmiechen, *Saving Power*, 135. He will later (140) note that Moltmann seems to imply only one nature in Christ at times—e.g., in *CG*, 231–34—but does not attempt to constructively reconcile these two observations.

12. See Neal, "Jürgen Moltmann," 375; also see Neal, *Theology as Hope*, 47–48.

complicated relationship to christological tradition.[13] Especially in light of our foregoing examination of Moltmann's theological methodology, it must be said that Schmiechen has most clearly detected the key controlling principle for Moltmann. Though often critical of traditional theology, Moltmann makes it fairly clear if he patently rejects some aspect of it (e.g., divine impassibility[14]), and no such patent rejection can be found for the two-natures conception *per se*.[15] Ryan Neal's citations of Moltmann—which are meant to support his judgment that Moltmann "rejects" the two-natures framework— all refer to passages where Moltmann is discussing how, in his estimation, two-natures Christology can be or has been problematic for a deep understanding of the cross, insofar as the human nature alone suffers and thus safeguards the divine nature from being affected.[16] But none of these passages from Moltmann features an outright *rejection* of a two-natures framework. Moltmann never declares that his Christology is anti-Chalcedonian, and he has had many opportunities to do so. As noted, he rarely rejects any revered part of theological tradition in a sweeping or wholesale fashion. Instead he will absorb traditional formulations into some new, unique synthesis, thus retaining them in some form.[17]

In light of this, both Schweitzer and Neal appear to be partially on-target in their evaluations. As we will see clearly in this chapter's ensuing discussion, Moltmann *affirms both the deity and the humanity* of Christ, but he does so in ways that resist direct parallel to a standard Chalcedonian account. Nevertheless, some version of a two-natures conception (or at least comfort with such a conception) is latent in Moltmann, and Neal may recognize this, for, even in the midst of discussing his own assessment that Moltmann rejects two-natures Christology,[18] he does quote

13. Bauckham is quite right to state the matter simply as "Moltmann is not content with the way in which Chalcedonian Christology could speak of God's suffering and death" (*Theology*, 54), but he does not then go on to delineate any more precisely how Moltmann handles the "two natures" in light of that discontentment.

14. See *CG*, esp. 273–74; Moltmann, "Theology of the Cross Today," 67–71; *TK*, especially chapter 2.

15. Moltmann certainly critiques some traditional understandings of the divine-human-person model, but saying that he "rejects" the framework, without qualification, may be going beyond the evidence. Note Neal's ameliorating comments in his related footnote, 154n11.

16. Neal cites the following: *WJC*, xiii–xv, 53, 136ff.; *CG*, 227–35; *FC*, 62–64.

17. Bauckham also notes this methodological trend: *Theology*, 200.

18. See Neal, *Theology as Hope*, 47; he references also John Webster's critique of Moltmann's view of two-natures Christology: Webster, "Jürgen Moltmann," 5. However,

the following passage from Moltmann's writing: "the cleavage [*der Riß*] of death on the cross goes right through God himself, and not merely through the divine and human [*gottmenschliche*] person of Christ."[19] This mention of an assumed divine-human person for Christ is significant (and seems to be the sort of declaration which fuels Schweitzer's interpretation of Moltmann on this score).

Furthermore, in *The Way of Jesus Christ*, after presenting his pneumatological Christology, Moltmann quickly moves to state that "Spirit Christology is not directed against the doctrine of the two natures."[20] Both of these quotations come in passages where Moltmann could easily dismiss the two-natures model, had he a mind to do so.[21] In this sense, then, while Schweitzer's comment that Moltmann "assumes" the two-natures model is too simple, it hints at the retaining-yet-modifying approach that Moltmann adopts. The most significant example of such an approach to the doctrine is still to be found in *Crucified God*.[22] There we find Moltmann, after criticizing traditional formulations (which he sees as functioning mainly to protect the ostensible impassibility of Christ's divinity), speaking approvingly of Luther's expanded conception of the *communicatio idiomatum*, but noting that Luther saw the entwinement of the divine and human histories

---

Webster stops short of saying Moltmann rejects the two-natures formulation outright, and he clearly detects the specific issues that Moltmann takes with the doctrine's past uses; Webster's analysis is largely compatible, therefore, with the more holistic analysis of Moltmann's stance that I am favoring here.

19. Moltmann, "Theology of the Cross Today," 65 (German: 73). See also Neal's comments on this passage: *Theology as Hope*, 48.

20. My translation. German: "Geist-Christologie ist auch nicht gegen die Zwei-Naturen-Lehre gerichtet" (93). Moltmann is inclined to make this point often—that Logos Christology and Spirit Christology correspond rather than conflict. See his major work on pneumatology, *SpL*, 17, 72, 232–34. The recent work of Myk Habets is among the most successful, nuanced presentations of these two (Spirit and Logos) christological paradigms working in tandem; see *The Anointed Son*. Significantly, Moltmann is a very consistent interlocutor for Habets in this work. Ian McFarland has recently theorized a "pneumatic Chalcedonian" that offers several insights along these lines, though McFarland is not relying on Moltmann to make them: "Spirit and Incarnation."

21. In the passage from *FC* (65), for instance, Moltmann continues to emphasize "going beyond" the two-natures model, seeming to want to retain the doctrine, but formulate it afresh and in the midst of new concerns and concepts—and, notably, without a commitment to a "classical" conception of the immutable, impassible divine nature.

22. See *CG*, 227–35. Webster's analysis is helpful here, though he is critical of Moltmann's view of the doctrinal history: "Jürgen Moltmann," 5.

inconsistently, mainly as a result of his under-developed trinitarianism.[23] Such discussion invites the notion that if the two-natures conception can be preserved apart from a classical, apathetic model of theism, Moltmann is willing to let it stand.[24]

We might then hold together the three disparate interpretations of Moltmann as follows: Since two-natures Christology is a traditional doctrine, Moltmann dialogues with it, assumes the truth that he detects in it (Schweitzer), rejects the interpretations of it that he finds problematic (Neal[25]), and incorporates it into a wider eschatological, trinitarian perspective (Schmiechen). And, in fact, Moltmann himself makes this fairly clear: "The ancient church's doctrine of the two natures [of Christ] will have to be taken up once again in the framework of the postmodern, ecological paradigm, and will have to be newly interpreted."[26]

But what precisely is this "new interpretation" that Moltmann offers? We must leave this question aside for the moment, for the answer he provides acquires both its force and clarity from the intersecting layers of his multi-dimensioned Christology. The full exposition of this Christology, including its nuanced (and often implicit) view on the kenosis of Christ, will be the subject of the remainder of this chapter and the entirety of Part III.

Kenosis as Key to Moltmann's Incarnational Thought

Put simply, a holistic survey of Moltmann's major published works reveals a "kenotic logic" at the heart of both his trinitarian thinking and his Christology proper. However, this logic rarely reveals itself in an outright or straightforward way. One must navigate the other topics that are more characteristic

---

23. Scholarship on Luther's view of the *communicatio* has been vexed, with some scholars arguing that Luther is innovative if inconsistent (similar to Moltmann's analysis) and others arguing that he is traditional, albeit rhetorically unclear. See the excellent work by Luy, *Dominus Mortus,* especially the Introduction and chapter 3.

24. This will be further demonstrated when we examine Moltmann's particular outlook on kenosis in forthcoming discussion.

25. Neal eventually describes Moltmann as avoiding the establishment of "a firewall, a static separation of human and divine effectively keeping suffering from the divine and the divine from suffering" (47). This is a fair summation of Moltmann's worries with this tradition, especially in *Crucified God* and *Future of Creation.* Rob Lister notes this as well: *God Is Impassible,* 136–37.

26. *WJC,* 215.

of Moltmann's theological concerns to unfold this underlying grammar. In this case, those topics are *perichoresis* and *Shekinah*.

Two Natures and Perichoresis

For Moltmann, as for Wolfhart Pannenberg, christological thinking that takes a metaphysically construed incarnation as its primary point of departure seems to run into various impasses, as illustrated, in their view, by the dogmatic history of the patristic, scholastic, and Reformation eras.[27] Moltmann mines the doctrinal progressions in less detail than Pannenberg, eschewing much of their historical and philosophical minutiae in order to state his general reservations about traditional christological approaches.

First, he finds the notion of the *anhypostasia*[28] of the human nature crippling to any meaningful understanding of Christ's *vere homo*.[29] Second, in the two-natures conceptuality of the ancient dogmas, Moltmann detects a difficulty in understanding the redemptive efficacy of Christ's death: In his sinless human nature, how could he die at all, and how could the divinity of Christ be operative in that redemptive death if the divine nature cannot have suffering predicated of it?[30] Third, and far more foundationally than either of the two foregoing points, Moltmann notes the decidedly divinity-focused history of the doctrine; he finds most traditional Christology focused so

27. See, e.g., Pannenberg, *Jesus,* 283-7. Moltmann assumes much of Pannenberg's critique and highlights various aspects of it with his own emphases; see Moltmann, *Way of Jesus Christ,* 51-55 (Pannenberg is referenced at 51n21).

28. The doctrine of *anhypostasis* argues that the only "person" (*hypostasis*) in the incarnation is a *divine* person; the divine nature and the divine person unite with a human nature, but not with a human person. The lack of human *hypostasis* was deemed important for the purposes of avoiding Nestorianism, since the presence of two persons in the identity of Jesus would seemingly amount to two Christs.

29. *WJC,* 51: "If the eternal Logos assumed a non-personal [*anhypostatic*] human nature, he cannot then be viewed as a historical person, and we cannot talk about 'Jesus of Nazareth.' The human nature that was assumed would then seem to be like the human garment of the eternal Son—something which he put on when he walked on earth. It becomes difficult to find an identity here between this human nature and our own." See also *CG,* 231-32. *Anhypostasis* and the attendant doctrine of *enhypostasis* have received able defense (e.g., in Barth), but can still smack of docetism. See the appreciably nuanced discussions in Gunton, *Christ and Creation,* 47-51, and Brown, *Divine Trinity,* 227, who resonate with Moltmann's concerns. For a counterpoint, see Crisp, "Desiderata," 30, 35-36.

30. *WJC,* 52. Early on, he claimed that Luther's understanding of the *communicatio idiomatum* had made headway here, though it was still inadequate, *CG,* 232-35.

profoundly on the "vertical history" between the divine and human natures that it largely neglects *the lived, embodied life and historical, enacted achievements* of Jesus of Nazareth: "It is no doubt due to this one-sided viewpoint that the prophetic proclamation of Jesus and his earthly ministry are not so much as mentioned in either the Apostles' or the Nicene creed. Between his birth from a virgin and his death under Pontius Pilate, the dogmatic history tells us *almost nothing.*"[31] In this kind of commentary, Moltmann basically reiterates the accusation of *docetism* against traditional Christology,[32] and sees this lack of focus on the concrete, historical, personal, and social contours of Jesus' life as the unfortunate correlative of an overt focus on the classical divine attributes rooted in Hellenistic thought.[33]

Despite this litany of reservations, Moltmann still does not present any explicit rejection of the basic conceptual framework of the two-natures-in-one-person. Rather, his conflict is with traditional Christology insofar as it has been construed to reflect the issues we just enumerated. Even a commentator like Ryan Neal, who claims that Moltmann "rejects" the tradition at this point,[34] still concedes that Moltmann's motivation is "to avoid an essentially oversimplified Apollinarian Christology"[35] and to not posit a "firewall" between the divine and human natures.[36] It emerges from these statements that Moltmann cannot be charged with an emphatic denial of the two natures as such; Moltmann is rather concerned with rearticulating *the natures' relationship to each other and to Christ's lived life*, and thus he is assuming the presence of the two natures in the person of Christ in some sense. By way of example we can note a critical question that Moltmann poses to ancient Christology, on the basis of Mark 15:34: "Was it really necessary to dissolve the personal union of the two natures [*personale Einheit der beiden Naturen*] in Christ in his cry of desolation?"[37] It is evident in

---

31. *WJC*, 52; see also Neal, *Theology as Hope*, 154. This contrasts somewhat with Robert Jenson, who states that Nicea safeguarded the church from "abstracting" any notion of deity apart from Jesus' "death or his career or his birth or his family or his Jewishness or his maleness or his teaching" (*Systematic Theology*, 103).

32. Explicitly in *CG*, 89, 227.

33. *WJC*, 53. T. D. Herbert emphasizes that this reservation is one of the major distinctives between the kenotic and trinitarian dimensions in Moltmann and both Barth and Balthasar (see *Kenosis and Priesthood*, 67–68).

34. E.g., Neal, *Theology as Hope*, 47, 154–55.

35. Neal, *Theology as Hope*, 154–55n11.

36. *CG*, 47.

37. *CG*, 229 (German: 216).

how he formulates this question that Moltmann is concerned that the *union* of the two natures not be *dissolved* [*auflösen*] by a non-biblical notion of impassibility. And this is a concern that Moltmann *cannot have* if he rejects the notion of two natures.

Similar, then, to the radical kenoticists (whom we discussed in chapter 3), Moltmann is concerned that dogmatic history has tended toward two christological oversights: reducing Christ's humanity or fracturing his person into disparate divine-human centers (which would also, in its own way, reduce or distort the humanity). So, Moltmann's early work shies away from any constructive statement about the relation between Christ's two natures, leading Schmiechen to note that, at least in *The Crucified God*, Moltmann can make "it sound like there is but one nature in Jesus."[38] This reminds us that a more radical view of christological kenosis is never that far from Wolfgang Gess, whose vision of Christ's kenosis was almost avidly monophysite.[39] But does Moltmann's lack of comfort with the two-natures tradition, alongside his clear comfort with kenosis, lead him to this sort of position? I argue that it does not, owing at least partly to Moltmann's deployment of *perichoresis* in his understanding of the two natures in Christ.

Perichoresis is a concept originally appropriated by Moltmann in order to frame his understanding of an intensely relational, communal Trinity.[40] Derived from the teaching of John Damascene and Richard of St. Victor, perichoresis has come to refer to a circulatory, interpenetrating, relational sharing between two realities or forms of existence, to the point where they co-define each other and share attributes.[41] In reference to Christology, perichoresis was traditionally seen as a *one-way* interpenetration and exchange between the two natures, flowing solely from the divine to the human—the classic image was the piece of iron (the humanity) heated red by fire (the divinity).[42] But much like his trinitarian radicalization of the Lutheran *communicatio idiomata*,[43] Moltmann posits a *reciprocal* exchange

38. Schmiechen, *Saving Power*, 140.

39. See Brown, *Divine Humanity*, 62–69, for a detailed recent treatment of Gess.

40. E.g., *TK*, 150, 155–58, 198–200; *GC*, 16–17, 234–43; *ET*, 316–20 (closely paralleled in Moltmann, *Sun of Righteousness*, 153–57); *SW*, 117–18.

41. See further Bonzo, *Indwelling*, 32–33.

42. The image emerges initially in Origen (*De Principiis*, II, 6, 6); it is also found in Gregory of Nyssa (*Oratio Catechetica*, 10). See Elert, *Der Ausgang der altkirchlichen Christologie*, 227–28. Pannenberg well notes the different ends to which this image could be employed in christological discourse (*Jesus*, 297nn40–41).

43. *CG*, 231–47. On the related importance of this strong reading of the

in his articulations of perichoresis. For him, perichoresis becomes the great binary blurring device; it is, in essence, the supreme form of "both/and" (rather than "either/or") reasoning.[44] Dualisms dissolve and conceptual dichotomies disintegrate as perichoretic logic argues for unity and diversity to co-participate as mutually-shaping realities.[45]

In Moltmann's trinitarianism, perichoresis involves a clear *kenotic* element. His use of kenosis here bespeaks the necessary *limitations* inherent in *relationship,* rather than a divestiture of some attribute or another. Moltmann will speak of the trinitarian persons "making room" for each other; they are three distinct persons, and yet are united in all things, through the hospitable perfection of kenotic love.[46]

> Each one of [the three Persons] is *active* and *passive, giving* and *receiving* at the same time. By giving themselves to each other, the perichoretic community is also a *kenotic community.* The Persons are *emptying* themselves into each other. . . . It is divine love which draws a Person so much out of himself, that it exists "in" the other.[47]

It is the self-emptying of the three persons in this perichoretic exchange that Moltmann relies on to deflect the charge of tri-theism, which often assails his social trinitarian outlook.[48] Though many of Moltmann's more

communication of attributes in Thomasius' kenotic thinking as well, see Welch, *Protestant Thought,* 235–36.

44. For a recent exploration of this dimension of perichoresis as reflected in the created order, see Leithart, *Traces of the Trinity.*

45. E.g., in reference to the Trinity: "The doctrine of the perichoresis links together in a brilliant way the threeness and the unity, with reducing the threeness to the unity, or dissolving the unity in the threeness" (*TK,* 175). See also *ET,* 318–20.

46. Ted Peters, referring to some similar movements in Pannenberg's trinitarian outlook, refers to "reciprocal self-dedication" (*God as Trinity,* 137). Pannenberg goes quite further than Moltmann on some points, but retains the same indebtedness, at this juncture at least, to the thinking of Hegel, whom Pannenberg credits with this inter-trinitarian notion of self-emptying—Peters, *God as Trinity,* 137n120; Pannenberg, *Jesus,* 179–83.

47. Moltmann, "Trinitarian Personhood," 312, emphasis original. It should be noted there is a slightly different semantic range to Moltmann's application of kenosis to the inner life of the Trinity. For Moltmann, all relationship (the "letting be" of something different from oneself) is essentially kenotic, insofar as it limits any subject or person from being the sole "absolute." But this relational dimension of kenosis does not clearly entail "suffering" limitations; that sort of limitation comes from God's kenotic relationship to, and redemption of, the world.

48. See the critiques and discussion in O'Donnell, *Trinity and Temporality,* 149–52;

impassioned descriptions of his perichoretic Trinity are striking, some scholars have objected to his sometimes inconsistent employment and qualification of such language.[49]

But more directly pertinent to our project is how Moltmann eventually applies the concept of perichoresis to his understanding of the two natures in Christ (which is how John Damascene initially employed it).[50] Explicit affirmation of this perichoretic unity of the natures has emerged in Moltmann's more recent work:

> Perichoresis describes the unity of Godhead and humanity in the person of Jesus Christ. This is not a matter of two who are by nature similar being bound together in inward community. Here are two different natures—that is, the one and the other. . . . In Christology, perichoresis describes the mutual interpenetration of two different natures [*die wechselseitige Durchdringung zweier verschiedender Naturen*], the divine and the human, in the God-human being Christ.[51]

Perichoresis, as we noted for his trinitarianism, is a *kenotic* reality for Moltmann. Thus, when we talk about Moltmann's kenotic Christology, we must recognize that we are dealing with a *dual-leveled* kenosis. One level is intra-trinitarian and refers to the continued kenotic relating between the divine persons; this is derived by Moltmann from the way in which Christ relates to the Father and the Spirit in the course of earthly life, as we will see in chapter 5. The other level of the kenosis is the relationship between Christ's divinity and humanity, and refers to the humiliation and lowliness undertaken by God in becoming human, as we will see below in

---

Lewis, *Between Cross and Resurrection,* 219; Bauckham, *One God in Trinity,* 130; Neal, *Theology as Hope,* 106–8 (and references). In his own defense, Moltmann has resolutely maintained that tri-theism is a "pseudo-issue" (see Peters, *God as Trinity,* 106; also Moltmann, *ET,* 382n30). Moltmann also makes a polemical point of his own, claiming that "the standard argument against 'tritheism' practically serves everywhere to disguise the writer's [own] modalism" (*TK,* 243n43).

49. E.g., Otto, "Use and Abuse," 366–84; the critique of Moltmann begins in earnest on 374. A related range of trinitarian critique finds Kathryn Tanner accusing Moltmann of maintaining "that the existence of the persons is distinct from their relations." But this seems to overstep Moltmann's actual conclusions in his attempt to balance an Eastern and Western view of interpersonal relation in the Trinitiy (see *TK,* 171–73). For Tanner's critique, see her "Trinity, Christology, and Community" 63–64.

50. In *De Fide Orthodoxa,* III.3–11. See Moltmann, *SW,* 117. See also Charles Twombly, *Perichoresis and Personhood.*

51. Moltmann, *Sun of Righteousness,* 113, 153 (German: 141).

chapter 6.[52] Both dimensions of this perichoretic kenosis are operative in his understanding of the incarnation, though they are not always explicitly highlighted and much of the specifics of their mutually exchanging interpenetration (especially any kind of specific ontological commentary) are left without speculation. Moltmann is comfortable to simply say: "This is undoubtedly God's *greatest mystery*: his closeness . . . Emmanuel, 'God with us'—with us, the godless and God-forsaken."[53]

Once these themes are balanced, we can see the truth in Gary Badcock's assessment that "Moltmann's position is best understood as a trinitarian intensification of the doctrine of the hypostatic union. . . . Moltmann's point is not to deny the divinity but to affirm its unity with the humanity, on the basis of his understanding of the unity of the economic and the immanent Trinity."[54] This is very close to spot-on, lacking only the emphasis on kenosis that defines both the Trinity and the incarnation in Moltmann's thought. This initial understanding of his kenosis as dual-leveled (one level: intra-trinitarian; another level: human realities and relationships) has quite concrete ramifications for certain specific aspects of Moltmann's doctrine of Christ. These will direct our attention in the next two chapters. But before embarking on those particulars, Moltmann's "kenotic logic" must be elucidated along one further line, and that is his understanding and application of the term *Logos* in christological contexts.

Logos and Shekinah

Any discussion of two-natures Christology must also deal with the proximate but discursively distinct topic of *Logos* Christology (that is, Christology that posits that the pre-existent person of the Logos was incarnate in the person Jesus of Nazareth). To consider the place of Logos Christology in Moltmann's thinking, we must not only place it in the context of his much-debated Spirit

---

52. Moltmann's eschatological panentheism comes to depend on a similar vision of perichoresis, applied to God and the world's eventual mutual interpenetration, see *Sun of Righteousness*, 30–32; *ET*, 315–16.

53. *ET*, 113, emphasis added. In more recent work, Moltmann has again made it clear that he holds to an unreservedly incarnational Christology by opposing himself to the thinking of Schleiermacher on this score: "[The] birth of God in the becoming human of Christ . . . [makes it] impossible to say that 'in Christ the being of God' consisted only of his 'unremettingly powerful God-consciousness,' as Friedrich Schleiermacher taught in his doctrine of faith" (Moltmann, "Is God Incarnate in All That Is?" 122–23).

54. Badcock, *Light of Truth*, 220.

Christology (which we broached and explored above in chapter 2), but also his unique thinking on the divine Shekinah.[55]

Colin Greene has argued that Moltmann "substitutes" a pneumatological Christology for a Logos Christology,[56] and finds this alleged neglect of Logos Christology to be highly problematic. Greene argues that, for Moltmann, Christ's relationship to the Holy Spirit is what "establishes a basis for the confession of Jesus' divinity."[57] However, Greene's analysis of Moltmann is, overall, subservient to his overarching point of praising the Christology of Barth by contrast, and as such he neglects Moltmann's clear attempts to mediate between Spirit and Logos Christology and admit the strengths of each. We can demonstrate this in the course of three major observations.

In the first place, Moltmann's strong emphasis on Spirit Christology is meant to correct an underrepresented aspect of Christology in church tradition.[58] He claims that a Christology that is more fully trinitarian will need to make prominent space for the Spirit's role in the history of Jesus, and that this will "make it possible to absorb the exclusive christomonism of a Christology of the God-human being into the fullness of trinitarian Christology, with its wealth of relationships."[59]

Secondly, over and against Greene's point that Moltmann thinks it to be the Spirit that establishes Jesus' deity, Moltmann explicitly *denies* the ability of Spirit Christology to secure any "essential unity [*wesentliche Einheit*]" between Jesus and the Father, since all purely pneumatological Christologies tend toward adoptionism.[60] The deity of Jesus consists in the incarnation of the Second Person of the Trinity, which, as I have shown, Moltmann

55. The divine Shekinah refers to God's *tangible presence* in the Old Testament, his physical glory that dwelt with and among his covenant people.

56. Greene, *Christology in Cultural Perspective*, 329. He also refers to Spirit Christology as Moltmann's "alternative to Logos Christology" (335). Both of Greene's designations do not reflect Moltmann's own discussions of Logos Christology, however.

57. Greene, *Christology in Cultural Perspective*, 331. He cites *WJC*, 93, in support of this assessment, but the passage does not say this; it says only that the Holy Spirit "takes up its dwelling" in Jesus. Such language is commonplace in New Testament pneumatology, applied regularly to believers (with no presumption of their "divinity" by way of it), e.g., 1 Cor 3:16, 6:19; 2 Cor 6:16; Rom 8:9, 11; 2 Tim 1:14.

58. *SpL*, 70–73.

59. *WJC*, 74. This is a partial emphasis even in *CG*, 235–49. Further, Moltmann sees a Spirit Christology as an important element of ecumenical discussion of the *filioque*: *TK*, 169–70; *ABP*, 87.

60. *TK*, 132 (German: 147–48).

affirms.[61] The eternal Son, who is "one in substance or essence with the Father,"[62] through whom all things were made, becomes incarnate. The particular contours of Moltmann's incarnational doctrine may be debatable, but his repeated affirmations of the incarnation itself should not be.

Thirdly, Moltmann states directly that Spirit Christology and Logos/incarnation Christology ought not be opposed to one another, and that he does not intend to place them in a conflictual relationship: "I developed a Spirit Christology designed to be a necessary complement [*notwendige Ergänzung*]—not an alternative—to Logos Christology."[63] The Son is eternally the Son; Moltmann affirms his pre-existence, and he articulates it, as we might expect, in thickly relational trinitarian terms: "the Father creates the world *through the Son* in the energies of the Holy Spirit . . . *the Son is sent* into the world by the Father through the Holy Spirit."[64] Thus, as far as Logos Christology goes, Moltmann is working against one-sidedness in understanding the trinitarian ramifications of the incarnation.[65] These efforts could be argued to give rise to a certain one-sidedness of Moltmann's own, but a zealous corrective emphasis is different from the total replacing of one paradigm by another.

Now, certainly, Moltmann does not detail the Son's pre-existence in a straightforward manner in his most important work on Christology, *The Way of Jesus Christ*. Richard Bauckham effectively circumscribes the issue: "Moltmann's focus on pneumatological Christology evidently enables him to side step a classic christological issue [namely, that of pre-existence]; it is less clear that his own trinitarian theology ought to allow him to evade it."[66] This is an important consideration; it is not always *clear* how Moltmann is linking Logos and Spirit Christology together, or how his Christology can be described in light of both these perspectives at the same time. Peter Schmiechen approvingly avers that "Moltmann explicitly

61. *TK*, 114–18, 166–68.

62. *TK*, 166.

63. *SpL*, 17 (German: 31). Moreover: "Spirit Christology is not set up in opposition to incarnation Christology, for every doctrine of the incarnation begins with the statement 'conceived by the Holy Spirit'" (*WJC*, 74). This same adding-not-subtracting method also attends Moltmann's discussion of Wisdom Christology alongside Logos Christology (see *ET*, 310–11; Moltmann, *In the End*, 11–12).

64. *ET*, 310. See also *TK*, 71, 74, 87; Moltmann, *History and the Triune God*, 37–40.

65. *CPS*, 73.

66. Bauckham, *Theology*, 208. Greene appropriates this same passage from Bauckham in his critique of Moltmann (*Christology in Cultural Perspective*, 331).

combines the themes of incarnation of the Word and adoption by the Spirit."[67] This is true. Yet it should be said that such a combination appears to be assumed and acknowledged rather than *explained* by Moltmann. Some unifying thematic principle seems to be implicit that links his Logos-christological presuppositions (the pre-existence of the Son) with his Spirit-christological emphases (the reliance of the Son upon the Spirit). One hope I have is that my ensuing discussion demonstrates the possibility that Moltmann's *understanding of christological kenosis* conjoins these seemingly frictional themes.

Now, and finally, we must highlight a fundamental category for understanding Moltmann's incarnational Christology in all its aspects: his *Shekinah theology*. This is not a standard category of dogmatic reflection in most Christologies, yet given his preoccupation with Judaism, it is little surprise that the concept of the Shekinah has been formative for Moltmann ever since *The Crucified God*.[68] In that work, as is well-known, Moltmann famously attacked the concept of divine impassibility via a staurocentric theology. But what is less well-known, and certainly less analyzed, is that he also drew on the work of Abraham Heschel in order to argue that God has *always* (not just at the cross) been passionately involved in the world's travail through his immanent presence, the *Shekinah*. Whereas Shekinah theology among the rabbis originally concerned God's presence in the ark of the covenant, the Tabernacle, and the Temple, Moltmann (following Jewish thinkers like Heschel and Franz Rosenzweig) radicalizes it into a general pattern of God's participatory, self-limiting providence and presence.[69] But though the divine Shekinah originally functions in Moltmann's thought as an extension of his concern for God's genuine passibility throughout history, it also becomes a fundamental and unique formulation for describing God's indwelling of the created order and his self-limitation in the midst of that indwelling. Again drawing on Heschel, Moltmann writes,

> In his *pathos* the Almighty goes out of himself, entering into the people whom he has chosen. He makes himself a partner in a covenant with his people. In this *pathos*, this feeling for the people which bears his name and upholds his honour in the world, the Almighty is himself ultimately affected by Israel's experience, its acts, its sins and its sufferings. In the fellowship of his covenant with Israel, God

67. Schmiechen, *Saving Power*, 136.

68. *CG*, 272–74.

69. Johnson, "Shekinah," 144.

becomes capable of suffering. . . . The Almighty humiliates himself to the end of the world. He is high and lifted up—and looks upon the lowly. He reigns in heaven—and dwells with widows and orphans. Like a servant he bears the torch before Israel in the desert. Like a slave he carries the people with their sins.[70]

For Moltmann, God's concern for, and immanent presence in, the world makes history a truly operative category in which God himself participates.[71] God's relationship to history and the world is *kenotic*, self-limiting, vulnerable, relational.

In essence, then, this kenotic Shekinah theology revolves around two mutually-reinforcing thematics: *entrance* and *limitation*. The divine enters the world in concrete, space-time ways and such entry involves the taking-on of certain limitations and sufferings.[72] We see both sorts of language in the quotation just given: God "enters [*eingeht*]" among his people and "humiliates [*erniedrigt*]" himself.[73] The logic of the entering, or indwelling, entails a sympathetic co-suffering reality that is thereby embraced by God.[74] But there is also a third thematic that eventually emerges in Moltmann's discourses on the Shekinah: *redemption*, or, better, *redemptive transformation*. The Shekinah does not merely co-suffer; as God's immanent presence in the world, it also "presses toward its return to the holy city from its exile," and will eventually bring "the full glory of God into the city and the new creation."[75] Not incidentally, this is where Moltmann makes a key break with the paradigm of thinkers like Hegel and Hans Jonas: God's immanent history does not ultimately depend on human effort for any kind of self-completion or self-realization.[76] God remains sovereign over himself

70. *TK*, 25, 27

71. "The history of the world is God's passion, not the process of his self-realization," (*TK*, 166); Moltmann comes close to Hegel here, but maintains this key distinction. See also *CG*, 326–30 to find even more distance created between Moltmann's views and those of Hegel.

72. See Moltmann, *Sun of Righteousness*, 91–92.

73. *TK* (German), 40–41, 43.

74. *TK*, 118–19: "[Through] his Shekinah God participates in man's destiny, making the sufferings of his people his own. . . . [Divine love] cannot compel a response by violence. For the sake of freedom, and the love responded to in freedom, God limits and empties himself. He *withdraws his omnipotence* because he has confidence in the free response of men and women." See also the discussion in *SRA*, 102–5.

75. *SRA*, 105.

76. *SRA*, 106–9. See also Moltmann's discussion of the relation between God's being and *Zukunft* (future) in "Theology as Eschatology," 12–13.

even in his sympathetic dwelling with the world, and he enters into that sympathy in order to transform afflicted circumstances. Moltmann quotes the following passage from Isaiah as illustrative: "He [Yahweh] lifted them up and carried them all the days of old" (63:9).[77] The Shekinah *limits* itself, *enters into* human situations, and then *effectuates transformation* of the created order from within that indwelt created order. All three ideas interrelate. God is the subject of his own history; he simply chooses to unite that history with ours in kenotic love.

This threefold understanding of the Shekinah, defined in terms of *entry, limitation, and transformation*, is significant for us because *Moltmann has presented a firm equation between incarnation and Shekinah*, seeing them as mutually reflective of the selfsame work of the triune God. What we have in the incarnation of the Logos and the indwelling of the Spirit in the theology of the New Testament is, for Moltmann, a concentrated and concrete radicalization of Shekinah theology. The Shekinah is explicitly linked with the kenotic hymn (Phil 2:5–11) by Moltmann,[78] and thereafter he explicates the intersection between Shekinah theology and incarnational kenotic Christology:

> There [in the Old Testament] the Shekinah is in the people of Israel—here [it is] in the person of Jesus Christ. . . . There the Shekinah suffers out of solidarity with the people, and leads the people home—here the Shekinah dies and is raised. . . . There by virtue of his indwelling, the Eternal One delivers scattered Israel—here the Incarnate One gives himself up to death for the redemption of the world.[79]

This is a foundational dimension of Moltmann's kenotic Christology. Rather than operating like the radical kenoticists of the nineteenth-century, who posited an abandonment of some aspects of the divine life, Moltmann sees Christ *exemplifying and revealing most deeply and fully the God who has always been entering into the world, suffering on its behalf, and leading it toward redemption.* This is how Moltmann articulates his Shekinah theology, which he strikingly calls the "presupposition for the Christian idea of Christ's *kenosis*, and its Jewish equivalent."[80] Moltmann describes this fundamental thematic

---

77. *SRA*, 104.

78. *SRA*, 110.

79. *SRA*, 112, 114.

80. *SW*, 58. Moltmann has occasionally been accused of supersessionism, though his reading of Rom 11 and Rosenzweig's influence on him seem to preclude this (see

link as a deepening of God's redemptive acts; incarnation and Shekinah are both revelatory of God and God's work:

> Through his self-humiliation and his emptying of himself, the eternal Logos "took the form of a servant," in order, like the Shekinah, to share the sufferings of those who are his, as their Brother, and through his sufferings on the cross to redeem them. In order to save the concept of God's unalterability, later Christology replaced the idea of kenosis by the idea of the *assumption* of human nature by the eternal Logos. Both ideas lead to the conception of a unique community of the indwelling God with human nature and its history, which he indwells; and both thus deepen Shekinah theology.[81]

In short, Shekinah entails incarnational thinking, incarnation "deepens" or extends Shekinah thinking,[82] and both are deeply reflective of Moltmann's kenotic logic: "According to Christian theology, *incarnation and indwelling are grounded in the kenosis of God. By virtue of his lowering of himself, the infinite God is able to indwell the finite being of creation.*"[83]

Now, it should be re-emphasized at this point that these discussions, concerning notions like perichoresis and Shekinah, merely reflect Moltmann's naming of what he believes to be enacted space-time realities in the material world. In short, they are not presented as abstractions. Perichoresis is how he *describes* the relations of the divine persons as they emerge in scriptural history; it is not a mere piece of dogma developed apart from historical referent. Also, apart from his relatively short defenses of himself against tri-theism, Moltmann does not use the doctrine to apologetic ends. Likewise, Shekinah theology, as it has been in Jewish

---

Zathureczky, *Messianic Disruption*, 29; Moltmann, *CG*, 196–98). His discussions of certain Old Testament ideas as Jewish precursors or anticipations of incarnational thinking fall in line with some recent scholarship on divine embodiment in the Hebrew Bible. See, e.g., Hamori, "Divine Embodiment," 161–83; Wyschogrod, "Jewish Perspective on Incarnation," 195–209. Hamori is comfortable arguing that the "Christian concept of incarnation has its roots in Israelite thought. . . . This is an indigenous Israelite idea" ("Divine Embodiment," 180, 181).

81. *CG*, 303–4. I note, in passing, Moltmann's generous treatment of the kenosis vs. assumption debate in this passage.

82. Compare further *SW*, chapter 4; *SpL*, 48. Bingaman also notes the correspondence between incarnation and Shekinah, though he does not dwell on it nor link it to kenosis: *All Things New*, 115–16.

83. *ET*, 316, emphasis added.

thinking, is seen to be clearly reflected (or implied) in Temple theology,[84] and in prophetic discourse about God's immanence. In a parallel sense, the recent work of N. T. Wright, among others, continues to make a non-speculative place for articulating doctrinally significant Christology via the thick categories of Temple theology.[85]

Conclusion: Toward the Kenotic Life of Christ

This chapter has sought to distill many core themes of Moltmann's incarnational and kenotic thought. I detailed how Moltmann attempts to embrace the two-natures conceptuality via a textured understanding of kenotic perichoresis; the person of the Son embraces a kenotic exchange with the Father, the Spirit, and the vicissitudes of human existence via his incarnation. (What this *looks like*, concretely, in the life of Christ, is the subject of our next chapters). This is all fundamentally grounded in Moltmann's view of the incarnation as reflective of a deeply immanent view of Shekinah theology, in which the Shekinah kenotically *enters* into the world, is thereby *limited* in the course of that entering, and works toward *redeeming* the world from within that limiting (and co-suffering) relationship.

We can combine all these elements in Moltmann's thought quite readily by replacing or equating Shekinah with "the Son" in regards to the incarnation (which is what Moltmann does) and understanding the kenotic perichoresis between the divine and human natures in the same way that Moltmann describes the Shekinah's relationship to the creation. Thus, we posit that the foundational orientation of Moltmann's kenotic Christology is *that the Son willingly enters into the kenotic limitations of human existence in order to work redemption in the midst of those limitations.* This is fully in keeping with the radical revelatory understanding that Moltmann espouses in relation to the kenosis hymn, which we detailed in chapter 3. Though rarely presented in detail by Moltmann, this pivotal outlook on the christological kenosis is brought to light in a key passage from *Trinity and the Kingdom,* which we need to quote at length:

---

84. See, e.g., *SRA,* 102–5.

85. See, e.g., Wright, "Jesus Self-Understanding," 56–58; Perrin, *Jesus the Temple,* 106–113. Neither Wright nor Perrin, however, employs the related Jewish thinking on the Shekinah in the depth that Moltmann does. The importance of the Shekinah category for an understanding John 1:14 especially is well distilled in Raymond Brown, *The Gospel According to John,* 33. See also Stephen Um, *The Theme of Temple Christology,* 153–54.

> The divine kenosis which begins with the creation of the world
> reaches *its perfected and completed form* in the incarnation of the
> Son. . . . [We] also [see] God's humiliation of himself in connection
> with the *indwelling* of the Spirit and the divine Wisdom *in history*.
> For *through his Shekinah God participates in* man's destiny, *making
> the sufferings of his people his own*. . . . In the incarnation of the Son
> the triune God enters [*eingeht*] into the limited, finite situation
> [*die begrenzte, endliche Situation*]. . . . He does not merely *enter
> into this situation*; he also accepts and adopts it himself, making
> it part of his own eternal life. The kenosis is realized on the cross.
> Of course *it serves the reconciliation and redemption* of men and
> women, but it also contains in itself this other significance: God
> becomes the God who identifies himself with men and women to
> the point of death, and beyond.[86]

This triple sense of the kenosis as limiting, entering, and transformative
activity is clearly fundamental for Moltmann,[87] and will serve as the bed-
rock on which we construct our rendering of the varied textures of his
kenotic Christology as they manifest themselves in the life of Christ in
the following chapters.

---

86. *TK*, 118–19 (German: 133–34). Emphasis mine.

87. This can be construed in two ways: Either self-limitation is necessary in order to
effect the redemptive entering, or the entering itself brings about a redemptively significant limitation.

PART III

The Life of Christ in Kenotic Key

5

The Way of the Kenotic Christ (I)

Father and Spirit

I AM NOW POSITIONED to explore the actual *content* of Moltmann's kenotic Christology as it relates to the historical life of Jesus as conveyed by the gospel witness. To anticipate: I have already broached the notion of Christ's kenosis as dual-leveled in Moltmann's thought—one level being intra-trinitarian (the Son's relation to the Father and Spirit) and one level relating to the distinct textures of human existence. These two levels of the kenosis are not simply a heuristic division. As reflected in the previous chapter, Moltmann sees divine kenosis itself to consist in these two levels: the kenotic, perichoretic life of the Trinity and the kenotic, sacrificial, loving activity marking God's interactions with the created order. Christ participates in, exemplifies, and radicalizes both of these levels. (It is worth noting, though beyond the scope of this present book, that Moltmann's eschatology entails that both of these levels of kenosis will eventually collapse into one, as creation is drawn into the divine life, into the very relationships of the Trinity.)

Christ is the divine-human person embedded in this dual-leveled kenosis. The christological kenosis, in Moltmann's vision, consists of the following four kenotic relationships: (1) patriological (concerning Christ's *obedient* relation to the Father), (2) pneumatological (concerning Christ's *dependent* relation to the Spirit), (3) social (concerning Christ's *identification* with the oppressed masses); and (4) physical (concerning his *vulnerability* in relation to the mortal "flesh" of human materiality).

While other kenotic thinkers occasionally emphasize some version of one or possibly two of these dimensions (especially relating to the Father or the Spirit) Moltmann's thinking reveals its singularity by the manner in which these four themes are historically grounded, thematically interrelated, mutually informative, and creatively synthesized throughout his

Christology. This wide-ranging, relational-kenotic Christology is effectively prefaced when Moltmann states that

> The complex dimensions of Jesus' life history are obscured if we talk about it in only one of these dimensions—Jesus and God, or God and Jesus—so as to see him either as the heavenly God-man or as the earthly man of God. If Christology starts by way of pneumatology, this offers the approach for a trinitarian Christology, in which the Being of Jesus Christ is from the very outset a Being-in-relationship [Sein-in-Beziehungen], and where his actions are from the very beginning interactions, and his efficacies co-efficacies.[1]

In short, Moltmann's multi-dimensioned kenotic Christology views the history of Jesus Christ as a developmental journey of ever-progressing surrender and self-emptying in the full warp and weft of his manifold relationality. In this chapter, we focus on the first two of these kenotic relations—the Father and the Spirit.

Kenotic Mission: The Will of the Father

The progression of the messianic ministry, from baptism to resurrection, is thoroughly animated by Jesus' unique relationship to God the Father, which Moltmann describes as "familiar, intimate, and tender" consisting in "basic trust" and a "real nearness . . . by which Jesus lived and acted."[2] Because of his concrete focus on the united and historical *person* of Jesus Christ, Moltmann spends little time discussing a relation between Christ's divine and human natures. He explores the divine-human relationship in terms of Jesus Christ's relationship to the one he unfailingly called "my Father" and even *Abba*, the language of assured familial standing and closeness.[3] Shunning any speculative musing on the two natures, and ascribing "legendary" status to the doctrine of the virgin birth,[4] Moltmann prefers to use Jesus' own references to God and clues from Jesus' own ministry to explicate his self-understanding and relation to God: "The relationship to God described by the name Abba evidently influenced Jesus' understanding of himself quite essentially, for the

1. *WJC*, 74 (German: 94).
2. Moltmann, "I Believe in God the Father," 11.
3. *TK*, 74–75; *WJC*, 142–45; *ET*, 325–26.
4. A point on which I disagree with Moltmann, though the discussion need not detain us here. His longest discussion on it can be found in *WJC*, 78–87. See also Pannenberg, *Jesus*, 141–50.

results of this relationship to God are clearly evident in the scandalous behavior passed down to us by tradition."[5]

However, it should be realized that these considerations do not stop Moltmann from affirming the *pre-existent* nature of the Father-Son relationship, for the intimate term Abba and the specificity of the expression "*my* Father" (rather than the corporately possessive *our* Father or generally designative *the* Father) indicate to Moltmann both a constitutive and originating force for Jesus' attested relationship to his God.[6] N. T. Wright and Ben Witherington, among others, have affirmed that the Abba-designation (the "filial consciousness") of Jesus to be both historically *unique* within his Jewish context as well as hugely *formative* for his messianic self-understanding.[7]

But Jesus' full humanity means that he must *come to learn* his identity, role, and mission; he must "learn" his relationship to his Father and what he is meant to do in history (we designated this earlier as a key aspect of Moltmann's "developmental Christology"). Support for the notion of Jesus' mental and vocational development derives quite readily from the christological statements of Luke's gospel, which famously records that Jesus increases in wisdom, maturity, human favor, and divine favor (Luke 2:52).[8] Moltmann says that Jesus "received his revelation and mission" from the Father, and he pinpoints the baptism as the moment of Jesus' unique filial call.[9] I will return to this notion of the messianic call of Jesus shortly. What emerges clearly at this point is that Moltmann affirms: (1) the incarnation of the Second Person of the Trinity (as I have demonstrated at various points in previous chapters), (2) the real development and learning of that incarnate, historical person, and (3) the Father's will as constitutive for that

5. *WJC*, 143. Pannenberg, "[One] cannot properly understand Jesus' Sonship without taking his relation to God the Father as the point of departure. . . . This is the common mistake of all theories that attempt to conceive the unity of God and man in Jesus on the basis of the concept of the incarnation of the Logos" (*Jesus*, 334).

6. The complex, ambiguous discussion emerges at greatest length in *WJC*, 142–43.

7. It is now relatively common to find biblical scholarship downplaying the use of Abba by Jesus, and in particular to barb the work of J. Jeremias, usually with reference to the critiques raised by James Barr. Against this, see Wright, *Jesus and the Victory*, 648–49; Witherington, *Christology*, 215–21; Thompson, *Promise of the Father*, chapter 1, especially 25–34.

8. I have taken *hēlikia* as "maturity" here, but even if this translation is not followed for this term, the passage clearly affirms both increasing *wisdom and favor* before humans and before God.

9. Moltmann, "I Believe in God the Father," 11.

development and learning. In short, we perceive a distinct kenosis of will, in which the incarnate Son submits to the Father, obeys him, and receives from him his directives, mission, and even sayings. Such kenotic reasoning reverberates powerfully with statements typical of John's gospel: "When you have lifted up the Son of Man, then you will realize that I am he, and that *I do* nothing on my own, but *I speak* these things as the Father *instructed me*. And the one who *sent me* is with me; he has not left me alone, for *I always do* what is pleasing to him" (John 8:28–29).

It is worth noting, again, that this is not seen by Moltmann to be any *exception* in the divine relations; it is radically kenotic, yes, but it is revelatory rather than exceptional: "[In this] obedience to God . . . the *self-realization* of the Son of God is also accomplished. . . . There is no imaginable condition of the Son of God in which he would not exist in this self-emptying surrendering."[10] Though Moltmann rarely provides any exhaustive listing of gospel texts to correlate with these suppositions, there are many that resound with these thematics, wherein Christ claims to only "do" what he "sees his Father doing," as well as claiming that he was "sent to do the will of the Father," and "to complete the work" that his Father had given him to do (John 4:43; 5:19–25). "By myself," says Christ, "I can do nothing," and he confesses explicitly to not seek his "own will" but rather "the will of him who sent me" (John 5:30).

Colin Gunton has well noted that Christologies which take this obedient-submission-of-the-Son motif seriously in terms of Christ's relation to the Father prove their relevance by sustaining what the old doctrine of dyotheletism intended to preserve:

> Were only the divine will being done in the ministry of Jesus with God, so to speak, forcing Jesus into a pattern of behaviour against his will, not only would the gospel stories be falsified, but the real humanity of Jesus would disappear. . . . [In the gospel accounts] we are given the picture of one who was willing to bring it about that his will was also the Father's so that in his freely accepted obedience both his will and the Father's are done. . . . [The] dyothelite doctrine, for all its apparent abstractness, was developed in order to preserve the reality of the gospel's claim that through the human career of a man the saving purposes of God were made real in time.[11]

10. Moltmann, "God Is Unselfish Love," 118–19.

11. Gunton, *Yesterday and Today*, 91–92. To make the point clear, both Moltmann and Gunton are articulating a version of dyotheletism in which the two wills are (1)

This makes good sense against the backdrop of Moltmann's consistent attestations; Christ is willing to do the Father's will; he is not forced into obedience. At times, Moltmann will even resist the language of "obedience and submission" in preference for "freedom and participation"—in Jesus' relation to the Father, he wants to do what the Father wants; he wants to please him; their relationship is real and living, reciprocal and mutually contributory:[12] "He is the child of God, the God whom he calls Abba, dear Father. As the child of God, he lives wholly in God, and God wholly in him [*lebt er ganz in Gott und Gott Ganz in ihm*]."[13]

There is a firmly kenotic dimension to the obedient submission here; the Son's divine-human person willingly does the will of another (the Father), rather than his own will (again John 8:28). However, for Moltmann, the *extremis* of this dimension of Christ's kenotic relationality emerges with clarity in the passion narratives, where Gethsemane and Golgotha serve as the deepest realizations of Christ's kenosis-of-will in relation to the Father.[14] From the tortured prayer in Gethsemane to the death-cry on the cross, Moltmann develops what he calls his "theology of surrender [*Hingabe*]." The Father *surrenders* the Son to death, and the Son himself *surrenders* to that surrendering movement. It is in the Gethsemane prayer of the synoptic gospels that Moltmann finds the greatest expression of Christ's kenosis-of-will: "Jesus threw himself on the ground and prayed that, if it were possible, the hour might pass from him. He said, 'Abba, Father, for you all things are possible; remove this cup from me; yet, not what I want, but what you want,'" (Mark 14:35–36 // Matt 26:39 // Luke 22:42).[15] Moltmann's exposition of this is arresting in its starkness: "It is only by *firmly contradicting his very self* [*Widerspruch gegen sich selbst*

---

the will of the Son and (2) the will of the Father. They are not advocating for two wills "within" Jesus; they are critical of that, admittedly more traditional, position. For a summary of issues with that traditional rendering of the doctrine, see Pannenberg's commentary on the problems of dyotheletism for "tearing apart Jesus' unity": *Jesus*, 294. For technical background on the promotion of dyothelitism, see Hovorun, *Will, Action and Freedom*, 103–62.

12. *TK*, 51–52; 71–74.

13. *WJC*, 149 (German: 171).

14. "The stories of Gethsemane and Golgotha tell the history of the passion which takes place between the Father and the Son" (*TK*, 76).

15. See also John 18:11: "Shall I not drink the cup the Father has given me?"

fest] that Jesus clings to fellowship with the God who as Father withdraws from him: 'Not what I will, but what thou wilt.'"[16]

Moltmann returns to this theology of surrender often throughout his major works, and every time, to varying degrees, he is sure to emphasize the darkness and suffering entailed by the christological kenosis-of-will. On a popular level, Christian believers sometimes suppose that Christ's suffering in Gethsemane is due to his fear of pain and death. And Moltmann, out of concern for the *vere homo*, certainly does not want to say that Christ did not feel *any* fear of his oncoming physical pain.[17] But he does underscore that the extent of Jesus' agony in the garden cannot be derived from a simple anticipation of physical suffering. Many are the martyrs and warriors in history, after all, who have faced bodily torment and death bravely in their human strength. Moltmann states of Christ that

> [We] would be . . . foolish to see him as an especially sensitive person who was overcome by self-pity at the prospect of the torments of death awaiting him. In the fear that laid hold of him and lacerated his soul, what he suffered from was God. *Abandonment by God is the "cup" which does not pass from him.* The appalling silence of the Father in response to the Son's prayer in Gethsemane is more than the silence of death.[18]

For Moltmann this divine silence, this darkness, this relational abandonment, all convey the true *agon* of Christ's darkest moments,[19] both in the prayer in the garden and the cry on the cross. Moltmann emphasizes that Christ is "helpless" and "forsaken" on the cross,[20] and that a true separation, however ineffable, has taken place between the Father and the Son. Moltmann claims that the "Epistle to the Hebrews still retains this remembrance, that 'far from God—*chōris theou*—he tasted death for us all' (2:9)."[21]

16. *TK*, 76 (German: 92), emphasis added; Kohl's translation slightly modified. See also *WJC* where Moltmann refers to Christ's "denying of himself" in this moment (166).

17. *TK*, 77; also *JCTW*, 33; *EG*, 46.

18. *TK*, 77, emphasis added.

19. Moltmann, *Power of the Powerless*, 115–19; Moltmann, "Come Holy Spirit!" 75–77.

20. *WJC*, 110.

21. *WJC*, 166. Moltmann is here favoring the textual variant of this passage that preserves *chōris* ("far from" or "apart from") rather than *charis* ("grace")—the latter variant yields the more-standard translation: "By the grace of God, he tasted death for us all." Both variants have strong support in the textual tradition of Hebrews. For discussion, see Ellingworth, *Epistle to the Hebrews*, 155–57. Ellingworth also favors the *chōris* reading

Moltmann has been accused of excessive rhetoric in his more impassioned descriptions of the theology of surrender. Perhaps most flagrant is his early statement that, on the cross, we see "the breakdown of the relationship that constitutes the very life of the Trinity."[22] This phrasing casts considerable question over the preservation of divinity at the cross,[23] and could also be seen to imply the dissolution of the Godhead into a historical event, thus rendering the Godhead itself in need of redemptive reconstitution.[24] Myk Habets is certainly correct to note that, in this early expression of his staurology, "Moltmann overstates his case when he mentions a separation within God—'God against God' using the concept of *stasis*."[25] However, Moltmann has tempered this part of his theology in later work, saying in *Jesus Christ for Today's World* that "God is the one who gives Christ up to death in God-forsakenness, and is yet at the same time the one who *exists and is present* in Christ."[26] This later statement reflects Moltmann allowing 2 Cor 5:19 to exercise greater control over his mature staurology.[27]

This theme of kenotic surrender to the will of the Father also has trinitarian implications, for in Rom 8:32[28] Moltmann notes that the Father is the one who *gives the Son up* to death, to be sin, to be cursed, for the sake of the world.[29] The underlying Greek term *paradidōmi*, Moltmann emphasizes, is also used to describe the "giving up" of sinners to godforsakenness in divine judgment (Rom 1:24)—it is an unyielding term of abandonment.[30] It is owed mainly to this part of his argument, wherein Moltmann expresses (in biblical terms) the Father's active role in the Son's passion, that accusations of divine sadism have been leveled against Moltmann's staurology

---

"with some hesitation" (156).

22. *TK*, 80.

23. A criticism raised aggressively by Jowers, "Theology of the Cross," 248–50.

24. Blocher takes exception to the "enmity within God" (Moltmann's phrasing in *CG*), as well as to Moltmann's Hegelian indebtedness; see Blocher, *Evil and the Cross*, 72–76.

25. Habets, *Anointed Son*, 167n189.

26. *JCTW*, 37.

27. "God was in Christ reconciling the world to himself." See also Moltmann, *IEB*, 69–70.

28. "He who did not spare his own Son but delivered him up for us all, will he not also give us all things in him?" This same "delivering" logic is seen by Moltmann to also underlie other key staurocentric passages (2 Cor 5:21; Gal 3:13; John 3:16).

29. *CG*, 242–43.

30. *CG*, 241–42. The term has "an unequivocally negative sense" (*TK*, 80).

(most famously by Dorothee Sölle[31]). But we have already seen the element of Moltmann's perspective that deflects this criticism; the Son himself *willingly* surrenders to the Father's surrendering of him—it is a *mutual surrender* insofar as the Son is kenotically willing and desires the Father's will in obedience, even as the Father's will is to give him up:

> As Rom 8.32 and Gal 2.20 show, Paul already described the god-forsakenness of Jesus as a surrender and his surrender as love. Johannine theology sums this up in the sentence: "God so loved the world that he gave his only-begotten Son that all who believe in him should not perish but have everlasting life" (3.16). . . . Thus in the concepts of earlier systematic theology it is possible to talk of a *homoousion*, in respect of an identity of substance, the community of will [*Willensgemeinschaft*] of the Father and the Son on the cross. However, the unity contains not only identity of substance but also the wholly and utterly different character and inequality of the event on the cross.[32]

This intense "community of will" is kenotic, for Jesus the Son limits his own desire (for the cup to pass) in order to align his will with that of the Father (that Jesus should embody the kingdom all the way to an unjust crucifixion). But it is not only the Son's suffering that is in view here; passibility, passion, and relational trinitarian involvement all animate the cross. Thus, for the Son to suffer death, the Father must suffer the death of the Son as the death of one that he loves.[33] The suffering of the loved Son afflicts the Father, and is also a constitutive part of the Father's surrender—it costs the Son *and the Father* greatly: "In the cross, Father and Son are most *deeply separated* in forsakenness and at the same time are most *inwardly one* in their surrender."[34] This suffering of mutual surrender gives rise to Moltmann's notion of "patricompassionism"—the loving suffering of the Father that, unlike patripassian teaching, differs *in kind* from the suffering

---

31. See Sölle, *Suffering*, 26–32.

32. *CG*, 244 (German: 231).

33. "And if Paul speaks emphatically of God's 'own Son,' the not-sparing and abandoning also involves that Father himself. In the forsakenness of the Son the Father also forsakes himself. In the surrender of the Son the Father also surrenders himself, though not in the same way. . . . The Father who abandons him and delivers him up suffers the death of the Son in the infinite grief of love" (*CG*, 243). See Moltmann's refinements of these notions in *TK*, 80–83; *JCTW*, 36–38; "God With the Human Face," 77–78.

34. *CG*, 244, emphasis added (German: 231). See also *CPS*, 95.

of the Son.[35] Moltmann's mature description of this kenotic sacrifice takes the following shape: "[The] giving up of the Son reveals the giving up of the Father. In the suffering of the Son, the pain of the Father finds a voice. The *self-emptying of the Son* also expresses the *self-emptying of the Father*. Christ is crucified 'in the weakness of God' (2 Cor 13:4). . . . 'In the surrender of the Son the Father also surrenders himself.'"[36]

But if Moltmann's trinitarian Christology is afoot in this theology of surrender, then what does he say of the Spirit? This mutual suffering of the Father and Son in the passion is first developed in the context of Moltmann's early pneumatology, which was deficient insofar as the Spirit was not envisioned as much more than the *vinculum amoris* between the Son and Father.[37] Eventually, as Moltmann's pneumatology gains strength and becomes directive for much of his later theology, the Spirit's co-surrendering role at the cross also materializes: "The surrender through the Father and the offering of the Son take place 'through the Spirit' [Heb 9:14]. The Holy Spirit is therefore the link in the separation [between Father and Son]."[38] Moltmann goes on to describe the Spirit not only as the bond of suffering-separation, but as the partner and power in Christ's active self-surrender: "It is Christ himself who is the truly active one, through the operation of the divine Spirit who acts in him [*Kraft des göttlichen Geistes, der in ihm wirkt*]. In 'the theology of surrender,' Christ is made the determining subject of his suffering and death through the Spirit of God."[39] Indeed, not only Christ's death but also his ministry through and

---

35. Moltmann, "Theology of the Cross Today," 73; *CG*, 243; *ABP*, 196. See also Herbert, *Kenosis and Priesthood*, 65–66.

36. *WJC*, 176–77, emphasis added; Moltmann is here drawing on a (slightly modified) passage from *CG*, 243.

37. See *CG*, 252, 256, 275–78. Indeed, at this stage Moltmann's understanding of the Spirit's personhood is too under-developed (and Augustinian) to allow for a full-blown trinitarian theology of the cross; see on this point McDougall, *Pilgrimage*, 48; Bauckham, *Theology*, 152–54—Neal's commentary is also helpful: *TH*, 182–86. Moltmann himself later pinpoints this shortcoming in Augustine's pneumatology and corrects his own; see Moltmann, "Trinitarian Personhood," 313; also *ET*, 317; *TK*, 169. Moltmann was also eventually able to sharpen his critique of Barth's trinitarianism, highlighting an alleged lack of personhood ascribed to the Spirit in the *Dogmatics*: see *TK*, 142–44.

38. *TK*, 82. The reference to Heb 9:14 and the Spirit's role at the cross is earlier highlighted in *CPS*, 95, 37n61.

39. *SpL*, 63 (German: 76). See the combination of pneumatological themes with the significance of the cross in *SoL*, 16–18.

in the power of the Spirit is the next pivotal dimension in understanding Moltmann's kenotic Christology.

Kenotic Efficacy: The Power of the Spirit

As the Johannine testimony emphasizes Jesus' obedience to his Father's will, the synoptic testimonies emphasize *his dependence on the Spirit's power*. This is the second dimension of the christological kenosis in Moltmann's thought: Christ's reliance on the Spirit as "the Spirit-imbued human being who comes from the Spirit, is led by the Spirit, acts and ministers in the Spirit."[40] In stark contrast to his earlier, more limited role for the Spirit in the life of Christ, Moltmann's work following *The Crucified God* is highly concerned with the "trinitarian history" of Jesus, and it thus consistently highlights the radical relational dependence of the Son on the Spirit.[41] If the kenosis in relation to the Father is a kenosis of will (seen in the obedient submission of the Son), then the kenosis in relation to the Spirit is a kenosis of efficacy and action, displayed in Christ's openness to and reliance upon the Spirit's energies. We shall here briefly trace the extent of Moltmann's thought on this "Spirit-history" of Jesus, which he glosses as "the coming, the presence, and the efficacy of the Spirit in, through, and with Jesus."[42]

Moltmann sees the "efficacy [*Wirken*] of the divine Spirit" as the "first facet of the mystery of Jesus"[43] and preserves the notion of Jesus' "conception by the Spirit" or his "coming from" the Spirit,[44] though, as I have mentioned, he is strongly reluctant to ascribe any historical value to the notion of the virginal conception.[45] For Moltmann, the virgin birth and its relevant *loci* (Matt 1:18–23; Luke 2:1–7) were intended to secure certain doctrinal anchors for Christ's divinity[46] as well as preserve the

40. *SpL*, 58; also *WJC*, 73.

41. *TK*, 19, chapter 3; *WJC*, chapters 3 and 4; *SpL*, chapter 3. "The history of Christ is a trinitarian history of the reciprocal relationships and mutual workings of the Father, the Spirit and the Son" (*WJC*, 86).

42. *WJC*, 73. On the "history with the Spirit," see *SoL*, 15.

43. *WJC*, 73 (German: 92).

44. *TK*, 293; *WJC*, 81–82.

45. The only extended treatment in his major works comes in *WJC*, 79–87; in a later reflection he says simply that he "took a Protestant view of the virgin birth as 'birth in the Spirit'" (*ABP*, 345).

46. Namely "that [Jesus] is the messianic Son of God and the Lord of the messianic kingdom not only since his resurrection . . . and not merely since his baptism . . . but

true humanity in the face of early gnostic (i.e., docetic) speculation. But this latter goal, Moltmann declares, is today better served if we "stress the *non*-virginal character of Christ's birth."[47] This is a debatable point on Moltmann's part. However, Peter Althouse, in his work on Moltmann's pneumatology, rightly notes that Moltmann still acknowledges a "miracle" in the birth of Jesus; there is, after all, the incarnation of the preexistent Son when Jesus is conceived, and this is brought about by what Moltmann calls the "motherhood of the Holy Spirit."[48]

Jesus' unique, efficacious, and seemingly public endowment with the Spirit takes place when the Spirit descends on him.[49] The synoptics portray this as occurring immediately after the baptism by John in the Jordan, but the Johannine testimony interestingly preserves *only* the Spirit's descent on Jesus (John 1:32). According to Gary Burge this Johannine omission of the baptism indicates that the Spirit, not the water, is "all that matters,"[50] a point with which Moltmann would seem to concur. The Spirit-endowment is taken by Moltmann to be what Jesus is referring to when he says that the Father has "given the Spirit [to me] without measure" (John 3:34), and it appears to be likewise interpreted in the early church's kerygma as God's anointing of Jesus "with the Holy Spirit and with power" (Acts 10:38).[51] From this anointing onward, highlighted especially in the Lukan tradition, Jesus is compelled in all things by the Spirit: "The Spirit 'leads' him into the temptations in the desert. The Spirit thrusts him along the path from Galilee to Jerusalem."[52]

---

by his heavenly origin and from his earthly beginnings. . . . [The] aim is not to report a gynaecological miracle. The aim is to confess Jesus as the messianic Son of God and to point at the very beginning of his life to the divine origin of his person" (*WJC*, 81–82).

47. *WJC*, 84. Pannenberg says much the same: *Jesus*, 146; further 141–50.

48. Althouse, *Spirit of the Last Days*, 133. Said differently, Moltmann believes Christ to be the divine Son of God incarnate, whether he is conceived seminally or not. Ian McFarland similarly discusses the virgin birth as an attendant miraculous account that is not a necessity for an establishment of Jesus' divine ontology: *From Nothing*, 102(n39).

49. Mark 1:9–11; Matt 3:13–17; Luke 3:21–22; John's gospel does not recount the event of water baptism but only John the Baptist's testimony of the Holy Spirit's descent (John 1:32).

50. Burge, *Anointed Community*, 52, 59.

51. *WJC*, 89–90.

52. *WJC*, 73. The language of the Spirit's actions in relation to Jesus is forceful in the gospel text—see Mark 1:12: "The Spirit drove (*ekballei*—propelled, threw) him into the desert." This is the verb often employed for the "casting out" of demons during exorcisms in the gospels.

We should be clear; this is a kenotic relationship on the part of Christ—he *relies and depends* on the Spirit; he does not enact his startling signs and wonder under his own (divine) power. He has chosen to be empty of this power; and thus he must rely on the Spirit's power in kenotic dependence and trust. In fact, we can identify at least *four distinct ways* in which Moltmann portrays the Spirit's efficacy in the life of Jesus, wherein the Spirit accomplishes things through him that, in his kenotic human life, he could *not* accomplish unaided. There is no standardized, categorical description of these four "efficacies of the Spirit" in Moltmann's writing; rather I have excavated them via a careful synchronic reading of his major pneumato-christological passages.

Firstly, as we might anticipate, the Spirit empowers Jesus in the working of his miraculous acts: "*[In] the power of the Spirit* [Jesus] drives out demons and heals the sick. . . . The Spirit lends [Christ's] acts . . . the divine *power* that is theirs."[53] For many expositions of kenotic and/or pneumatological Christology, this is the major extent of the Spirit's work during the Son's incarnate life; rather than attribute the miracles and obedience to the powers of the Second Person of the Trinity, they are attributed instead to the Third.[54]

But Moltmann's description of the Spirit's activity goes far deeper than this. Secondly, he claims that the Spirit effectuates Christ's ministry to "sinners" and empowers him to bring "the kingdom of God to the poor."[55] That is, the Spirit enables not just his miracles, but also his prophetic and compassionate mission (as seems to be the major force of Isa 61:1 in Luke 4:18).[56] This means, importantly, that *the kenotic reliance on the Spirit is also empowering Christ's kenosis to the Father.* It is by the Spirit's power that the Son is enabled to be perfectly obedient to the Father. (On a critical note, Moltmann provides very little consideration for the Spirit's role in Jesus' life before his baptism—his discomfort with the virginal conception and his complete neglect of the temple incident with the boy Jesus [Luke 2:41–50] are doubtlessly at the root of this lacuna.[57])

53. *SpL*, 61, 63, emphasis original.

54. See, e.g., Bruce Ware, "Christ's Atonement," 180–82.

55. *SpL*, 61.

56. "[The Spirit's] energy was the worker of all his works," (*WJC*, 91). See also Althouse, "Implications of the Kenosis," 155.

57. I would echo Greg Liston's pointed question: "Before the indwelling [at the baptism], how did Jesus remain sinless; how did he grow and develop spiritually?" (*Anointed Church*, 46). The Spirit must be operative in some sense on the human Jesus—albeit in

There is a key interrelation between these first two aspects of the keno-sis of efficacy that is well formulated by Michael Welker. In an analysis that closely parallels Moltmann's in many respects,[58] Welker emphasizes that though the Spirit's power is manifested in remarkable ways in Jesus' actions, those actions are still distinctly *limited*. The Messiah does not, for instance, disband all demonic oppression and illness from all the faithful throughout the whole land of Israel with a single word. Rather "[Jesus] enters into a variety of individual, concrete stories and experiences of suffering. In the relative weakness and laboriousness of individual concrete acts and encoun-ters, the Messiah intervenes in disfigured, suffering, woe-generating life."[59] The public ministry, empowered mightily by the Spirit, is thus still *kenotic*; it proceeds in a limited manner conditioned by the progressions, vicissitudes, and frustrations of human encounter.[60]

Such expansion of pneumatological Christology into both interper-sonal and kerygmatic action is reflective of what Max Turner has identified as the scholarly consensus on the extent of the Spirit's effects in the Lukan tradition.[61] It also represents the utter limit of the Spirit's Christ-centered activity in the vast majority of biblically-driven Spirit Christologies. For in-stance, Klaus Issler focuses his own "Spirit Christology" almost entirely on the notion of "resources" (referring to the *power and knowledge* that Jesus acquires through his dependence on the Spirit) while simultaneously main-taining that Christ's "own divine power" could have been utilized, though only "infrequently."[62] As I show in the following paragraphs, Moltmann's thought goes significantly beyond even this in its understanding of Christ's radical dependence on the Spirit's efficacy.

---

a different mode than post-anointing—starting from birth, or, indeed, *conception* (Luke 1:35). This reasoning aligns with the rigorous examination given in MacDonald, "Prob-lems of Pneumatology," 129–48.

58. Welker is of course highly influenced by Moltmann, as an erstwhile student of his.

59. Welker, *God the Spirit,* 202.

60. This is at least one aspect of what Moltmann means in his discussions on the "kenosis of the Spirit," e.g., *SpL,* 61–63.

61. Turner, *Holy Spirit,* 37–41; see also the discussion in Strauss, "Jesus and the Spirit," 268–70.

62. Issler, "Jesus' Example," 199–217; on Christ's possible-if-infrequent use of his own divine power, see 202–5. See also Strauss' article which, in dialogue with Hawthorne, mainly focuses also on resources and abilities (power and knowledge), "Jesus and the Spirit," 273–83.

Thirdly, the Spirit enhances and guides Christ's epistemic position; it reveals things to him and leads him into truths. Moltmann avers that the baptism not only makes Christ aware of his messianic office but also enters him into his "unique" Abba-consciousness,[63] for the heavenly voice says: "You are my *beloved* Son" (Mark 1:11; cf. Matt 3:17).[64] Moltmann specifies the pneumatological efficacy here, saying that the "Spirit *allows [läßt]* the Son to say 'Abba, beloved Father.'"[65] In short, Christ's consciousness of the immediacy of the Father, and of his incredible communion with the Father, is *mediated* by the Spirit.[66] For Moltmann, this Spirit-mediated Abba-communion firmly distinguishes Jesus from foregoing prophets and ensures that his proclamation of the kingdom is not solely about obedience to God (in contrast to John the Baptist's call to repentance) but also about love, intimacy, and adoption into the Father's care:[67] "This theology makes it understandable why Jesus does not merely proclaim as prophet the far-off, sovereign kingdom of God the Lord, but now proclaims as brother the imminent, loving kingdom of his Father."[68] This dimension of the Son's Spirit-history, his awareness of his relationship to the Father, has been explicated at depth in the work of James Dunn,[69] though Dunn does not necessarily share all of Moltmann's important "incarnational" commitments. And Gerald Hawthorne certainly discusses the Abba-relation, even stating at one point that the Spirit "enlightened [Jesus'] mind so that he might understand his unique relationship with the Father,"[70] but he does not explicate this dimension of his pneumato-Christology with nearly as much significance for Jesus' ministry as does Moltmann. For Moltmann, this efficacy of the Spirit is operative in Jesus even as the impending darkness of the cross looms: "In Gethsemane too Jesus utters this Abba prayer *in the Spirit of God*."[71]

63. *WJC*, 90–91.

64. I would locate the dawning of Jesus' Abba-consciousness earlier than Moltmann, since he refers to God as "my Father" in the boyhood temple incident (see Luke 2:49).

65. *TK*, 74 (German: 90), emphasis added.

66. Habets, *Anointed Son*, also makes this point, with consistent reliance on Moltmann (see 136–38). Liston also makes it, *Anointed Church*, 131–32; he is strongly reliant on Habets, and thus on Moltmann by extension.

67. "I Believe in Jesus Christ," 35–36; also *SoL*, 125; *TK*, 163.

68. *WJC*, 90. See also Habets, *Anointed Son*, 131–32(n51–52).

69. See, e.g., Dunn, *Jesus and the Spirit*, 15–67.

70. Hawthorne, *Presence and the Power*, 179.

71. *SpL*, 63, emphasis added. Althouse, in dependence on Moltmann, states that "the

This brings us to the fourth, and most distinctive, element of Moltmann's understanding of Christ's kenosis of efficacy. While Myk Habets notes correctly that theological scholarship has often "overlooked [the] role the Holy Spirit plays . . . in the death, resurrection, and exaltation,"[72] the death of Jesus has quite possibly been the most pneumatologically neglected of these three topics.[73] Fittingly, the Spirit's relation to Christ's death is also the last element of Moltmann's pneumatological Christology to come into focus, hinted at in *The Way of Jesus Christ* and developed fully only in *The Spirit of Life*.[74] We have already noted the intense kenosis of will outlined by Moltmann in terms of the Son's relationship to the Father, which reaches its crescendo at the cross. That dimension of the kenosis concerns surrender and obedience. So, in keeping with a parallel kenosis of efficacy (or of power), we would expect to find Christ's kenosis with the Spirit expressed in terms of powerlessness on the cross. And this is precisely how Moltmann treats it:

> The real theological difficulty of the stories about Jesus' healings, however, is raised by his passion and his death in helplessness on the cross. "He saved others; let him save himself, if he is the Christ of God, his Chosen One" (Luke 23:35). *But this is just what Jesus apparently cannot do.* The healing powers that emanate [*ausgeht*] from him, and the "authority" which he has over the demons, are given him not for himself but only for others. They act through him, but they are not at his disposal [*Sie wirken durch ihn, aber er hat sie nicht zur Verfügung*].[75]

As Lyle Dabney (another past student of Moltmann's) has made clear, a *pneumatologia crucis*, a place for the Spirit at the cross, has been difficult to come by in theological history.[76] The difficulty persists today, in large measure. An incisive expositor of pneumatological Christology like Hawthorne, for instance, seems to completely pass over this dimensionality in his otherwise robust analysis; Hawthorne states simply that the gospels

---

Spirit reveals to Jesus that he is the Son of the Father" ("Implications," 162).

72. Habets, *Anointed Son*, 161.

73. See the trenchant analysis by Dabney, "*Pneumatologia Crucis*," 515–23.

74. See further on this development in Moltmann's pneumatology: Althouse, "Implications," 161–63.

75. *WJC*, 109–10 (German: 130), emphasis mine.

76. See Dabney, "Naming the Spirit," 30–40.

"have nothing to say" about the Spirit and Jesus at the cross.[77] But this lack of something to say is surely of great import when, as Hawthorne's study (among many others) makes clear, the gospels (especially Luke) express the Spirit's efficacy in *every other* dimension of Christ's lived mission.[78] Why, then, is the Spirit not referenced during the passion, which Jesus' public and Spirit-driven career had inexorably precipitated? It is this strange silence that grants Moltmann's thesis at least some plausibility: the Spirit is not mentioned at the cross because its christological efficacies are trammeled or withheld in some sense; the Spirit and Jesus are relating in a different manner than before; the efficacy has become an absence of efficacy.[79] In a way, this fourth dimension of the christo-pneumatological kenosis can be seen as an inversion of the first, and it thus highlights in sharp relief just what kenotic dependence means: *Jesus' power depends on another's agency, the Spirit's agency.*

But there is also in Moltmann a concurrent, important sense in which Jesus, in his powerless self-surrender, does not *will* to partake of the Spirit's energies. This is not a case of the Son "wanting" the Spirit to empower him and the Spirit refusing (or vice versa). There is no reason to see Jesus as somehow abandoned by or in conflict with the Spirit on the cross. In fact, a strong reading of Heb 9:14 drives Moltmann to bind together staurological suffering and pneumatological empowerment of the will.[80] As he comes to discuss it in *Spirit of Life*, Jesus' kenosis of will even unto death is *facilitated* by the Spirit: "Jesus goes in the Spirit and through the Spirit to his death."[81] When Christ in the garden states that "the Spirit is willing but the flesh is weak" (Mark 14:38), Moltmann sees this as an affirmation that the Holy Spirit is present and that it even "frames [*formt*]" the kenotic response of

---

77. Hawthorne, *Presence and the Power*, 180.

78. "[The evangelists] agree that Jesus was dependent upon the Spirit for the successful completion of the work God had given him to do in this world throughout *the whole of his life* (cf. John 17:4)" (Hawthorne, *Presence and the Power*, 179, emphasis mine).

79. Myk Habets takes this cue from Moltmann and focuses intensely on the Spirit's role at the cross: *Anointed Son*, 165–70.

80. The key phrase refers to "the blood of Christ, who through the eternal Spirit offered himself without blemish to God." *Pneuma* lacks the definite article in this passage, and so some interpreters have argued against seeing "the Spirit" here. However, Hawthorne provides strong reasoning for a fully pneumatological reading, see *Presence and Power*, 180–84. See also Motyer, "Spirit in Hebrews," 226–27.

81. *SpL*, 64.

the Son: "Not my will, but thine be done."[82] The Spirit empowers the kenosis of will by continuing to effect those realities which we've already noted (consciousness of filial relation, enablement of obedience, etc.), while the more obvious miraculous efficacies are withdrawn in the helplessness of the cross. As Kornel Zathureczky incisively puts it, "The power of the Spirit . . . is the power that makes the kenotic surrender of the Son possible."[83] This is the groundwork for Moltmann's *pneumatologia crucis,* in which a "kenosis of the Spirit" parallels the kenosis of Christ:

> [If] the Spirit accompanies him, then it is drawn into his sufferings, and becomes his *companion* in suffering. The path the Son takes in his passion is then at the same time the path taken by the Spirit, whose strength will be proved in Jesus' weakness. The Spirit is the transcendent side of Jesus' immanent way of suffering. *So the "condescendence" of the Spirit leads to the progressive kenosis of the Spirit, together with Jesus.* Although the Spirit fills Jesus with the divine, living energies through which the sick are healed, it does not turn him into a superman. It participates in his human suffering to the point of his death on the cross.[84]

This is a hugely clarifying development in Moltmann's Christology and pneumatology.[85] This now fully trinitarian outlook on the cross echoes the patricompassionist language we have seen already, but it is now inclusive of the Spirit: "[The] story of the suffering of the messianic Son of God is the story of the suffering of God's Spirit too. But the Spirit does not suffer in the same way. . . . On Golgotha the Spirit suffers the suffering and death of the Son, without dying with him."[86] This stands at the apex of Moltmann's fully-orbed theology of surrender,[87] which fun-

82. *SpL,* 64. (German: 77).

83. Zathureczky, *Messianic Disruption,* 133.

84. *SpL,* 62 (emphasis original). Moltmann identifies a substantial debt to Dabney's work on these points (*SpL,* xi, 64n15). Dabney's major arguments on the Spirit's kenosis can be found in Dabney, *Die Kenosis des Geistes.* See also the comments in Althouse, "Implications," 163–64.

85. Though some commentators do not think this distances Moltmann enough from an Augustinian *vinculum amoris* pneumatology. E.g., Kim, "Jürgen Moltmann," 247; Jowers, "Theology of the Cross," 245–66.

86. *SpL,* 62, emphasis added. See also Dabney, "Naming the Spirit," 53–58. The appropriate neologism for this kenotic co-suffering on the part of the Spirit would seemingly be "pneumacompassionism," though Moltmann does not employ this particular term.

87. Moltmann also calls it "the theology of *divine co-suffering* or *compassion*" (*WJC,* 178, emphasis original).

damentally binds together inter-trinitarian christological kenosis with inter-trinitarian staurological passibility.

Conclusion: Messiah-in-Process

In my foregoing discussions in chapters 3 and 4, I noted that the kenosis of Christ in Moltmann's thought possesses a dual-leveled dimensionality. This present chapter has focused on the first level: the trinitarian. The divine Son is kenotically obedient to the Father and kenotically dependent on the Spirit throughout his human life. While these are radical and pivotal dimensions of Christ's kenosis, they are only half the story. The other half—what we can call the second level of kenosis in Moltmann's Christology—involves two other distinctive dimensions: Christ's kenotic relationship to other people and his kenotic relationship to his own body.

6

The Way of the Kenotic Christ (II)

Others and Flesh

THE INCARNATE LIFE OF Jesus always invites two prominent avenues of theological reflection. The first avenue is God-focused and often somewhat abstract: what does it mean for Christ to be *divine*, especially if that divinity is "trinitarian"? The second avenue is human-focused, worldly, concrete: what does it mean for Christ to be *human*, especially a poor Palestinian living under an oppressive political reality in the first-century?

Heuristically, there's little harm in treating these avenues separately, so long as such an approach is simply a tool for understanding and in no way enabled to become some definitive road to lopsided doctrine, emphasizing one avenue at the expense of the other. In fact, even this statement is too dichotomous. These two avenues *only* exist heuristically. The true life of the Incarnate is *real, historical, unified, embodied*, and, indeed, *ongoing*. I have treated the first heuristic avenue in chapter 5—kenosis as it relates to Christ's divine-trinitarian relationships. The second occupies my analysis in the present chapter—kenosis as it relates to Christ's human-worldly relationships. Then, in my final chapter, I will purposely collapse that heuristic dichotomy, in-step with Moltmann's own aims, to discuss the life of Christ *undivided* and thus as the holistic foundation of a church called into the warp and weft of life *in the world*.

But that is to anticipate. In what follows here, I closely track Moltmann's analysis of two dimensions of the life of Christ that many other late-twentieth century kenotic Christologies neglect: Christ's "human" relationships—to *others* in the midst of societal and communal structures and, perhaps most radically, to *his very self*, his body, his flesh.

Kenotic Identity: The Community of the Poor

In *The Way of Jesus Christ* Moltmann pursues what he calls "an emphatically *social* Christology."[1] Traditional Christology has focused largely on the abstract relation between the divine and human natures, and Enlightenment-era "quest" Christology tended to focus on the relations between the private interiority of Jesus and his cultural-historical environment, or perhaps on the relation between the distant, vague past figure of Jesus and the allegedly embellished icon of the church's kerygma. But Moltmann moves past these sorts of analyses into a thickly relational accounting of Jesus. He claims that feminist theology in particular compels him to "look at the 'social' person of Jesus . . . his fellowship with the poor and the sick, with the people, with the women, and with Israel."[2] What is to be found at this stage of the Christology is an active *kenosis-of-identity* in which he who possessed a glorious existence "before the world began" (John 17:5) takes on the form of a *slave* (*doulos*—Phil 2:7), a term that Moltmann takes very seriously in its sociopolitical implications.[3] It is in fact this dimension of the christological kenosis that informs one of Moltmann's earliest references to the Phil 2 hymn:

> [P]easants [and] slaves find in [Jesus] the brother who put off his divine form and took on the form of a slave (Phil. 2), to be with them and to love them. They find in him a God who does not torture them, as their masters do, but who becomes their brother and companion. Where their own lives have been deprived of freedom, dignity and humanity, they find in fellowship with him respect, recognition, human dignity and hope. They find this, their true identity, hidden and guaranteed in the Christ who suffers with them, so that no one can deprive them of this identity.[4]

Like the foregoing two aspects of his kenotic Christology, this dimension is active and participatory. It involves Christ's entry as a first-century man into risky social and cultural milieus and his willing embrace of *lowly, unclean, and even accursed status* within those milieus. This is a kenotic

1. *WJC*, 71.

2. *WJC*, 71.

3. On the fact and manner of the humiliating and brutal crucifixion of slaves and criminals under the Roman Empire, see Martin Hengel, *Crucifixion in the Ancient World*, 51–63.

4. *CG*, 49. See further Bauckham, *Messianic Theology*, 69–70.

Christology about what Christ *does*, and in the doing, in the living, he reveals the God that he *is*.

Moltmann avers that Jesus "becomes poor himself" in community with the poor.[5] As he develops his theologically freighted understanding of poverty, Moltmann's schematic range is expansive. Drawing on Korean Minjung theology to interpret the Greek term *ochlos* (variously "people," "crowds") in the gospels, Moltmann sees the poor as "the addressee of Jesus' mission; he came on behalf of the people, his messianic kingdom is meant for the poor, his love is for the many."[6] Moltmann provides a survey of the use of *ochlos* in the synoptic gospels and finds it to include the "hungry, the unemployed, the sick, the discouraged . . . the sad . . . the suffering . . . the subjected, oppressed, and humiliated people . . . [the] sick, crippled, homeless. . . . The poor are 'non-persons,' 'sub-human,' 'dehumanized,' 'human fodder.'"[7] And it is these that Christ willingly takes on as "his people" and "his family,"[8] his dining companions, those whom he seeks out, touches, and heals. Moltmann is fond of noting that the gospel is "partisan [*parteiergreifenden*]" in this way; it is on the side of the *ochlos*.[9] In his radically kenotic identification Jesus "is one of them"[10] and when he heals the sick and ritually impure in their midst "he too becomes unclean."[11]

This becomes one of the most repeated aspects of Moltmann's Christology in its later formulations (that is, in the period subsequent to *The Trinity and the Kingdom*). We have already identified it in chapter 2 as his "solidarity" Christology, though he will also refer to it as the *Freundschaft*, *Gemeinschaft*, and *Bruderschaft* of Jesus,[12] all entailing an intimacy with the downtrodden that is not only representative or illustrative, but that goes all the way to the point of Christ's personal *identification*. Jesus does not simply "represent" the poor and the unclean; he *is* poor; he enters into uncleanness. This kenosis of identity is then "realized" or completed by

5. *WJC*, 100.

6. *ET*, 254.

7. *WJC*, 99.

8. *JCTW*, 19; *WJC*, 102.

9. *WJC*, 101 (German: 121); see also *CPS*, 78–80; "Justice for Victims and Perpetrators," 47–48; *JCTW*, 17–18; *CG*, 53.

10. *WJC*, 102.

11. *WJC*, 106.

12. Friendship, community, brotherhood: *Freundschaft* in *CPS* (German), 134–37; *Gemeinschaft* in *JCTW* (German), 18–19; *Bruderschaft* in *TK* (German), 103, 130.

Jesus' degrading public execution on the cross, in which he experienced social, religious, and political violence, as well as the divine silence so often characteristic of human suffering.[13] His death at the hands of violent men echoes the situation of the *ochlos* itself, for "men of violence" prey on the *ochlos* often in the scriptural accounts.[14]

The self-emptying here is absolute, as Jesus identifies to the very nadir of human spiritual, relational, and existential suffering:

> "He emptied himself" says the Letter to the Philippians. Betrayed, denied, and left alone by the men who had been his disciples; cru-cified by the Romans as an enemy of the state, and indeed of the human race; forsaken by God on the cross—so divested [*solchen Entäußerung*], he arrives at the point of our own most profound desolation [*tiefste Elend*]. . . . His history is first of all an expression of God's solidarity with the victims of torture and violence.[15]

> Astonishingly, the . . . hymn about Christ in Phil 2 says that the form of the Son of God, Jesus Christ, who humiliated himself, was "the form of the slave." If this is a reference to Jesus' humble origins among the humiliated people (*ochlos*) of Galilee, then in his suf-fering and death Jesus shared the fate of these enslaved people. Wretched and stripped of their rights as they were, it was their misery which Jesus experienced in his own body [*dessen Elend und dessen Entrechtung erfuhr er an seinem Leibe*].[16]

In order to most fully identify with the oppressed, Jesus' kenosis of identity effectuates the abandonment of several layers of communal security, four of which are discussed often and powerfully by Moltmann. Characteristi-cally, Moltmann does not provide a taxonomy of these emphases in any one place, but my reading of his major works has unearthed each of them as a distinct stratum of discourse.

The first layer of Jesus' foregone security we have alluded to already: Jesus foregoes and never pursues) *financial security or stability*; he is economically poor. He is born into a poor household (Luke 2:22–24 records Mary making the appropriate sacrifice for the impoverished—"a pair of turtledoves"; see Lev 12:8). In Matt 17:24–27 Jesus has to provide his and Peter's temple tax

13. See Hengel, *Crucifixion in the Ancient World*, 84–90.

14. *CPS*, 79–80; *WJC*, 99–100.

15. *JCTW*, 65, (German: 59), also 38–39. "The God of the poor is manifested in Christ, who emptied himself 'unto death, even death on the cross'" (*ET*, 233).

16. *WJC*, 168 (German: 190).

via a miracle. Jesus lacks a coin with which to make his point about paying tax to Caesar; one must be brought to him (Matt 22:17–22). Jesus is buried in Joseph of Arimathea's tomb (implying that his own family is not wealthy enough for a family tomb). The expensive burial spices for Jesus seem to be provided by Nicodemus (John 19:38–42). Jesus himself emphasizes his destitute and itinerant status,[17] and his ministry depended on charitable donations.[18] Moltmann states plainly the lack of financial security that attended the course of Jesus' life: "[He] himself lived as one of the poor . . . without any income or provision for the future (Luke 9:58)."[19]

Second, Moltmann emphasizes the aspect of Jesus' career that was probably the most scandalous among the masses: he relinquishes the *security of his family* and even, to some extent, his *national heritage*. His public vocation engenders tension with his family (Mark 3:21), a tension which reaches a point of culmination when he disassociates himself from them in full hearing of a public audience: "Jesus said, 'Who are my mother and my brothers?' And looking around on those who sat about him, he said, 'Here are my mother and my brothers!'" (Mark 3:33–34).[20] Culturally speaking, this moment would likely not have been seen as a mere rhetorical point or throwaway line on the part of Jesus.[21] Rather, it has the character of "a formal secession from his family" and, moreover, implies some sort of purposive separation from his Jewish lineage, for "it is a Jewish mother that makes a person a Jew."[22] N. T. Wright's recent work has, in fact, argued that Jesus was hereby challenging and symbolically reconstructing many of the assumed familial and ethnic assumptions of his culture.[23] It is this scandalous behavior of Jesus, a seemingly "deliberate breach of the fifth

17. "Foxes have holes, and birds of the air have nests; but the Son of Man has nowhere to lay his head" (Luke 9:58).

18. On the poverty of Jesus, see further Ellacuría, "Political Nature," 85–89. He emphasizes the "fundamental theological value" of Jesus' poverty, claiming that it "has a sociotheological meaning of the first importance" (87).

19. *WJC*, 100.

20. Moltmann notes the alleged parallels in the other synoptics, but Luke's account (8:19–21) may well be a separate occurrence, and Matthew characteristically softens the scandal by dropping the accusation that Jesus was "out of his mind" (12:46–50). See also Dunn, *Jesus Remembered*, 595.

21. Against Dunn, who calls Jesus' pronouncement to the crowd simply part of a "vivid repartee" as well as a "molehill" out of which should not be made a "theological mountain" (*Jesus Remembered*, 596).

22. *WJC*, 143, 144; also *ET*, 254.

23. See, e.g., Wright, *Jesus and the Victory of God*, 398–402, 430–32.

commandment,"[24] that enables Moltmann to say that Jesus was "without the protection of a family"[25] as a furtherance of his solidarity with the most outcast members of society.

Third, and perhaps the most obvious, is Jesus' lack of *political security*. The course of his public ministry issued a direct challenge to the imperial *status quo*. Such activity would have been clearly "*politisch hochgefährlich*."[26] Examples abound: according to the gospels Jesus publicly denounces Herod the puppet-king as a "fox" (Luke 13:32), and he processes into Jerusalem with donkey and foal, an act that excites messianic fervor to such a degree that the Jewish populace calls urgently for liberation: *Hosanna! (Save us!)*[27] (see Mark 11:1–10 and parallels). Such actions bear persecutorial fruit, for we see in the midst of the show trial before the authorities that Jesus is charged with setting himself up as the messianic king (Luke 23:2).[28] To claim royal status was seditious and worthy of Rome's attention—John records soldiers among those who arrest Christ at the Mount of Olives (John 18:3), and Mark also preserves the political charge, in ironic fashion, when Jesus himself asks why he is being arrested in the night as if he were a "bandit" (*lēstēs*—Mark 14:48).[29] This term is the same one applied to the political rebels who are crucified alongside him (Mark 15:27) as well as to Barabbas, the violent revolutionary for whom the crowd trades his life (Mark 15:7 and parallels).[30] And it is his alleged rebellious claim to kingship that is finally inscribed upon the *titulum crucis*—"King of the Jews"—a point preserved in all four gospels. It stands as the political seal upon his degrading death. In short, claims Moltmann, like so many of the Jewish people in his day, Jesus

24. This is Ben-Chorin's point, which Moltmann follows. See Ben-Chorin, *Mirjam— Mutter Jesu*, 99ff, referenced in *WJC*, 143 (also in *HTG*, 12). These perspectives, as well as that of N. T. Wright, stand in some contrast to an assessment like Dunn's (see *Jesus Remembered*, 595–97), which argues against "a severe rupture" between Jesus and his family, since the family is present among the disciples in Acts 1:14.

25. *WJC*, 100.

26. "Politically dangerous," *WJC* (German), 184. Kohl colorfully translates this as "political dynamite" (English: 163).

27. On the messianic import of the action and the crowds' reactions, see *WJC*, 160–61; also Wright, *Jesus and the Victory of God*, 490–93; Witherington, *Christology of Jesus*, 106–7.

28. On this show trial, see William Herzog, *Jesus, Justice, and the Reign of God*, chapter 10; Paul Winter, *On the Trial of Jesus*, chapters 3 and 5.

29. *WJC*, 161.

30. See also Luke 23:19; Wright, *Jesus and the Victory of God*, 419–20, 549.

"was a victim of Rome's despotic rule over Israel"[31] and he "suffered the fate of many enslaved poor in the Roman empire."[32]

Fourth, and finally, Moltmann emphasizes that Jesus willingly contested his own *socioreligious security* by virtue of his scandalous actions and message. Not only did he repeatedly render himself ritually impure through his association with the sickly, immoral, and unclean,[33] but his theological claims also constituted the depth of his social self-emptying of identity, for it is what led to the most repeated charge against him: *blasphemer*. Jesus' revelation of the character and grace of God, the God with whom he implied nonpareil closeness and from whom he claimed to derive his authority, directly provoked not only some of the crowd, who accused him of "making himself equal to God" (John 10:33),[34] but also the religious leaders, who accused him of blasphemy directly (e.g., Mark 2:7; 14:64). Moltmann thus finds in Jesus an abandonment of the security of religious tradition, a true vulnerability on the stage of first-century Jewish theology, a self-emptying of rabbinical prestige and religiously construed honor:

> The conflict [with the religious leaders] was provoked not by his incomprehensible claim to authority as such, but by the discrepancy between a claim which arrogated to itself the righteousness of God and his unprotected and therefore vulnerable humanity. For one "without office or dignities" to abandon the tradition and lay claim to the office and dignity of God himself, and to reveal divine righteousness in a "wholly other" way by the forgiveness of sins, was a provocation of the guardians of the law.[35]

Not only did Jesus collide with the Torah and its authoritative interpreters, but he also emptied his messianic identity of all its assumed

31. *WJC*, 163. John 19:12 highlights the political justification of Jesus' swift execution when Pilate is told that he "is no friend of Caesar" if he does not administer death to Jesus.

32. *WJC*, 100. Moltmann explicitly mentions the Phil 2 hymn ("form of a slave") in this same context; see also Gorringe, *Redeeming Time*: "[Phil 2:5–11] depicts Jesus again refusing to 'snatch at' or hang on to glory, but opting for the lot of the great majority of the Roman world, the lot of a slave, and dying the death which was reserved for them, crucifixion" (56).

33. Many examples could be named, but most notably the interactions with the hemorrhaging woman (Mark 5:25–34 and parallels) and with the lepers (Mark 1:40–42 and parallels; 14:3).

34. *ōn poieis seauton theon*—literally "are making yourself God." The public attempts to stone Jesus are rooted in an assumed crime of blasphemy, e.g., John 8:59; 10:31.

35. *CG*, 130; see the whole discussion on these points, 128–34; further *WJC*, 162–63.

interpretations. Far from fulfilling any militaristic or political role, Jesus went to his death in every sense appearing like a "defeated" messianic pretender.[36] As N. T. Wright concisely puts it, "It was, after all, failed Messiahs who ended up on crosses."[37] In his apparent defeat, Jesus is emptied even of his followers and friends, for nearly all of them flee (Mark 14:50), abandoning him to ignominious agony.[38] For they had hoped "he would be the one to redeem Israel" (Luke 24:21) and so, as Moltmann states, "Jesus' helpless death on the cross [was] the end of their hope."[39]

Each one of these four dimensions of distinctive and finally deadly vulnerability—economic, familial, political, religious—expresses an element of the *social kenosis* of Jesus Christ, the kenosis of identity. His obedience to the Father's will and his dependence on the Spirit's efficacy drive him into a mission of unparalleled uniqueness, which proceeds at the fringes of society and challenges personal and communal categories of security. In this humbling of himself, Jesus travels through what Moltmann calls a "social and religious no-man's-land."[40]

In this light, it should come as no surprise when in the gospel accounts Jesus is moved to depart from company and pray alone (e.g., Luke 6:12).[41] This prayer life, this clear portrayal of a dependent human in need of divine support, typifies the self-emptying which animates the whole course of Jesus' career. He seeks strength and guidance because in his mission he is emptied of all social safeguards and takes his place alongside the most misunderstood and rejected: "He himself becomes a victim among other victims."[42]

These radical extensions of Christ's lived vulnerability all consist in communal, corporate, and social relationships. Yet the greatest depth of his vulnerability is reserved in Moltmann's thought for Christ's self-emptying in relation to the *created order* itself. Indeed Christ's *flesh* is the immediate locus of the bloodiest and most iconic depth of the kenosis: the stark

---

36. *CG*, 132–33.

37. Wright, *Jesus and the Victory of God*, 606; also see 658.

38. But see John's recounting, which seems to imply the presence of at least one disciple, as well as some of the women (John 19:25b–27).

39. *SRA*, 44.

40. *WJC*, 144.

41. See also Matt 14:23; Heb 5:7; John 17:1–26.

42. *SpL*, 130(–131).

suffering of Christ's flesh itself. We turn finally, then, to this aspect of Christ's kenosis in Moltmann's thought.

Kenotic Embodiment: The Frailty of the Flesh

The human person is a psychosomatic unity, animated by life which is inextricably and irreducibly composed of both material and spiritual aspects: this is axiomatic for Moltmann's understanding of anthropology and cosmology,[43] especially since the "greening" of his theology between 1972 and 1985.[44] Over and against the more common theological dualities prompted by modernity (mind vs. body, history vs. revelation, civiliation vs. nature, etc.[45]) Moltmann has striven to see—in the light thrown by emerging scientific discourse[46]—humanity as a part of nature whose embodied materiality is taken with resolute seriousness.[47] The fourth and final dimension of Moltmann's kenotic Christology reflects this, for it is concerned with Jesus' human body itself:

> Modern historical thinking set human history over against a nature without history. Newer thinking integrates human history in the natural conditions in which it is embedded. . . . Christology therefore directs its attention towards Christ's bodily nature [*die Leiblichkeit Christi*] and its significance for earthly nature [*irdische*

43. See *GC*, 247–70; *SW*, 47–51; *SRA*, chapters 6 and 7; also *JCTW*, 85–87. For a thoroughly integrated examination of Moltmann's wide-ranging anthropology, see Prooijen, *Limping but Blessed*, 330–55.

44. 1972 marked the West's first major oil crisis and catalyzed Moltmann's ecological theology, which emerged prominently in his paper "Creation as an Open System," (115–30) but reached its full expression in his Gifford Lectures (published as *GC*). See the discussions in *ABP*, 211–12, 295–301.

45. We have highlighted this aspect of his method earlier. See also Schmiechen, *Saving Power*, 139.

46. Excellent commentary on the philosophical and scientific movement away from soul/body dualism and its importance for Christology can be found in Shults, *Christology and Science*, 35–38.

47. See Davies, *Theology of Transformation*, 12–14, 29–30, 43–48. As Moltmann states it: "Personhood is nature structured by the reflection of the mind and spirit, and by history. Every individual person is a hypostasis of nature. There are no human persons without nature, and there is no human nature without personhood. To be a person is more than to be a subject of understanding and will. A person is a living body" (*WJC*, 256).

Natur], because embodiment is the existential point of intersection between history and nature in human beings.[48]

If Christ's physicality is part-and-parcel of his humanity, and if humanity is intrinsically and irreducibly embedded in the natural world, then it can be argued that the incarnation has cosmic (or *earthly* or *natural*) significance; the body of Jesus is then much more than simply the vehicle (or veil, or cloud, to use the more traditional concealment metaphors) that encapsulates a spiritual or "metaphysical" salvific reality. For Moltmann, what it means to appreciate Christ's ministry, especially those acts concerning the tangible healing of blatantly physical maladies,[49] is to take note of the "bodily character of salvation" and "the God who loves earthly life,"[50] and to follow Friedrich Oetinger in recognizing that "embodiment is the end of all God's works."[51]

Moltmann's theme of kenotic identification thus extends beyond the sociological and relational dimensions I've already detailed. In becoming a creaturely *human*, i.e., an interrelated element within the biological matrix of the created cosmos, God the Son inhabits the depths of vulnerable materiality and finitude that characterize the cosmic order.[52] Thus Moltmann would agree with numerous contemporary interpreters that the Word became "fallen" flesh upon the incarnation,[53] but he understands this fallenness to be manifested in the flesh's *frailty* and its subjection to the ravages of death, pain, and time, without any recourse to speculation about "original sin" or a causal connection between sin and physical death.[54] For Moltmann,

48. *WJC*, xvi (German: 14).

49. Skin diseases (Mark 1:40–45 and parallels; Luke 17:11–19); paralysis (Mark 2:3–12 and parallels; Matt 8:5–13 and parallels); hemorrhage (Mark 5:24–34 and parallels.); blindness (Mark 9:27–31; Luke 18:35–43; John 9:1–12); fever (Mark 1:29–31 and parallels); deafness (Mark 7:31–37); death itself (Mark 5:40–42 and parallels; Luke 7:11–16; John 11:38–44).

50. *WJC*, 107.

51. *GC*, chapter 10; *EthH*, 72–73. See also the constructive assessment, with reference to Moltmann, of Kärkkäinen, *Christ and Reconciliation*, 143–48.

52. In Bauckham's words, "the mortality characteristic of this present reality" (*Theology*, 197).

53. E.g., Barth, *Dogmatik*, I.2, 155–59; Weinandy, *In the Likeness*; Rae, "Baptism of Christ," especially 128–37. See Jeff McSwain's commentary on Barth and Bonhoeffer on this score, *Movements of Grace*, 78–79.

54. See *WJC*, 169–70. Here Moltmann explicitly favors Schleiermacher's view over and against what he calls the "Augustinian and Pauline" tradition. He locates the beginning of the "concrete history of human sin" in Cain's fratricide (Moltmann, "Justice for

death is a "tragedy in creation," though this enigmatic phrase places death in no clear relation to sin itself, and the question of the origination of death in the midst of God's good creation is left hanging quite prominently in Moltmann's thought.[55] But we can leave this particular ambiguity aside in order to see Moltmann's larger christological point.[56]

As the incarnate one, God the Son *became a creature*.[57] As a creature, he was comprised of material elements necessarily animated by natural laws relating to energy and matter.[58] That is, like all elements of the physical created order, Christ was constituted in and by a nexus of *corporeal relations*. Colin Gunton's Christology aligns, at least partially, with Moltmann here, for Gunton claims that "no Christology is adequate which tries . . . to evade the material determinateness of Jesus" and that "Jesus was, as we are, a creature in relations of 'horizontal' reciprocal constitution with other people *and the world*."[59]

For Moltmann, this deepening of the concept of incarnation delves beyond the assumption of human nature *in abstracto* in order to engage earnestly with the assumption of human *flesh* (and to, in fact, closely conflate the two). Jesus of Nazareth was born innately mortal, and that means that he suffered in the flesh what all flesh suffers—the law of natural death: "Jesus died *the death of all the living*, for he was mortal and would one day have died even if he had not been executed. Through his death struggle he participated in the fate of everything that lives—not merely the fate of human beings; for all living things desire to live and have to die."[60] Here emerges the key to this aspect of the kenotic Christology: the kenosis of Christ takes

---

Victims," *HTG*, 45). While many points about this can be made compelling, I think that Moltmann's rendering of sin in this way is, at best, under-developed and partial. Sin is *at least* rooted in our natural, doomed-to-die selves, but this does not describe sin *in total*.

55. Höhne raises some critical points on this score, "Moltmann on Salvation," 160. See also McDougall, *Pilgrimage*, 148–50.

56. An interpreter who has consistently called attention to Moltmann's underdeveloped doctrine of sin is McDougall (e.g., "Trinitarian Praxis," 201–2; *Pilgrimage*, 148–51). Moltmann's reservations about traditional formulations of harmartiology appear with clarity in *SpL*, 125–28. There he supports the notion that sin should be treated nonabstractly and only insofar as it can produce marked "therapeutic" value in the healing of human brokenness (127–28). See also his comments in his Foreword to *Pilgrimage*, xiv.

57. Höhne, "Moltmann on Salvation," 160, with parenthetical reference to Col 1:15–17. See also Gunton, *Christ and Creation*, chapter 2.

58. Gunton, *Christ and Creation*, 36–37.

59. Gunton, *Christ and Creation*, 41, 43, emphasis added.

60. *WJC*, 169.

the divine Son all the way to an *embrace of cosmic vulnerability*, of dying material existence; he suffers nature's kind of suffering, both in life and on the cross.[61] The one who in his divine form became a slave (Phil 2:7) was self-emptied to the point of death, death being the fate of all things in the present created order. Jesus was "enslaved," via his incarnation, to a "body of death" like the one Paul bemoans in Rom 7:24. This willing enslavement, this self-emptying, fetters Christ's flesh to the powers of the old and broken creation—namely, the powers of dissolution, entropy, and death; indeed he was, as we are, "subjected to futility" (Rom 8:20).

This also forms an important and hitherto unmentioned facet of Moltmann's theology of surrender, for it answers the question of *what Christ was surrendered to*. Moltmann's answer is simply *death*: creaturely finitude; the sickness of pain and transitoriness that runs through all flesh. Jesus "was handed over to death" (Rom 4:25),[62] for death is the ruling power with dominion over the Adamic creation (Rom 5:12–21) and it is that dominion that was broken by his resurrection (Rom 6:9). Sin and death had to be "condemned in the flesh" by Christ who was sent "in the likeness of sinful flesh" (Rom 8:4). In various moments in the history of the church, these passages have been treated as though their major referent is *spiritual* death, but Moltmann, in line with his focus on cosmology and embodiment, takes them as referring to the *physical* death that characterizes all life on this side of the new creation,[63] and thus he sees Christ's subjection to it not only on the cross, but in the incarnation as a whole. God the Son did not only become poor, unclean, outcast, and abandoned; he became *sarx* itself (*sarx* = flesh; see John 1:14), and so went the way of all flesh, at the nadir of his self-emptying. It is the cross—fleshly, bloody, corporeal death—that realizes (or completes) this kenosis.[64] Christ's kenotic identification with the broken, interrelated material order allows the cross to be the place where he suffers the sufferings of all creation, for all flesh plummets toward death.[65] This is one of the most sustained points

61. WJC, 154–59, 193–97, 253, 255, 258; also Schmiechen, *Saving Power*, 138–39; Neal, *Theology as Hope*, 157–59; Bauckham, *Theology*, 210.

62. Moltmann states: "The Son is given over to the power of death, a power contrary to God" (CPS, 95).

63. JCTW, 84–87.

64. TK, 119. See Kärkkäinen, "The self-surrender to the death on the cross and the cry . . . was the ultimate point of his self-distinction and self-emptying" (*Christ and Reconciliation*, 165).

65. WJC, 154–59, 169–70, 193–97, 253, 255, 258.

THE WAY OF THE KENOTIC CHRIST (II)

in *The Way of Jesus Christ* and also one of the most prominent developments in Moltmann's staurology since *The Crucified God*.

> Jesus died the death of all living things. That is, he did not only die "the death of the sinner" or merely his own "natural death." He died in solidarity with the whole sighing creation, human and non-human—the creation that "sighs" because it is subject to transience [*Vergänglichkeit unterworfenen*]. He died the death of everything that lives. . . . The sufferings of Christ are therefore also "the sufferings of this present time" (Rom 8.18), which are endured by everything that lives.[66]

This has then brought us to the cosmological—or we might say *sarxiological*—extent of the christological kenosis in Moltmann. When the Phil 2 hymn talks about "being born in human likeness [*homoiōmati*]" and "being found in human form [*schēmati*]" (Phil 2:7), these should be seen as standing alongside the consistent New Testament claim of divine *enfleshment*. We are told that "the Word became flesh [*sarkos*]" (John 1:14), and that the Son "through whom God created the worlds" also participated in what is referred to as "the days of the flesh [*tais hēmerais tēs sarkos*]" (Heb 1:2; 5:7).[67] Moltmann takes this flesh to be all-embracing; *sarx* does not simply refer to "sinful" flesh but to flesh itself and the conditions of fleshly existence. The scholarship of N. H. Gregersen lends support to such a view, saying that *sarx* "refers to the realm of materiality in its most general extension, perhaps with a note of frailty and transitoriness."[68]

Gregersen's christological work has recently engendered a school of thought known as "deep incarnation," which further expounds the significance of Christ's flesh by re-formulating Anselm's famous christological question. Anselm asked *cur Deus homo?* (Why the God-man?), but deep incarnation asks *cur Deus caro* (Why the God-flesh?). This question's implications are expanded as, "What in the world has the *body* of Jesus to do with the vast body of *cosmos*?"[69] Those who have advocated for the idea of deep incarnation[70] propose that in Jesus the divine and the creaturely are

---

66. *WJC*, 169–70 (German: 191).

67. See also Heb 2:14, where Christ is said to share in *haimatos kai sarkos*.

68. Gregersen, "Idea of Deep Incarnation," 328, see also 321. So also Moltmann, "Is God Incarnate in All That Is?" 126–28. This understanding of *sarx* is strongly advocated by J. A. T. Robinson as well: *The Body*, 17–26.

69. Gregersen, "Cur Deus *Caro*," 375.

70. Aside from Gregersen, Celia Deane-Drummond and Elizabeth Johnson have

"conjoin[ed] so intensely together that there can be a future also for a material world characterized by decomposition, frailty, and suffering" and that "incarnation is about a radical divine self-embodiment that reaches into the roots (*radices*) of biological existence."[71] For Gregersen, as in Moltmann, "the flesh assumed in Jesus includes the entire human race (women and men), as well as the nonhuman creatureliness"[72]—in short, the Logos' coming-as-flesh has meaning for "the entire matrix of materiality."[73]

In a recent volume of essays focused on this deep incarnation motif, Moltmann himself has in fact been able to interact with some of the major exponents of the perspective, and has iterated his agreement with it explicitly: "God assumes the whole vulnerable, mortal nature in his becoming human, in order that it may be healed, reconciled, and glorified."[74] There is thus prevalent accord between the idea of deep incarnation and our explication of Moltmann's view of Christ's kenotic relation to the vulnerable human body. Along these lines, Christopher Southgate has rightly noted that Moltmann's discourse on this co-suffering solidarity with the whole created order reflects "Christ's ultimate act of kenosis."[75] An effective summation of this kenotic theme is also provided by Zathureczky:

> Moltmann's Christ is not the ontological abstraction of the metaphysics of two natures. He is the Messiah who identifies with the decay of existence and through his kenotic identification, rescues creation from its ultimate decay. The Messiah redeems the incomplete by identifying with it. . . . The connection between the cross of Christ and the materiality of existence is an essential determining factor of Moltmann's soteriological schema.[76]

made use of the ideas. See also the recent work from Moritz, "Deep Incarnation," 436–43; Cole-Turner, "Incarnation Deep and Wide," 424–35, as well as the recent anthology, Gregerson, *Incarnation*.

71. Gregersen, "Cur Deus *Caro*," 375.

72. Gregersen, "Cur Deus *Caro*," 383.

73. Gregersen, "Deep Incarnation and *Kenosis*," 252.

74. Moltmann, "Is God Incarnate in All That Is?" 128. See also his comments in *EthH*: "The biblical word 'flesh' (*kol' basar*) means 'all the living,' and embraces human life together with all the living on earth. The 'becoming flesh of the Word' (John 1:14) [is] not meant anthropocentrically" (62).

75. Southgate, *Groaning of Creation*, 76. Southgate also claims a debt to Gregersen's work on deep incarnation (76–77).

76. Zathureczky, *Messianic Disruption*, 131. Though Southgate and Zathureczky both mention the kenotic co-identification with materiality, they do not explicate it at any length beyond these quotations here, nor do they weave it into the larger dimensions of

Eschatology never far from view, Moltmann will declare in his later works that, though we are tempted to "flee from the mortality of the body" with its "infirmities and frailties," it is Jesus who "brings and makes a truly living life [the] harbinger and beginning of the bodily life of the new creation."[77] The point is this: Christ's kenosis does not simply designate the depths of suffering solidarity but is, for Moltmann, the literal *manner* of the world's transformation. The path from old creation to new creation—through the cross to the resurrection—is *a kenotic path.*

Conclusion: An Empathetic and Suffering Christ

This chapter completes my explication of the major themes of Moltmann's kenotic Christology. Chapters 5 and 6 have been pressed, most essentially, to answer this question: *What does kenosis mean for Moltmann's doctrine of Christ?*

Fundamentally, as I have shown, kenosis designates a radical, revelatory, and relational reality. In line with almost all formulations of contemporary theological anthropology, Christ is understood as constituted by, identified with, and animated by an interweaving matrix of relations. In each of the four relational categories that frame the incarnate life—relation to the Father, Spirit, others, and cosmos (flesh)—kenosis is principal and operative. The relations of Christ are kenotic; therefore Christ is kenotic.

What remains to be undertaken in this study is an all-too-brief examination of some of the *implications* of this Moltmannian Christology. In particular, what does this understanding of such a radically kenotic Messiah potentially mean for Christ's *ongoing work* in the world? And what does it mean for his *church*? What does it mean, then, to *follow* him?

Moltmann's kenotic doctrine of Christ.

77. *EthH*, 54.

7

Following the Way of the Kenotic Christ

Moltmann's Christology and Its Horizons

HAVING NOW THOROUGHLY ANALYZED and described Moltmann's unique fourfold vision of Christ's kenosis, this final chapter directs itself to two modest tasks: (1) Summarizing and synthesizing the Christology as it has been described throughout this book, answering remaining questions and clarifying issues along the way; and (2) pointing to further christo-logical and, indeed, *ecclesiological* work that may be helpfully propelled by Moltmann's doctrine of Christ.

Summarizing the Christology: The Whole Self-Emptying

Given the radical extent to which Moltmann proves willing to follow his reading of Christ's kenotic relations, the Christology finds itself staring headlong at a classic question, one which I do not want to sidestep in my analysis. And, in fact, by not sidestepping it, the question itself opens a broad stage upon which Moltmann's christological ideas might be more clearly examined.

The question is this: What is to be made of Jesus' *self-understanding* and his "messianic consciousness" in the gospels? That is, what did Jesus think of himself? Or again, who and what did he understand himself to be, and how does the progression of his ministry relate to that understanding?

As would be expected, Moltmann does not undertake any answer to such questions via consideration of the two natures *in abstracto* or through some fracturing of the consciousness of Jesus into "divine" and "human" components.[1] Rather, it is the concrete historical accomplishments and

1. For examples of both strategies, see, e.g., Morris, *Logic of God Incarnate,* chapters 4, 6; also Swinburne, *Christian God,* 199–209.

progressions of the life of Jesus that help to inform an implicit suggestion (rather than an overt philosophical or psychological declaration) about his self-understanding; this is part of what Moltmann means when he claims to be pursuing a "narrative Christology."[2] The gospel events, the *enacted* moments, scaffold this christological reasoning, not speculative assumptions imported from elsewhere.

The baptism of Jesus, as the catalyst for his public ministry, is a definitive scriptural moment for Moltmann, and one that illustrates a core distinctive of his christological narrative: Jesus experiences *stages* of his self-understanding and vocational outlook; he "grows" into his messiahship; he has a "*being-in-history,* and [a] 'learning process' [*Lernprozeß*] of his life and ministry."[3] The kenotic dependence upon the Spirit emerges as a clear element here, for if Jesus needs the Spirit's energies and influence to help him know both his mission and who he is before the Father; the kenosis in relation to the Spirit *facilitates* the kenosis in relation to the Father: "It is therefore the Spirit who 'leads' Jesus into the mutual history between himself and God his Father, in which 'through obedience' (Heb 5:8) he will 'learn' his role as the messianic Son."[4] Thus, Moltmann's pneumatological and developmental Christology (as themes) must be understood concurrently with the kenosis of efficacy, which enables and sustains the kenosis of will and which further forms the basis of Moltmann's "messianic" and "firstborn" christological thematics.

As Jesus embraces his role as Messiah, empowered by the Spirit and submitted to the Father, further stages can be detected in his self-understanding. While Jesus may have come to understand himself as Messiah around the time of his baptism, the question still remains of *what sort of Messiah* he understood himself to be. It was, after all, a time of messianic fervor in Israel.[5] There were many expectations and hopes that took on particular messianic shapes, and Jesus would no doubt have been exposed to the varied contours of this *Zeitgeist* in the course of his childhood and maturation. The temptations in the desert (Matt 4:1–11 and parallels), no matter how they are construed in terms of historical event, at the very least

---

2. *WJC,* xv. See also McDougall, *Pilgrimage,* 11–13 (nn45–46), 65.

3. *WJC,* 136 (German: 158). The most important section on this is *WJC,* 136–50. See also *SpL,* 60–65.

4. *SpL,* 61.

5. For a thorough historical survey of messianic formulations, movements, figures, and expectations, see Oegema, *Anointed and His People,* 103–47, 294–303.

illustrate Jesus' clash with messianic expectations that were defined by displays of power, grandeur, and standard images of rulership.[6] In the important christological work *Freedom Made Flesh*, Ignacio Ellacuría discusses the reality of "the key temptation of false messianism" as a persistent and publicly manifested challenge in the life of Jesus.[7] As evidenced by his accomplished victory over such temptation, Jesus is aware (or becomes aware) that his "way" must be different from any heretofore expected militaristic or political Messiah. This Messiah is a self-emptying one: the kenosis of identity in solidarity with the poor and the kenosis of body in a vulnerable and humiliating death are key to his inhabitation of this *countercultural* messianic role. For Moltmann, then, the kenosis of Christ's vulnerable identity is what funds his theme of messianic Christology.

The full knowledge of his kenotic messianic calling dawned upon Jesus over time. In generalized terms, both Luke and Hebrews tell us of the *learning of Christ* (e.g., Luke 2:52; Heb 5:8). In specific terms, Moltmann emphasizes that Jesus is dependent on and grows through his social relations.[8] The interactions with women especially seem to push Jesus beyond himself to new realizations; the woman with the hemorrhage (Mark 5:25–34) and the Canaanite woman (Matt 15:22–28) both impress Jesus with their faith, and it seems that "Jesus himself grows from the expectation and faith of these women. He surpasses himself as we say—he grows beyond himself [*er wächst über sich hinaus*]. But it would be more exact to say: he grows into the One whom he will be, God's messiah."[9] Said differently, and slightly less drastically, these stories of the women (among others) can be seen as providential encounters that teach Jesus about himself and the role into which the Father beckons him and toward which the Spirit compels him.

Though Moltmann himself does not make this express point, we might add that the prayer life of Jesus seems to demonstrate interpersonal and vocational development, for the act of private prayer on his part (Matt 14:23, 26:36–44; Luke 5:16; 6:12; 9:28) seems strongly to indicate a seeking

6. *CG*, 142; *SpL*, 61; *WJC*, 92. See further Wright, *Jesus and the Victory of God*, 457–59; Habets (who, again, is heavily reliant on Moltmann), *Anointed Son*, 143. See also the helpful summative discussion in Stein, *Jesus the Messiah*, 102–11.

7. Ellacuría, *Freedom Made Flesh*, 54–60.

8. *WJC*, 71. Furthermore, at least twice in the gospel narratives, Jesus is said to be "amazed" (*thaumazō*) by an encounter with others—once by the faith of the centurion (Luke 7:9) and again by the lack of faith in his hometown (Mark 6:6)—an expression that certainly implies a *new realization* or *surprising noetic experience* on the part of Jesus.

9. *WJC*, 111 (German: 131); also see 146–47.

of *personal guidance, instruction, and edification.*[10] As Myk Habets rightly notes, this practice of private prayer has often been a "puzzle" and a "mystery" to traditionally rendered Christologies.[11] By contrast, Moltmann's unique form of kenotic Christology renders it deeply meaningful and coherent rather than baffling.

Not only the prayer life of Jesus, but also his forty-day fast in the wilderness can be taken to illustrate this, for an analysis of fasting, based on the few Old Testament texts concerning the practice, readily concludes that the two most general and consistently attested purposes of Jewish fasting were either (1) as mourning or expiation relating to death, destruction, or sin (e.g., Neh 9:1; Esth 4:3; Joel 2:12) or (2) as an "auxiliary to prayer" in order to seek divine assistance and revelation (Isa 58:4; Dan 9:3).[12] Given a lack of clear contextual rationale for why (1) would apply in Jesus' case,[13] (2) seems the more obvious justification for his fasting in the wilderness. The fast's placement between the baptism and the beginning of his ministry makes good sense of this. Jesus undertakes the practice of fasting *in order to seek divine illumination as to the true meaning of his just-declared messianic status.* This line of thinking echoes Donald MacKinnon's thought that in the desert narrative we may well be reading "a recollection of what Jesus himself may have said concerning his own most strenuous self-interrogation, as if he had first put to himself the question: 'What think you of Christ?' before he could put it to others."[14] This certainly would also explain the narratival force of the recounted devilish temptations *all involving distinctly messianic pretexts.*[15]

---

10. Dunn, *Jesus and the Spirit,* 19–20; Anna Wierzbicka, *What Did Jesus Mean?* 147–48.

11. Habets, *Anointed Son,* 265.

12. See further Diamond, *Holy Men and Hunger Artists,* 94–95 (n20); Brongers, "Fasting in Israel," 3.

13. This is not to say that the baptism itself (rather than the act of fasting) did not entail some thematic of (possibly representational) repentance; see Webb, "Jesus' Baptism by John," 133–35.

14. Mackinnon, "Myth of God Incarnate," 143.

15. See Stein, *Jesus the Messiah,* 106–10. Michael Welker says that Jesus is not *denying* the grasping of power but rather *demonstrating* the power he already has. There doesn't seem to be any reason, though, why both readings cannot stand side-by-side, since there is an undeniable difference between the sort of power Christ refuses and the sort of power he demonstrates in so refusing. See Welker, *God the Spirit,* 187.

If this fasting-and-temptation narrative displays Jesus' "initial victory" over such false messianic ambitions,[16] then it is the confrontation with Peter at Caesarea Philippi that unveils the matured contours of Jesus' messianic self-understanding (see Mark 8:27–33). Here, Peter rightly identifies Jesus as Messiah, but he does not understand *the kind of Messiah* that Jesus is called to be, and he is rebuked for it, as well as pejoratively identified with that initial source of messianic misconstrual, the "satan" (8:33).[17] This climactic moment in Jesus' history, for Moltmann, is what points to the true "messianic secret," which is the secret of a *suffering* Messiah, whose way is a way of humiliation, limit, and apparent loss; a hidden victory if ever there was one. (It is here that we perceive how the kenosis is fundamental to Moltmann's theme of "solidarity" Christology and his emphasis on Christ's *Leidenschaft*, his passionate suffering.) Moreover and pivotally, it is only *after* this revealing moment at Caesarea Philippi that Jesus begins to speak of his impending death (e.g., Mark 8:31; 9:31; 10:33–34; 14:27). He now knows that he is the kind of Messiah who is called to die and be raised; rather than do battle against pagan powers or be "made king" in any political sense,[18] he is called to kenotically suffer for the sake of the world's transformation.

But even after this there remains his dark struggle with this messianic calling-unto-death in Gethsemane, and here Ellacuría again provides reasoning that is consonant with Moltmann's paradigm: "[Jesus'] messianism must be interpreted in terms of apparent failure and ruin, and it is this realization that leads to his bloody sweat and agony in the garden. . . . *It costs him a great deal to see this.*"[19] For Moltmann, this means that Jesus speaks and acts in a dawning or gradual assurance of the full depths of his radically kenotic calling:

---

16. Wright, *Jesus and the Victory of God*, 457–59; MacDonald, "Problems of Pneumatology," 149–51.

17. The link between "satan" and false messianism may also be represented in the character of Judas. There are grounds for suspecting Judas Iscariot to be a Zealot, and ahead of his betrayal of Jesus it is said that "Satan entered into him" (John 13:27; compare Luke 22:3). See *CG*, 139. Wright also links all three of these events—the desert, Caesarea Philippi, and the betrayal—within the matrix of satanic temptation and false messianic thinking (see *Jesus and the Victory of God*, 463).

18. See, e.g., John 6:15, where Jesus anticipates and avoids a Jewish mob's attempt to "make him king by force."

19. Ellacuría, *Freedom Made Flesh*, 60, emphasis added.

If Jesus holds fast to his endowment with the Spirit, dispensing with the economic, political and religious methods of forcible rule, then all he can do is to suffer the forces that oppose him, and then he must die in weakness. But this is the way along which the Spirit "leads" him, so this is also the way in which he is assured of his messiahship [*seiner Messianität gewiß wird*]. It is as he follows the path that he comes to understand the messianic role that God's Spirit has assigned him.[20]

Thus, it emerges with acute clarity how every thematic dimension of Moltmann's Christology not only requires but *presupposes* the varied dimensions of Christ's kenosis. The messianic ministry is developed, informed, and constituted by an array of kenotic relationships (with the Father, Spirit, society, the created order, etc.). And this is what Moltmann refers to summatively as the "whole self-emptying," the whole kenosis:

> [Jesus] neither affirms nor denies the title of the Christ with which Peter acknowledges him [at Caesarea-Philippi). He suspends this answer, giving himself and the disciples an answer of his own: the announcement of his suffering. Who he truly is, is to be manifested in his death and resurrection. . . . The sequence is: suffering—great suffering—rejection—death at the hands of others; and this sequence shows step by step the total loss of self, the whole self-emptying [*die totalen Selbstverlust, die gänzliche Selbstentleerung*], the loss of strength, the loss of dignity, the loss of human relationships, the loss of life. It is the road into a no-man's-land where there is no longer any sustaining tradition or human community—nothing but the God whom Jesus trusts.[21]

This is the sum of Moltmann's kenotic Christology as it relates to Christ's past life, his life as recounted in the gospel narratives. In trinitarian relation and in genuine humanity, the eternal Son casts himself into an existence completely defined by others, by limitation, and by suffering, and he must grow into this missional existence as the "Messiah in becoming."

Gunton offers an analysis that accords strongly with some aspects of this, saying that "Jesus' particular humanity is perfected by the Spirit, who respects his freedom by enabling him to be what he was called through his baptism to be. That sacrificial offering can be understood in its fullness if it is seen to consist not only in the life laid down, but in the whole pattern of a

20. *SpL*, 62 [German: 75]; also Althouse, *Spirit of the Last Days*, 133–34; Wright, *Jesus and the Victory of God*, 527–38.

21. *WJC*, 138 (German: 159).

life leading to passion and death."[22] Moltmann claims that, throughout every stage of his self-emptying, Christ participates in a "co-instrumentality" with the Father and Spirit—"his life history is at heart a 'trinitarian history of God'"[23] and also, as we've seen, the Father and Spirit each experience their own forms of co-kenosis alongside Jesus.[24]

So how did Jesus understand himself? No less an eminent and creedally committed scholar than N. T. Wright has suggested that Jesus, in his truly human and dependent existence, would have had to consider "the serious possibility that he might be totally deluded" about his own identity.[25] But, in surprising contrast to this sort of assessment, Moltmann's thickly trinitarian and narratival view of Christ's kenosis allows Jesus *a deep assurance of mission once that mission is learned,* even in the agony of the crucifixion.[26] But this does not lessen the kenosis or the depths of Christ's limitation and suffering. The Son of God on a rebel's cross is never anything other than a kenotic reality for Moltmann, and it is this kenosis that "reveals the divinity of God":[27]

> Israel's messiah king goes his way to the Roman cross. The Son of God empties himself of his divinity and takes the way of a poor slave to the point of death on the cross. If we look at the divine power and sovereignty, this is a path of self-emptying [*ein Weg der Entäußerung*]. If we look at the solidarity with the helpless and poor which it manifests, it is the path of the divine love in its essential nature.[28]

> This is solidarity Christology: Christ with us, the God-forsaken. The Gospels describe Jesus' passion as the story of his path into an ever-deeper self-emptying. This path ends with his execution on the Roman cross.[29]

22. Gunton, *Christ and Creation,* 57.

23. *WJC,* 74.

24. The christological self-emptying of the Father: *WJC,* 176, *TK,* 82–83; the christological kenosis of the Spirit: *SpL,* 62–63. See Habets' discussion of the co-kenosis of the Spirit with the Son (*Anointed Son,* 143–44, 165–67) and his suggestive commentary on the co-kenosis of the Father, at least during the death of Christ (168n193).

25. Wright, *Jesus and the Victory of God,* 606.

26. See *SpL,* 65.

27. *IEB,* 70–71.

28. *WJC,* 178 (German: 200).

29. *IEB,* 69.

The Christology's Horizon: Constructive Trajectories

This study has been, naturally, limited. It has focused on articulating the principal methods, themes, hermeneutics, and arguments that shape Moltmann's unique iteration of kenotic Christology. All robust Christologies, however, push beyond such doctrinal analysis. Christology should always, more than any other arena of Christian reflection, push us toward the "now," the present and ongoing context of all those who would claim to be followers of Christ. As Moltmann says, Christology and praxis, doctrine of Christ and the living of Christian life, must go together.

So, the final and all-too-brief movement of this study shifts to the present tense. It concerns *the present Christ*; Christ now, alive and ascended, and his relation to the world. This movement is funded by one of Moltmann's core impulses, which I described in some detail back in chapter 1: Moltmann cares about theology not for the sake of abstraction, but for the sake *of the church in the world.* Theology must correlate; theology must make a difference. When speaking of the church, the theological locus that matters most is Christology, for the church is "the body of Christ." In moving from Christology to ministry, Christology to ecclesiology, or Christology to ethics, certain insights become truly pivotal. In what follows I circumscribe some of these insights, noting how Moltmann's unique thought points forward to future constructive projects in which his Christology could play a vital part.

From Christ to Life: Soteriology

How did Christ change the world? That is, what has been changed, *specifically and concretely*, about the human situation by the birth, life, death, resurrection, ascension, and ongoing life of Christ? Or, said differently again: *What did Christ achieve?* These provocative queries are housed within soteriology, the study of salvation. In Christologies, kenotic or otherwise, that have focused overmuch on an abstraction of the two natures and their ontological unity in the person of Christ, the answers to the question of Christ's accomplishment have too often been similarly abstract: "Christ reconciled us to the Father"; "Christ made possible our redemption"; "Christ paid our debt of sin"; and so on. None of these renderings are, strictly speaking, wrong, but they appear increasingly irrelevant and/or cryptic to our contemporary world. What is needed, now more than ever, is a *concrete soteriology*—a soteriology that can name, in detailed and specific ways, the distinct and revolutionary alterations to human life Christ has effected. Since Moltmann's kenotic Christology is robustly, almost aggressively, concrete in its focus on actual events, narratives, history, and developments, it could serve as a distinct partner in the pursuit of a relevant and practical rendering of Christian soteriology. At its core, the chief contribution of Moltmann along these lines would be how *each dimension of Christ's kenosis brings about a distinctive transformation of human reality.* This would produce, in short, a holistic, multifaceted, and distinctly kenotic vision of soteriology and redemption.

From Christ to Church: Ecclesiology

I must admit that my study of Moltmann's Christology, as it appears in this present book, is missing an important element: Moltmann's reflections on *the ascension of Christ and his current presence in the world.*[30] It is well-recognized that the course of Christ's life reached a threshold at his ascension. Due to the clear scriptural portrayal of Christ's withdrawn visible presence (Luke 24:51; Acts 1:9; 1:22; 1 Tim 3:16) and yet equally clear scriptural conviction of his continuing and efficacious presence,[31] the state of the ascended Jesus summons critical reflection about its relationship to his mortal life. This scriptural difficulty, compounded by the cosmological and historical theses of the Enlightenment,[32] has given rise to a situation in which, according to Kärkäinnen, "by and large contemporary theology . . . has ignored the topic of the ascension."[33] But the foundational importance of the ascension is well summed by Christoph Schönborn: "[The exaltation] is in a sense the christological article that has the most ecclesiological

30. My doctoral dissertation, on which much of this present book is based, contains substantial material on these topics. That material will likely emerge in later published work along the lines described in these sections.

31. See Davies, "Interrupted Body," 50. This is especially evident scripturally in statements of Christ being "with" individuals and the church (e.g., Matt 18:20; 28:20; Acts 18:10) and statements of Christ being "in" individuals and the church (e.g., Col 1:27) or individuals or the church described as "in" Christ (e.g., Eph 2:10).

32. In addition to Davies' description of these factors (e.g., *Theology of Transformation,* 35–43), see Farrow, *Ascension and Ecclesia,* 165–71; *Ascension Theology.* esp. 25–31. Farrow's emphasis is more philosophical and anthropological while Davies' is more cosmological, but both assessments are largely consonant.

33. Kärkäinnen, *Christ and Reconciliation,* 357; Kärkäinen makes the statement more radical further on, claiming that "Western theology has ignored the ascension with its focus on the cross" (363). Kapic and Lugt are more measured, saying that the ascension is "given relatively little attention in comparison with the cross and resurrection," ("Ascension of Jesus," 23).

relevance. . . . That is not surprising, since it has to do precisely with the *present* relationship of Christ to his Church."[34] In short, an underdeveloped Christology (by way of neglecting the exaltation) results in an impoverished ecclesiology and thus a vitiated perspective on Christian life and acting in the world.[35]

Given Moltmann's focus on embodiment in his kenotic Christology, the ascension is a topic of distinctive importance and potential contribution from his thought. Though I lack the space to detail it here, Moltmann does make a radical suggestion relating to the ascended Christ. It is this: Christ's life is *still kenotic.* That is, Christ's fourfold kenotic relationships have not ceased in his ascension; they have altered, to some degree, in their expression and implications, but they are nonetheless real and pivotal for the church's ongoing relationship to him. Following in line from what I said about soteriology, Moltmann implies not only that Christ's kenosis bring about *past* transformations of worldly reality, but that his ongoing kenosis effectuates transformations of *present* worldly reality. This lends powerful support to the notion that, if the church is the *body* of Christ, and if Christ is still living and working in a *kenotic* manner, then the church must be a *kenotic body.* Many have undertaken to talk about a kenotic, sacrificial, or "cruciform" church, but very few have grounded this in *the ongoing kenotic life of the ascended Christ.* Moltmann's potential contributions along such lines are substantial.

From Christ to Ministry: Praxis

Moltmann repeatedly affirms that every Christology entails a "christopraxis."[36] He is not alone in this; many are the theologians who have affirmed a deep and irreducible link between Christology and ethical praxis in the Christian life (one thinks of Bonhoeffer and liberation theology, among other voices).[37] Accordingly, every rendering of Christ in doctrine entails a relation to Christ in our lived lives. In light of this, it is hardly strange that in the wake of Moltmann's unique kenotic Christology a

34. Schönborn, *God Sent His Son*, 344.

35. This point is perhaps best made in Farrow, *Ascension & Ecclesia*, especially chapters 5–6; also *Ascension Theology*, especially chapters 4–5.

36. *WJC*, 41–43, 118–19, 215.

37. Bonhoeffer, *Christ the Center*; Sobrino, *Christology at the Crossroad*; Ellacuría, *Freedom Made Flesh.*

similarly unique articulation of Christian praxis would be enabled, rooted in a Moltmannian kenotic ecclesiology.

Moltmann himself has presented some clear hints of this in his later work, but his statements on Christ's mediation to the church via the Spirit imply a perspective possibly even more radical and daring than he himself has (thus far) promulgated. Based on my work in Moltmann, only some of which has been published in this present volume, I believe that his thought could support the following praxiological link between Christ and Christians: *Christ's ongoing kenosis is extended, via the Holy Spirit, as the lived activity of the church.* Or, with a slightly different emphasis: *the church serves as the pneumatic, kenotic extension of Christ's own ongoing ministry to the world.* The horizons opened by such an articulation are manifold, and hold considerable potential for a church that has lost much of its cultural power in the West and must, to a significant degree, rediscover what it means to be "a church under the cross."[38]

Conclusion: The Kenotic Christ in Moltmann's Thought

Though it has often been treated in a piecemeal fashion in secondary scholarship, Moltmann's doctrine of Christ demonstrates both robustness and singularity when its diverse thematics and kenotic motifs are brought holistically together. Moreover, in this chapter we have duly noted the horizons that Moltmann's Christology opens for constructive theological and ecclesial work. I myself hope to pursue some or all of these noted horizons in future projects.

T. R. Thompson, in an excellent essay focused on the development of kenotic Christology, interestingly comments that while Moltmann is keen on expressing a generally kenotic *theism*, he

> does not expressly entertain this same fruitful move [i.e., kenosis] in the Incarnation of the Son. My point here is this: the classic kenotic approach in principle seems to me not only eminently compatible with Moltmann's Christology, but his Christology

---

38. Work along this wavelength would doubtlessly need to integrate with the headway already established in Herbert, *Kenosis and Priesthood*; and Oden, *Transformative Church*. It would also stand in interesting and dialogical tension with the good work of Andrew Root (*Christopraxis*), insofar as Root's "practical theology of the cross" is Barthian in its foundation, rather than Moltmannian.

actually appears to presuppose it. [So why does Moltmann] shy away from the issue?[39]

The contribution of this book ultimately reveals both what is right and what is wrong with such an assessment of Moltmann's Christology. Thompson is right insofar as a certain form of kenosis is *presupposed* by Moltmann's Christology, and I have spent significant portions of this book unveiling the unique contours of it. But, as has been demonstrated, it would be wrong to suggest as Thompson does that Moltmann's kenotic Christology is remotely equivalent to "the classic approach" (i.e., nineteenth century radical German models). Moltmann is *critical* of classic kenoticism. However, he retains and employs certain strengths of it in his own rendering of a relational, biblically driven, non-speculative rendering of kenotic Christology. Moreover, Moltmann is hardly "shy" about his views of christological kenosis; his work is replete with explicit discussion and implicit utilization of such a framework in his doctrine of Christ, as I have made evident here.

But as unique as his kenotic Christology is, it would be relegated to the status of mere intellectual curiosity if not for that quality of Moltmann's thought I noted on the first page of this study: *fecundity*. Moltmann's theology spreads; it grows; it influences; it fertilizes. In the past half-century it has demonstrated an impact that far outstrips its tendencies toward overstatement and idiosyncracy. In him, we find christological intuitions and arguments that point toward constructive doctrinal movements for a church that wishes to be "clothed with Christ" (Gal 2:7) and to follow him on his kenotic way.

39. Thompson, "Nineteenth Century," 109.

Bibliography

Althaus, Paul. *The Theology of Martin Luther*. Philadelphia: Fortress, 1966.

Althouse, Peter. "Implications of the Kenosis of the Spirit for a Creational Eschatology: A Pentecostal Engagement with Jürgen Moltmann." In *The Spirt Renews the Face of the Earth*, edited by A. Yong, 155–73. Eugene, OR: Pickwick, 2009.

———. *Spirit of the Last Days: Pentecostal Eschatology in Dialogue with Jürgen Moltmann*. London: T. & T. Clark, 2003.

Ansell, Nicolas. *The Annihilation of Hell: Universal Salvation and the Redemption of Time in the Eschatology of Jürgen Moltmann*. Eugene, OR: Pickwick, 2013.

Athanasius. *Orationes I*. In *The Orations of St. Athanasius: Against the Arians*, translated by W. Bright, 1–67. Oxford: Clarendon, 1873.

Augustine. *Sermons 4 & 5*. In *Sermones de vetere testamento*, Corpus Christianorum Series Latina 41. Belgium: Brepols, 1961.

Badcock, Gary. *Light of Truth and Fire of Love: A Theology of the Holy Spirit*. Grand Rapids: Eerdmans, 1997.

Balthasar, Hans Urs von. *Mysterium Paschale*. Translated by Aidan Nichols. Edinburgh: T. & T. Clark, 1990.

Barth, Karl. *Church Dogmatics*. Vol. 4.1. Translated by G. W. Bromiley. Edinburgh: T. & T. Clark, 2010.

———. *The Epistle to the Philippians*. Translated by J. W. Leith. Richmond, VA: John Knox, 1962.

———. *The Humanity of God*. London: C. D. Deans, 1960.

Bauckham, Richard. "The Future of Jesus Christ." *Scottish Bulletin of Evangelical Theology* 16.2 (1997) 97–110.

———. *God Crucified: Monotheism and Christology in the New Testament*. Grand Rapids: Eerdmans, 1999.

———. *Jesus and the God of Israel: God Crucified and Other Studies on the New Testament's Christology of Divine Identity*. Grand Rapids: Eerdmans, 2009.

———. *Moltmann: Messianic Theology in the Making*. London: Marshall Pickering, 1987.

———. "Moltmann's Messianic Christology." *Scottish Journal of Theology* 44 (1991) 319–31.

———. *Theology of Jürgen Moltmann*. Edinburgh: T. & T. Clark, 1995.

Beck, T. David. *The Holy Spirit and the Renewal of All Things: Pneumatology in Paul and Jürgen Moltmann*. Eugene, OR: Pickwick, 2007.

Ben-Chorin, Schalom. *Mirjam—Mutter Jesu*. Munich: Guetersloher Verlagshaus, 1971.

Bingaman, Brock. *All Things New: The Trinitarian Nature of the Human Calling in Maximus the Confessor and Jürgen Moltmann*. Edinburgh: James Clarke, 2015.

Blocher, Henri. *Evil and the Cross: An Analytical Look at the Problem of Pain*. Grand Rapids: Kregel, 1994.

Bock, Darrell. *The NIV Application Commentary: Luke*. Grand Rapids: Zondervan, 1996.

Bonhoeffer, Dietrich. *Christ the Center*. Translated by E. H. Robertson. San Francisco: Harper, 1978.

Bonzo, J. Matthew. *Indwelling the Forsaken Other: The Trinitarian Ethics of Jürgen Moltmann*. Eugene, OR: Pickwick, 2009.

Brongers, H. A. "Fasting in Israel in Biblical and Post-Biblical Times." In *Instruction and Interpretation: Studies in Hebrew Language, Palestinian Archaeology and Biblical Exegesis*, edited by H. A. Brongers, 1–21. Leiden: E. J. Brill, 1977.

Brown, David. *Divine Humanity: Kenosis Explored and Defended*. London: SCM, 2010.

———. *The Divine Trinity*. London: Duckworth, 1985.

Bruce, A. B. *The Humiliation of Christ*. Edinburgh, T. & T. Clark, 1895.

Burge, Gary. *The Anointed Community: The Holy Spirit in the Johannine Tradition*. Grand Rapids: Eerdmans, 1987.

Buxton, Graham. "Moltmann on Creation." In *Jürgen Moltmann and Evangelical Theology: A Critical Engagement*, edited by S. W. Chung, 40–68. Eugene, OR: Pickwick, 2012.

Calvin, John. *Institutes of the Christian Religion*. Translated by H. Beveridge. Edinburgh: The Calvin Translation Society, 1845.

Chester, Timothy. *Mission and the Coming of God: Eschatology, the Trinity and Mission in the Theology of Jürgen Moltmann and Contemporary Evangelicalism*. Paternoster Theological Monographs. Eugene, OR: Wipf & Stock, 2006.

Chung, Sung Wook. "Moltmann on Scripture and Revelation." In *Jürgen Moltmann and Evangelical Theology: A Critical Engagement*, edited by S. W. Chung, 1–16. Eugene, OR: Pickwick, 2012.

Clarke, Antony. *A Cry in the Darkness: The Forsakenness of Jesus in Scripture, Theology, and Experience*. Macon, GA: Smyth & Helwys, 2002.

Clutterbuck, Richard. "Jürgen Moltmann as Doctrinal Theologian." *Scottish Journal of Theology* 48.4 (1995) 489–506.

Coakley, Sarah. "Does Kenosis Rest on a Mistake? Three Kenotic Models in Patristic Exegesis." In *Exploring Kenotic Christology*, edited by C. S. Evans, 246–64. Oxford University Press, 2006.

———. "*Kenosis* and Subversion." In *Powers and Submissions: Spirituality, Philosophy, and Gender*, 3–39. Oxford: Wiley-Blackwell, 2002.

———. *Powers and Submissions: Spirituality, Philosophy, and Gender*. Oxford: Wiley-Blackwell, 2002.

Cole-Turner, R. "Incarnation Deep and Wide: A Response to Niels Gregersen." *Theology and Science* 11.4 (2013) 424–35.

Congar, Yves. *I Believe in the Holy Spirit*. Translated by D. Smith. New York: Seabury, 1983.

Cowdell, Scott. *Is Jesus Unique? A Study of Recent Christology*. Mahwah, NJ: Paulist, 1996.

Crisp, Oliver. "Desiderata for Models of the Hypostatic Union." In *Christology: Ancient and Modern*, edited by O. Crisp and F. Sanders, 19–41. Grand Rapids: Zondervan, 2013.

Dabney, Lyle. *Die Kenosis des Geistes, Kontinuität zwischen Schöpfung und Erlösung im Werk des Heiligen Geistes*. Neukirchen-Vluyn: Neukirchener Verlag, 1997.

———. "Naming the Spirit: Towards a Pneumatology of the Cross." In *Starting with the Spirit*, edited by G. Preece and S. Pickard, 30–40. Sydney: Australian Theological Forum, 2001.

———. "*Pneumatologia Crucis*: Reclaiming *Theologia Crucis* for a Theology of the Spirit Today." *Scottish Journal of Theology* 53.4 (2000) 511–24.

Davies, Oliver. "The Interrupted Body." In *Transformation Theology*, 37–61. New York: T. & T. Clark, 2007.

———. *Theology of Transformation: Faith, Freedom, and the Christian Act*. Oxford: Oxford University Press, 2013.

Dawe, Donald. *The Form of a Servant: An Historical Analysis of the Kenotic Motif*. Philadelphia: Westminster, 1963.

Diamond, Eliezer. *Holy Men and Hunger Artists: Fasting and Asceticism in Rabbinic Culture*. Oxford: Oxford University Press, 2003.

Dunn, James D. G. "Christ, Adam, and Preexistence." In *Where Christology Began*, edited by R. P. Martin and B. J. Dodd, 74–83. Louisville, KY: Westminster John Knox, 1998.

———. *Jesus and the Spirit: A Study of the Religious and Charismatic Experience of Jesus and the First Christians as Reflected in the New Testament*. London: SCM, 1975.

———. *Jesus Remembered: Christianity in the Making*. Grand Rapids: Eerdmans, 2003.

Elert, Werner. *Der Ausgang der altkirchlichen Christologie*. Berlin: Lutherisches Verlaghaus, 1957.

Ellacuría, Ignacio. *Freedom Made Flesh: The Mission of Christ and His Church*. Maryknoll, NY: Orbis, 1976.

———. "The Political Nature of Jesus' Mission." In *Faces of Jesus: Latin American Christologies*, edited by José Míguez Bonino, 79–92. Maryknoll, NY: Orbis, 1984.

Ellingworth, Paul. *The Epistle to the Hebrews*. New International Greek Testament Commentary. Grand Rapids: Eerdmans, 1993.

Evans, C. S. *Exploring Kenotic Christology*. Oxford: Oxford University Press, 2006.

Farrow, Douglas. *Ascension & Ecclesia: On the Significance of the Doctrine of the Ascension for Ecclesiology and Christian Cosmology*. Edinburgh: T. & T. Clark, 1999.

———. *Ascension Theology*. New York: T. & T. Clark, 2011.

Fee, Gordon. *God's Empowering Presence: The Holy Spirit in the Letters of Paul*. Peabody, MA: Hendrickson, 1994.

———. "The New Testament and Kenosis Christology." In *Exploring Kenotic Christology*, edited by C. S. Evans, 25–44. Oxford: Oxford University Press, 2006.

———. *Paul's Letter to the Philippians*. New International Commentary on the New Testament. Grand Rapids: Eerdmans, 1995.

Feske, Millicent. "Christ and Suffering in Moltmann's Thought." *The Asbury Theological Journal* 55.1 (2000) 85–104.

Fiddes, Paul. *Participating in God: A Pastoral Doctrine of the Trinity*. Westminster John Knox, 2015.

Gibbs, John G. "The Relation Between Creation and Redemption According to Phil. II 5–11." *Novum Testamentum* 12.3 (1970) 270–83.

Gorman, Michael J. *Inhabiting the Cruciform God: Kenosis, Justification, and Theosis in Paul's Narrative Spirituality*. Cambridge: Eerdmans, 2009.

Gorringe, Timothy. *Redeeming Time: Atonement Through Education*. London: Dartman, Longman & Todd, 1986.

Greene, Colin. *Christology in Cultural Perspective*. Grand Rapids: Eerdmans, 2003.

Gregersen, N. H. "*Cur Deus Caro*: Jesus and the Cosmos Story." *Theology and Science* 11.4 (2013) 370–93.

———. Deep Incarnation and *Kenosis*: In, With, Under, and As: A Response to Ted Peters." *Dialog* 52.3 (2013) 251–62.

———. "The Idea of Deep Incarnation: Biblical and Patristic Resources." In *To Discern Creation in a Scattering World*, edited by F. Depoortere and J. Haers, 319–42. Leuven: Peeters, 2013.

———, ed. *Incarnation: On the Scope and Depth of Christology*. Minneapolis: Fortress, 2015.

Gregory of Elvira. *On the Faith*. In *Opera quae supersunt, Dubia et Spuria, Opera*. Corpus Christianorum Series Latina 69. Belgium: Brepols, 1967.

Grenz, Stanley, and Roger Olson. *20th Century Theology: God & the World in a Transitional Age*. Downers Grove, IL: InterVarsity, 1992.

———. *Rediscovering the Triune God*. Minneapolis: Augsberg Fortress, 2004.

Gunton, Colin. *Christ and Creation*. The Didsbury Lectures 1990. Eugene, OR: Wipf & Stock, 2005.

———. *Yesterday and Today: A Study of Continuities in Christology*. London: SPCK, 1997.

Gutierrez, Gustavo. *A Theology of Liberation*. Translated by Caridad Inda and John Eagleson. Maryknoll, NY: Orbis, 1973.

Guttesen, Poul, F. *Leaning Into the Future: The Kingdom of God in the Theology of Jürgen Moltmann and the Book of Revelation*. Princeton Theological Monograph Series 117. Eugene, OR: Pickwick, 2009.

Habets, Myk. *The Anointed Son: A Trinitarian Spirit Christology*. Eugene, OR: Pickwick, 2010.

Hamori, Esther J. "Divine Embodiment in the Hebrew Bible and Some Implications for Jewish and Christian Incarnational Theologies." In *Bodies, Embodiment, and Theology of the Hebrew Bible*, edited by S. T. Kamionkowski and Wonil Kim, 161–83. New York: T. & T. Clark, 2010.

Hanson, Bradley. *Christian Theology*. Minneapolis: Fortress Press, 1997.

Harteshorne, Charles. *Omnipotence and Other Theological Mistakes*. New York: SUNY, 1984.

Harvie, Timothy. *Jürgen Moltmann's Ethics of Hope*. Burlington, VT: Ashgate, 2009.

———. "Living the Future: The Kingdom of God in the Theologies of Jürgen Moltmann and Wolfhart Pannenberg." *International Journal of Systematic Theology* 10.2 (2008) 149–64.

Hawthorne, Gerald. "In the Form of God and Equal to God." In *Where Christology Began*, edited by R. P. Martin and B. J. Dodd, 96–110. Louisville, KY: Westminster John Knox, 1998.

———. *Philippians*. Word Biblical Commentary. Waco, TX: Word, 1983.

———. *The Presence and the Power: The Significance of the Holy Spirit in the Life and Ministry of Jesus*. Eugene, OR: Wipf & Stock, 1991.

Hengel, Martin. *Crucifixion in the Ancient World and the Folly of the Message of the Cross*. London: SCM, 1977.

Herbert, T. D. *Kenosis and Priesthood: Towards a Protestant Re-Evaluation of the Ordained Ministry*. Carlisle, UK: Paternoster, 2009.

Herzog, William. *Jesus, Justice, and the Reign of God: A Ministry of Liberation*. Louisville, KY: Westminster John Knox, 2001.

Höhne, David. "Moltmann on Salvation." In *Jürgen Moltmann and Evangelical Theology: A Critical Engagement*, edited by S. W. Chung, 152–73. Eugene, OR: Pickwick, 2012.

Hoover, Roy. "The Harpagmos Enigma: A Philological Solution." *Harvard Theological Review* 56 (1971) 95–119.

Horrell, David G. *Solidarity and Difference: A Contemporary Reading of Paul's Ethics*. New York: T. & T. Clark, 2005.

Horrell, J. Scott. "The Eternal Son of God in the Social Trinity." In *Jesus in Trinitarian Perspective*, edited by Fred Sanders and Klaus Issler, 44–79. Nashville: B&H, 2007.

Hovorun, Cyril. *Will, Action and Freedom: Christological Controversies in the Seventh Century*. Leiden: Brill, 2008.

Hunsinger, George. "The Crucified God and the Political Theology of Violence." *Heythrop Journal* 14 (1973) 266–79.

Hurtado, Larry. "Jesus as Lordly Example in Philippians 2:5–11." In *From Jesus to Paul*, edited by P. Richardson and J. C. Hurd, 113–26. Waterloo: Wilfred Laurier University Press, 1984.

Issler, Klaus. "Jesus' Example: Prototype of the Dependent, Spirit-Filled Life." In *Jesus in Trinitarian Perspective*, edited by Fred Sanders and Klaus Issler, 189–225. Nashville: B&H, 2007.

Janz, Paul. "What Is 'Transformation Theology'?" *American Theological Inquiry* 2.2 (2009) 9–28.

Jenson, Robert. *Systematic Theology*. Vol. 1, *The Triune God*. Oxford: Oxford University Press, 1997.

Jeroncic, A. "A Peaceable Logic of Self-Integration: Jürgen Moltmann's Theological Anthropology and the Postmodern Self." PhD diss., University of Chicago, 2008.

Johnson, A. J. "Shekinah: The Indwelling of God in the Theology of Jürgen Moltmann." PhD diss., Luther Seminary, 2003.

Jowers, Dennis. "The Theology of the Cross as Theology of the Trinity: A Critique of Jürgen Moltmann's Staurocentric Trinitarianism." *Tyndale Bulletin* 52.2 (2001) 248–50.

Kapic, Kelly M., and Wesley Vander Lugt. "The Ascension of Jesus and the Descent of the Holy Spirit in Patristic Perspective: A Theological Reading." *Evangelical Quarterly* 79 (2007) 23–33.

Kärkkäinen, Veli-Matti. *Christ and Reconciliation*. Grand Rapids: Eerdmans, 2013.

———. *Christology: A Global Introduction*. Grand Rapids: Baker Academic, 2003.

Käsemann, Ernst. "On the Subject of Primitive Christian Apocalypse." In *New Testament Questions for Today*, 122. Minneapolis: Fortress, 1969.

Kasper, Walter. *The God of Jesus Christ*. London: Continuum, 2012.

Kim, Grace Ji-Sun. "Jürgen Moltmann." In *Beyond the Pale: Reading Theology from the Margins*, edited by M. A. De La Torre and S. M. Floyd-Thomas, 245–54. Louisville, KY: Westminster John Knox, 2004.

Leithart, Peter J. *Traces of the Trinity: Signs of God in Creation and Human Experience*. Grand Rapids: Brazos, 2015.

Lewis, Alan. *Between Cross and Resurrection: A Theology of Holy Saturday*. Grand Rapids, MI: Eerdmans, 2001.

Linahan, Jane. "The Kenosis of God and Reverence for the Particular: A Conversation with Jürgen Moltmann." PhD diss., Marquette University, 1999.

Lister, Robert. *God Is Impassible and Impassioned: Toward a Theology of Divine Emotion*. Wheaton, IL: Crossway, 2013.

Liston, Gregory, J. *The Anointed Church: Toward a Third Article Ecclesiology.* Minneapolis: Fortress, 2015.

Long, D. Stephen. *Hebrews.* Louisville, KY: Westminster John Knox, 2011.

Loomer, B. "Paul Tillich's Theology of Correlation." *The Journal of Religion* 36.3 (1956) 150–56.

Lösel, Steffen. *Kreuzwege: Ein ökumenisches Gespräch mit Hans Urs von Balthasar.* Zürich: Ferdinand Schöningh, 2001.

Luther, Martin. "A Meditation on Christ's Passion." In *Martin Luther's Basic Theological Writing,* edited by T. F. Lull, 126–31. Minneapolis: Fortress, 2012.

Luy, David. *Dominus Mortus: Martin Luther on the Incorruptibility of God in Christ.* Minneapolis: Augsburg Fortress, 2014.

MacDonald, W. G. "Problems of Pneumatology in Christology." ThD diss., Southern Baptist Theological Seminary, 1970.

Mackinnon, Donald. "The Myth of God Incarnate." In *Themes in Theology: The Three-Fold Cord,* 137–44. Edinburgh: T. & T. Clark, 1987.

Macleod, Donald. *Jesus Is Lord: Christology Yesterday and Today.* Fearn, UK: Christian Focus, 2000.

Martin, Ralph P. *Carmen Christi.* Cambridge: Cambridge University Press, 1967.

———. *A Hymn of Christ: Philippians 2:5–11 in Recent Interpretation & in the Setting of Early Christian Worship.* Downers Grove, IL: InterVarsity, 1997.

———. *Philippians.* New Century Bible Commentary. Grand Rapids: Eerdmans, 1976.

McDougall, Joy Ann. *Pilgrimage of Love: Moltmann on Trinity and the Christian Life.* New York: Oxford University Press, 2005.

McFarland, Ian. *From Nothing: A Theology of Creation.* Louisville, KY: Westminster John Knox, 2014.

———. "Spirit and Incarnation: Toward a Pneumatic Chalcedonianism." *International Journal of Systematic Theology* 16.2 (2014) 143–58.

McGrath, Alister. *Luther's Theology of the Cross.* Oxford, UK: Blackwell, 1985.

———. *The Making of Modern German Christology: 1750–1990.* Eugene, OR: Wipf & Stock, 1994.

McSwain, Jeff. *Movements of Grace: The Dynamic Christo-Realism of Bonhoeffer, Barth, and the Torrances.* Eugene, OR: Wipf & Stock, 2010.

Meeks, Douglas. *Origins of the Theology of Hope.* Minneapolis: Fortress, 1974.

Mercedes, Anna. *Power For: Feminism and Christ's Self Giving.* Edinburgh: T. & T. Clark, 2011.

Moltmann, Jürgen. "Adventure of Theological Ideas." *Religious Studies Review* 22.2 (1996) 102–5.

———. "Antwort auf die kritik an 'Der gekreuzigte Gott.'" In *Diskussion über Jürgen Moltmanns Buch 'Der gekreuzigte Gott,'* edited by M. Welker, 165–90. Munich: Chr. Kaiser Verlag, 1979.

———. "An Autobiographical Note." *God, Hope, and History,* edited by A. J. Conyers, 203–19. Macon: Mercer University Press, 1988.

———. *A Broad Place: An Autobiography.* Minneapolis: Fortress, 2008.

———. "The Christian Hope—Messianic or Transcendent?" In *History and the Triune God,* translated by John Bowden, 91–109. London: SCM, 1991.

———. "Christian Theology and Its Problems Today." In *The Experiment Hope,* edited and translated by M. Douglas Meeks, 1–14. Philadelphia: Fortress, 1975.

------. *The Church in the Power of the Spirit.* Translated by Margaret Kohl. Minneapolis: Fortress, 1993.

------. "Come Holy Spirit! Renew the Whole of Creation." In *History and the Triune God*, translated by John Bowden, 70–79. London: SCM, 1991.

------. *The Coming of God.* Translated by Margaret Kohl. Minneapolis: Fortress, 2000.

------. "Creation as an Open System." In *Future of Creation: Collected Essays*, translated by Margaret Kohl, 115–30. Minneapolis: Fortress, 2007.

------. "Creation, Covenant, Glory." In *History and the Triune God*, translated by John Bowden, 125–42. London: SCM, 1991.

------. "The Cross as Military Symbol of Sacrifice." In *Cross Examinations*, edited by Marit Trelstad, 259–63. Minneapolis: Fortress, 2006.

------. *The Crucified God.* Translated by Margaret Kohl. Minneapolis: Fortress, 1993.

------. "The Crucified God and Apathetic Man." In *The Experiment Hope*, edited and translated by M. Douglas Meeks, 69–84. Philadelphia: Fortress, 1975.

------. "Die Kategorie Novum in Der Christlichen Theologie." In *Ernst Bloch Zu Ehren*, edited by Siegfried Unseld, 243–63. Frankfurt: Suhrkamp, 1965.

------. *Ethics of Hope.* Translated by Margaret Kohl. Minneapolis: Fortress, 2012.

------. *Experiences in Theology.* Translated by Margaret Kohl. Minneapolis: Fortress, 2000.

------. *Experiences of God.* Translated by Margaret Kohl. Minneapolis: Fortress, 2007.

------. *God for a Secular Society: The Public Relevance of Theology.* Translated by Margaret Kohl. Minneapolis: Fortress, 1999.

------. *God in Creation.* Translated by Margaret Kohl. Minneapolis: Fortress, 1993.

------. "God Is Unselfish Love." In *The Emptying God: A Buddhist-Jewish-Christian Conversation*, edited by J. B. Cobb and C. Ives, 116–24. Maryknoll, NY: Orbis, 1990.

------. "The God with the Human Face." In *Humanity in God*, by Jurgen Moltmann and Elisabeth Moltmann-Wendel, 55–106. New York: Pilgrim, 1983.

------. "Gottesoffenbarung und Wahrheitsfrage." In *Parrhesia: Karl Barth zum actzigsten Geburstag*, edited by Eberhard Busch, 149–72. Zurich: Evz-Verlag, 1966.

------. "I Believe in God the Father: Patriarchal or Non-Patriarchal Talk of God?" In *History and the Triune God*, translated by John Bowden, 1–18. London: SCM, 1991.

------. "I Believe in Jesus Christ, the Only Son of God: Brotherly Talk of Christ." In *History and the Triune God*, translated by John Bowden, 31–43. London: SCM, 1991.

------. *In the End, the Beginning: The Life of Hope.* Translated by Margaret Kohl. Minneapolis: Fortress, 2004.

------. "Is God Incarnate in All That Is?" In *Incarnation: On the Scope and Depth of Christology*, edited by N. H. Gregersen, 119–32. Minneapolis: Fortress, 2015.

------. *Jesus Christ for Today's World.* Translated by Margaret Kohl. Minneapolis: Fortress, 1994.

------. "Justice for Victims and Perpetrators." In *History and the Triune God*, translated by John Bowden, 44–56. London: SCM, 1991.

------. "Justification and the New Creation." In *Future of Creation: Collected Essays*, translated by Margaret Kohl, 149–71. Minneapolis: Fortress, 2007.

------. *On Human Dignity: Political Theology and Ethics.* Translated by M. D. Meeks. Minneapolis: Fortress, 2007.

------. *The Passion for Life: A Messianic Lifestyle.* Translated by Douglas Meeks. Minneapolis: Fortress, 2007.

------. *The Power of the Powerless.* Translated by Margaret Kohl. London: SCM, 1983.

———. *Science and Wisdom.* Translated by Margaret Kohl. Minneapolis: Fortress, 2003.

———. *The Source of Life: The Holy Spirit and the Theology of Life.* Translated by Margaret Kohl. Minneapolis: Fortress, 1997.

———. *The Spirit of Life.* Translated by Margaret Kohl. Minneapolis: Fortress, 2001.

———. *Sun of Righteousness, Arise! God's Future for Humanity and the Earth.* Translated by Margaret Kohl. Minneapolis: Fortress, 2010.

———. "Theologia Reformata et Semper Reformanda." In *Toward the Future of Reformed Theology,* edited by David Willis-Watkins, 120–35. Grand Rapids, MI: Eerdmans, 1998.

———. "Theology as Eschatology." In *The Future of Hope,* edited by F. Herzog, 1–24. New York: Herder & Herder, 1970.

———. *Theology of Hope.* Translated by James W. Leitch. Minneapolis: Fortress, 1993.

———. "The Theology of the Cross Today." In *Future of Creation: Collected Essays,* translated by Margaret Kohl, 59–79. Minneapolis: Fortress, 2007.

———. "Towards the Next Step in the Dialogue." In *The Future of Hope,* edited by F. Herzog, 154–64. New York: Herder & Herder, 1970.

———. "The Trinitarian History of God." In *Future of Creation: Collected Essays,* translated by Margaret Kohl, 80–96. Minneapolis: Fortress, 2007.

———. "Trinitarian Personhood of the Spirit." In *Advents of the Spirit: An Introduction to the Current Study of Pneumatology,* edited by Lyle Dabney and B. E. Hinze, 302–14. Milwaukee: Marquette University Press, 2001.

———. "The Trinitarian Story of Jesus." In *History and the Triune God,* translated by John Bowden, 70–89. London: SCM, 1991.

———. *The Trinity and the Kingdom.* Translated by Margaret Kohl. Minneapolis: Fortress, 1993.

———. *The Way of Jesus Christ.* Translated by Margaret Kohl. Minneapolis, Fortress, 1993.

Moltmann, Jürgen, and Elisabeth Moltmann-Wendell. *Humanity in God.* New York: Pilgrim, 1983.

Moltmann, Jürgen, and Pinchas Lapide. "Dialogue." In *Jewish Monotheism and Christian Trinitarian Doctrine,* translated by Leonard Swindler, 59–81. Minneapolis: Fortress, 1981.

Moritz, J. M. "Deep Incarnation and the *Imago Dei*: The Cosmic Scope of the Incarnation in Light of the Messiah as the Renewed Adam." *Theology and Science* 11.4 (2013) 436–43.

Morris, Thomas. *The Logic of God Incarnate.* Ithaca: Cornell University Press, 1986.

Motyer, Steven. "The Spirit in Hebrews: No Longer Forgotten?" In *The Spirit and Christ in the New Testament & Christian Theology,* edited by I. H. Marshall, V. Rabens, and C. Bennema, 213–27. Grand Rapids: Eerdmans, 2012.

Moule, C. F. D. "Further Reflexions on Philippians 2:5–11." In *Apostolic History and the Gospels,* edited by W. W. Gaque and R. P. Martin, 264–76. Grand Rapids: Eerdmans, 1970.

———. "The Manhood of Jesus in the New Testament." In *Christ, Faith, and History: Cambridge Studies in Christology,* edited by S. W. Sykes and J. P. Clayton, 95–110. Cambridge: Cambridge University Press, 1972.

Müller-Fahrenholz, Geiko. *The Kingdom and the Power: The Theology of Jürgen Moltmann.* Minneapolis: Fortress, 2001.

Murphy, Nancey, and George F. R. Ellis. *On the Moral Nature of the Universe: Theology, Cosmology, and Ethics.* Minneapolis: Augsburg Fortress, 1996.

Neal, Ryan. "Jürgen Moltmann." In *Companion to the Theologians*, edited by Ian S. Markham, 461–71. West Sussex, UK: Wiley-Blackwell, 2009.

———. *Theology as Hope.* Princeton Theological Monograph Series 99. Eugene, OR: Pickwick, 2008.

Ngien, Dennis. *The Suffering of God According to Martin Luther's "Theologia Crucis."* Vancouver, BC: Regent College, 2005.

O'Collins, Gerald. *The Tripersonal God.* Mahwah, NJ: Paulist, 2014.

Oden, Patrick David. *Transformative Church: New Ecclesial Models and the Theology of Jürgen Moltmann.* Minneapolis: Fortress, 2015.

O'Donnell, John. *Trinity and Temporality: The Christian Doctrine of God in the Light of Process Theology and the Theology of Hope.* Oxford: Oxford University Press, 1983.

Oegema, Gerbern. *The Anointed and His People: Messianic Expectations from the Maccabees to Bar Kochba.* Sheffield: Sheffield Academic Press, 1998.

Olson, Roger. *The Journey of Modern Theology: From Reconstruction to Deconstruction.* Downers Grove, IL: InterVarsity, 2013.

Otto, Randall E. *The God of Hope: The Trinitarian Vision of Jürgen Moltmann.* Lanham: University Press of America, 1991.

———. "The Use and Abuse of Perichoresis in Recent Theology." *Scottish Journal of Theology* 54 (2001) 366–84.

Pannenberg, Wolfhart. "Die Aufnahme des philosophischen Gottesbegriffs als dogmatisches Problem der frühchristlichen Theologie." In *Grundfragen systematischer Theologie*, vol. 1, 296–346. Göttingen: Vandenhoeck & Ruprecht, 1967.

———. *Jesus—God and Man.* Translated by L. L. Wilkins and D. A. Priebe. London, SCM, 1968.

Papanikolaou, Aristotle. "Person, *Kenosis*, and Abuse: Hans Urs von Balthasar and Feminist Theologies in Conversation." *Modern Theology* 19 (2003) 41–65.

Peters, Ted. *God as Trinity: Relationality and Temporality in Divine Life.* Louisville, KY: Westminster John Knox, 1993.

Prooijen, Ton van. *Limping but Blessed: Jürgen Moltmann's Search for a Liberating Anthropology.* Netherlands: Rodopi, 2004.

Quick, Oliver. "An Ethical Sermon." In *Doctrines of the Creed.* London: Nisbet, 1938.

Rae, Murray A. "The Baptism of Christ." In *The Person of Christ*, edited by Stephen R. Holmes and Murray A. Rae, 121–37. London: T. & T. Clark, 2005.

Robinson, J. A. T. *The Body: A Study in Pauline Theology.* London: SCM, 1982.

Schmiechen, Peter. *Saving Power: Theories of Atonement and Forms of the Church.* Grand Rapids: MI: Eerdmans, 2005.

Schönborn, Christoph. *God Sent His Son: A Contemporary Christology.* Translated by Henry Taylor. San Fransisco: Ignatius, 2010.

Schweitzer, Donald. *Contemporary Christologies.* Minneapolis: Fortress, 2010.

Sedmak, Clemens. "The Disruptive Power of World Hunger." In *Transformation Theology*, 115–41. London: T. & T. Clark, 2007.

Shults, F. LeRon. *Christology and Science.* Grand Rapids: Eerdmans, 2009.

Sobrino, Jon. *Christ the Liberator: A View from the Victims.* Translated by Paul Burns. Maryknoll: Orbis, 2001.

———. *Christology at the Crossroads.* Translated by John Drury. Maryknoll, NY: Orbis, 1978.

Sölle, Dorothee. *Suffering*. Philadelphia: Fortress, 1975.

Southgate, Christopher. *The Groaning of Creation: God, Evolution, and the Problem of Evil*. Louisville, KY: Westminster John Knox, 2008.

Steenburg, David. "The Case Against the Synonymity of *morphe* and *eikon*." *Journal for the Study of the New Testament* 34 (1988) 77–86.

Steffen, B. *Das Dogma vom Kreuz. Beitrag zu einer staurozentrischen Theologie,*. Güterloh: Bertelsmann, 1920.

Stein, Robert. *Jesus the Messiah: A Survey of the Life of Christ*. Downers Grove, IL: IVP Academic, 1996.

Strauss, Mark L. "Jesus and the Spirit in Biblical and Theological Perspective." In *The Spirit and Christ in the New Testament & Christian Theology*, edited by I. H. Marshall, V. Rabens, and C. Bennema, 266–84. Grand Rapids: Eerdmans, 2012.

Swinburne, Richard. *The Christian God*. Oxford: Clarendon, 1994.

Sykes, S. W. "The Strange Persistence of Kenotic Christology." In *Being and Truth: Essays in Honor of John Macquarrie*, edited by Alistair Kee and Eugene T. Long, 349–75. London: SCM, 1986.

Tang, Siu-Kwong. *God's History in the Theology of Jürgen Moltmann*. European University Studies XXIII. Berne: Peter Lang, 1996.

Tanner, Kathryn E. "Trinity, Christology, and Community." In *Christology and Ethics*, edited by Brent Waters and L. Leron Shults, 56–74. Grand Rapids: Eerdmans, 2010.

Thomasius, Gottfried. *Christi Person und Werk*. In *God and Incarnation in Mid-nineteenth Century German Theology*, edited by Claude Welch. Oxford: Oxford University Press, 1965.

Thompson, John. *Modern Trinitarian Perspectives*. Oxford: Oxford University Press, 1994.

Thompson, Marianne Meye. *The Promise of the Father: Jesus and God in the New Testament*. Louisville, KY: Westminster John Knox, 2000.

Thompson, T. R. "Nineteenth Century Kenotic Christology." In *Exploring Kenotic Christology*, edited by C. Stephen Evans, 74–111. Oxford: Oxford University Press, 2006.

Treat, Jeremy. "Exaltation In and Through Humiliation: Rethinking the States of Christ." In *Christology: Ancient and Modern*, edited by O. Crisp and F. Sanders, 96–114. Grand Rapids: Zondervan, 2013.

Turner, Max. *The Holy Spirit and Spiritual Gifts—Then and Now*. Carlisle: Paternoster, 1999.

Twombly, Charles Craig. *Perichoresis and Personhood: God, Christ, and Salvation in John of Damascus*. Eugene, OR: Pickwick, 2015.

Vidales, Raúl. "How Should We Speak of Jesus Today?" In *Faces of Jesus: Latin American Christologies*, edited by José Míguez Bonino, 137–61. Maryknoll, NY: Orbis, 1984.

Volf, Miroslav. "A Queen and a Beggar: Challenges and Prospects of Theology." In *The Future of Theology: Essays in Honor of Jürgen Moltmann*, edited by M. Volf, ix–xviii. Grand Rapids: Eerdmans, 1996.

Volf, Miroslav, and M. Welker. "Preface." In *God's Life in Trinity*, edited by M. Volf and M. Welker xii–xiv. Minneapolis: Augsburg Fortress, 2006.

Wanamaker, C. A. "Philippians 2:6–11: Son of God or Adam Christology?" *New Testament Studies* 33.2 (1987) 179–93.

Ward, Graham. "Kenosis: Death, Discourse and Resurrection." In *Balthasar at the End of Modernity*, edited by L. Gardiner, 15–68. Edinburgh: T. & T. Clark, 1999.

Ware, Bruce. "Christ's Atonement: A Work of the Trinity." In *Jesus in Trinitarian Perspective*, edited by Fred Sanders and Klaus Issler, 156–88. Nashville: B&H, 2007.

Watson, Hubert. *Towards a Relevant Christology in India Today: An Appraisal of the Christologies of John Hick, Jürgen Moltmann and Jon Sobrino*. Berlin: Peter Lang, 2002.

Webb, Robert. "Jesus' Baptism by John: Its Historiticity and Significance." In *Key Events in the Life of the Historical Jesus*, edited by Darrell Bock & Robert Webb. Grand Rapids, Eerdmans, 2010.

Webster, John. "Jürgen Moltmann: Trinity and Suffering." *Evangel* 3.2 (1985) 4–6.

Weinandy, Thomas. *In the Likeness of Sinful Flesh: An Essay on the Humanity of Christ*. Edinburgh: T. & T. Clark, 1993.

Welch, Claude, ed. *God and Incarnation in Mid-nineteenth Century German Theology*. Oxford: Oxford University Press, 1965.

———. *Protestant Thought in the Nineteenth Century*. Hartford: Yale University Press, 1972.

Welker, Michael, ed. *Diskussion über Jürgen Moltmann Buch "Der gekreuzigte Gott."* Munich: Chr. Kaiser, 1979.

———. *God the Spirit*. Translated by J. F. Hoffmeyer. Minneapolis: Fortress, 1994.

Wierzbicka, Anna. *What Did Jesus Mean? Explaining the Sermon on the Mount and the Parables in Simple and Universal Human Concepts*. Oxford: Oxford University Press, 2001.

Williams, Stephen. "Jürgen Moltmann: A Critical Introduction." In *Getting Your Bearings: Engaging with Contemporary Theologians*, edited by Philip Duce and Daniel Strange, 75–124. Downers Grove, IL: InterVarsity, 2009.

———. "Moltmann on Jesus Christ." In *Jürgen Moltmann and Evangelical Theology: A Critical Engagement*, edited by S. W. Chung, 104–25. Eugene, OR: Pickwick, 2012.

Winter, Paul. *On the Trial of Jesus*. Berlin: Walter De Gruyter, 1974.

Witherington, Ben. *The Christology of Jesus*. Minneapolis: Fortress, 1990.

———. *Friendship and Finances in Philippi*. Valley Forge, PA: Trinity, 1994.

Wright, Nigel G. *Disavowing Constantine: Mission, Church and Social Order in the Theologies of John Howard Yoder and Jürgen Moltmann*. Paternoster Theological Monographs. Eugene, OR: Wipf & Stock, 2007.

Wright, N. T. *Climax of the Covenant*. New York: T. & T. Clark, 1991.

———. *Jesus and the Victory of God*. Minneapolis: Fortress, 1996.

———. "The New Creation." In *The Crown and the Fire: Meditations on the Cross and the Life of the Spirit*, by N. T. Wright, 61–72. Grand Rapids: Eerdmans, 2014.

———. *The Resurrection of the Son of God*. Minneapolis: Fortress, 2003.

———. *Surprised by Hope: Rethinking Heaven, the Resurrection, and the Mission of the Church*. New York: HarperOne, 2008.

———. "That the World May Be Healed." In *The Crown and the Fire: Meditations on the Cross and the Life of the Spirit*, by N. T. Wright, 122–31. Grand Rapids: Eerdmans, 2014.

Wyschogrod, Michael. "A Jewish Perspective on Incarnation." *Modern Theology* 12.2 (1996) 195–209.

Zathureczky, Kornel. *The Messianic Disruption of Trinitarian Theology*. Lanham, MD: Lexington, 2009.

Index